Lorca, Alberti, and
the Theater of Popular Poetry

American University Studies

Series II
Romance Languages and Literature
Vol. 170

PETER LANG
New York • San Francisco • Bern
Frankfurt am Main • Paris • London

Sandra Cary Robertson

Lorca, Alberti, and
the Theater of Popular Poetry

PETER LANG
New York • San Francisco • Bern
Frankfurt am Main • Paris • London

Library of Congress Cataloging-in-Publication Data

Robertson, Sandra Cary
   Lorca, Alberti, and the theater of popular poetry
/ Sandra Cary Robertson.
      p. cm. — (American university studies. Series
II, Romance languages and literature ; v. 170)
      Includes bibliographical references.
      1. García Lorca, Federico, 1898-1936—Dramatic
works. 2. Alberti, Rafael, 1902- —Dramatic works.
3. Folklore in literature. I. Title. II. Series:
American university studies. Series II, Romance
languages and literature ; vol. 170.
PQ6613.A763Z6872 1991 862'.62—dc20 91-17755
ISBN 0-8204-1565-0   CIP
ISSN 0740-9257

Die Deutsche Bibliothek-CIP-Einheitsaufnahme

Robertson, Sandra Cary:
Lorca, Alberti, and the theater of popular poetry /
Sandra Cary Robertson.—New York; Berlin; Bern;
Frankfurt/M.; Paris; Wien: Lang, 1991
   (American university studies : Ser. 2, Romance
languages and literature ; Vol. 170)
   ISBN 0-8204-1565-0
NE: American university studies / 02

The paper in this book meets the guidelines for permanence and
durability of the Committee on Production Guidelines for
Book Longevity of the Council on Library Resources.

For Zach and Joan

Contents

Acknowledgments

There is a long, long road leading to this book, traversed by many people who have helped and encouraged me along the way. Here I can acknowledge only some of them. My primary debts are to Stephen Gilman, who first introduced me to the passions of the intellect; and to Diego Catalán, who knew better than I did just what I was after, and whose vast knowledge, as well as generosity of mind and spirit, I will never forget and can never repay.

I want to thank Antonio Sánchez Romeralo, Samuel G. Armistead, and Julian Palley for their careful readings of the manuscript and insightful comments along the way. To Andrew A. Anderson, Christopher Maurer, and Christian de Paepe, I owe much for their help and suggestions.

I am grateful to the University of San Diego for their support of this project. Special thanks to Monica Wagner, for seeing this work through many obstacles with admirable expertise. Thanks also to Juli Busse.

For the information in chapter 4, I am deeply indebted to Diego Catalán. A portion of chapter 5 was previously published in translation under the title, "*Mariana Pineda*: el Romance popular y su retrato teatral," in the *Boletín de la Fundación Federico García Lorca*, 3 (June, 1988), pp. 88–106. I am also grateful to the staffs of the Fundación García Lorca and the Instituto Seminario Menéndez Pidal in Madrid for their time and help.

Prologue

When Rafael Alberti stopped in Havana on his way to Mexico in early 1935 to give a talk in commemoration of the 300th anniversary of the death of Lope de Vega, he set out to do much more than pay homage to Lope (whose artistry he extols nonetheless: "Yo sé que Lope es todo")—he made use of the occasion to present himself and the poets of his generation as they stand in relation to Spain's literary history as a whole, and to demonstrate the largely unacknowledged debt, throughout that history, to the influence of popular poetry of oral tradition.

Members of the Generation of 1927, most notably Alberti and García Lorca, hold a unique position in the history of Spanish letters. They were the first generation in Spain to be fully integrated as plenary members of the European avant-garde; at the same time, they felt themselves to be the inheritors and the qualified interpreters of what Unamuno had termed Spain's *intrahistoria*, embodied in the *pueblo*. Between 1923 and 1935, they define themselves in relation to the "línea llanista" of popular poetry they consider part of the authentic Spanish tradition.

Indeed by now it has become a commonplace in literary criticism to say that, while indisputably members of the vanguard, the poets of the Generation of 1927 (and Alberti and García Lorca, in particular) sought inspiration for their work in traditional popular poetry. Many have pointed out, in general, the important role of "lo popular" in the literary production of the times. Yet these observations are, for the most part, remarks made in passing, which are then left aside in favor of some more easily demonstrable problem, thus adding to a stockpile of unexamined assertions concerning a unique period of Spain's literary history, and, furthermore, contributing nothing to the investigation of a long and pervasive cultural tradition that is still relatively unknown to the learned class of scholars.

My purpose is to defend the idea that a) this approach to "lo popular" in the works of Lorca and Alberti is an essential feature in their very conception of art, as well as of the function they attribute to themselves as "poetas cultos"; b) that their attitude in this respect demands a more rigorous explanation than the one usually limited to mere anecdote—one which firmly situates their "popularismo" within the cultural (and, to some extent, political) history of Spain; and c) that their affinity for popular and traditional literature is the key to understanding their attempts to explore the inherent dramatic qualities of popular lyric and narrative poetry for the stage.

My study necessarily includes not only major plays by these two poets, but minor dramatic works which have received less attention, yet which are fundamental demonstrations of their attraction to and repeated experiments with the poetry of oral tradition. In addition, I rely on their lectures and public presentations for information about their literary program, and for their view of themselves as participants in a dynamic relationship to the *pueblo*, mediated by popular and traditional art. When pertinent, I touch upon developments in the intellectual and political life of the period which affect their understanding of their endeavors on both artistic and social levels. The outcome of the Civil War puts an end to the trajectory drawn here, depriving us of an author in one case, and depriving the author of his audience in the other.

1

The Literary Manifesto within the Recourse
to Popular Traditional Art

The attraction to the materials and methods of popular art is an essential ingredient impossible to disregard in any definition of Lorca's and Alberti's work. The impact on the poets of 1927 "de ese tipo de poesía de la que el pueblo es guardador," as Alberti described it, was publicly announced and sustained by both poets in a number of lecture/demonstrations, many of which were presented before audiences abroad during the years 1929–1935.

Alberti's sense of mission is always explicit, as can be seen in the talk he gave at the Friedrich-Wilhelm Universität in Berlin on November 30, 1932, entitled "La poesía popular en la lírica española contemporánea."[1] The following April or May, 1933, he gave a lecture in Madrid (with the participation of García Lorca and the renowned dancer, 'La Argentinita'), which most probably repeated the substance of the Berlin lecture.[2] Again, in Havana, in April of 1935, he read "Lope de Vega y la poesía contemporánea," also based on his previous lecture.[3]

García Lorca's exposition of the importance of "lo popular" is less explicit than Alberti's, but underlies and justifies a number of his lectures. For instance, it is the point of departure for his talk, "Canciones de cuna españolas" (later retitled "Las nanas infantiles"), first performed by Lorca at the Residencia de Estudiantes in Madrid on December 13, 1928. It was presented again at Vassar College in New York sometime during the fall or winter of 1929–1930, and again finally in

Havana, on March 16, 1930.[4] His lecture, "Cómo canta una ciudad de noviembre a noviembre," illustrated by popular songs he sang and played on a piano, was presented during the poet's first trip abroad, in Havana, in March or April of 1930, and twice again during his second appearance in Latin America, in Buenos Aires on October 26, 1933, and with a slightly different title, "Granada y sus canciones," in Montevideo, Uruguay, in early February, 1934.[5] Other talks by Lorca which demonstrate his attraction to popular culture are the "Juego y teoría del duende,"[6] his early lecture on "El cante jondo: Primitivo canto andaluz,"[7] and the later "Arquitectura del cante jondo."[8]

To designate these public presentations as "lectures" is misleading. All of them are accompanied by numerous selections of popular poetry and song. But neither do they constitute mere "demonstrations" of the material. Rather they are better described as "pronouncements"—pronouncements, since the musical and poetical illustrations are consistently embedded in a theoretical approach to popular traditional poetry, comprising a kind of literary manifesto on the part of both poets. Curiously enough, neither Lorca nor Alberti had the scholarly training or profession to qualify them as critical theorists of their generation, yet by the early 1930's they have developed a sense of mission. They have meditated on their role in Spanish literary history, they have become fully conscious of that role, and they attempt to explain it to the public, both in Europe and Latin America. In these talks Lorca and Alberti evince a historical perspective, a global view of their national literature, within which they consciously insert themselves as principal proponents. They define and defend themselves in this role at the same time they define and defend Spain's particular poetic tradition.

Another significant aspect of these presentations is that they constitute an act, as opposed to a text, of personal introduction to audiences outside of Spain. Unlike the purely academic discourses of many poet-scholars of the generation, both Lorca and Alberti present themselves simultaneously as artists who are individuals and as typified representations of their culture as a whole. At the same time their consciousness of their two-fold role—as members of the European vanguard, and as young inheritors of a peculiarly Spanish literary tradition—determines the notably propagandistic element of these lectures. In essence they advertise Spanish literature while they examine themselves in relation to it.

The "Embestida" or Impact of the Art of Popular Tradition

As literary ambassador of Spain and poet of the avant-garde, it is natural that Rafael Alberti would be invited to talk at the conference in Havana organized in honor of Lope de Vega by José María Chacón y Calvo, who introduced Alberti as "un puro representante de la mejor poesía española, nutrido de la savia popular de Lope, [que] viene a decirnos cuánto deben a aquella vena inagotable los nuevos poetas españoles."[9]   However, considering the historical and personal circumstances surrounding the occasion, Alberti's decision to retain and repeat the substance of his lecture given two and a half years earlier in Berlin is certainly surprising.

In 1934 Alberti had made his second trip to Moscow, with María Teresa León, to attend the First Congress of Soviet Writers. Already actively affiliated with the Communist Party since 1932,[10] in Moscow he became acquainted with Gorky, Prokofiev, Eisenstein and André Malraux, among others.[11]   The rise of National Socialism in Germany had contributed to a climate of extreme political tension throughout Europe, but in Spain this tension reached a maximum point in October, 1934, with the brutal repression of the miners' strike in Asturias. Alberti and María Teresa, unable to return to Spain, traveled to America where Alberti gave poetry readings in an attempt to raise funds for the Asturian workers.[12]   It is during this year of exile that Alberti accepts the invitation to speak at Havana, and Chacón y Calvo recognizes Alberti's growing crisis of conscience when he adds to his introduction, "un poeta español representativo, lleno de la inquietud de nuestra hora."[13]

Alberti's increasing political activism, his contacts with the circle of Soviet and Marxist artists, and the violent political climate in his homeland, as well as in Europe generally, would all dictate a drastic revision of his earlier views on popular poetics. At a moment in history when he would have been likely to change his mind about the entire subject, he reaffirms his first point of view and continues to define himself and his generation in relation to the same subject.[14] His 1935 pronouncement on popular and traditional poetry occurs within a context of heightened political consciousness, personal and global. But in spite of the historical moment, and in spite of the different topic of the lecture, to commemorate Lope, Alberti retains the body and substance of his previous lecture, reiterating his position as a poet and as a member of a new generation of poets in Spain, tracing the same vital relationship he sees between these poets and the anonymous popular poetic tradition, and postulating the same definition of what that tradition is. In addition he chooses to conclude the lecture with a reading of *La pájara pinta*, his play of popular lyrics.

The nucleus of Alberti's exposition, both in Berlin and Havana, consists of defining himself as a poet "que recrea lo 'popular,' que lo toma, para devolverlo reinventado."[15] Within this definition he includes other members of the Generation of 1927, specifically Federico García Lorca and Fernando Villalón, a now almost forgotten poet who was active in the group until shortly before his death in 1930.[16] Yet, within this "recreación," he is quick to recognize the danger, for himself and for his generation, of creating poetry that might be purely an imitation of the authentic tradition. Choosing one of his favorite subjects, the bullfight,[17] he uses the metaphor "el torillo suelto de la poesía popular," to describe the particular magnetism popular poetry holds for poets such as himself, who are irresistibly drawn into the encounter: "su embestida llega hacia nosotros, nos alcanza, cogiéndonos, volteándonos." But at the same time he points out the dnager of this encounter for poets who insist on coming too close, i.e., who try to imitate the popular style: "cuyas cornadas pueden sernos mortales."[18] Therefore he defends the necessity of becoming conscious of this "torillo," and of confronting its "embestida," for, according to his view, the impact of poetry of the oral tradition cannot be disregarded in any panorama of Spanish literature.

Alberti takes recourse to "toros" (and, as we shall see, to other symbols of popular culture) in an attempt to describe what he cannot strictly define: the vibrant energy of traditional popular poetry, and its impact on the "poeta culto."[19] There is no question that he views himself and other members of his generation as learned, professional poets. What distinguishes them, he feels, is their relationship to "lo popular." Around this self-definition, Alberti groups his contemporaries and his observations on poets of previous centuries, creating a scaffolding out of the tradition of popular poetry which links and sustains them all.

Traditional Aesthetics: "A coger los aires"

The relationship of the "poeta culto" with "poesía popular" is based on an aesthetic attraction to the poetics of traditional popular poetry. Alberti's view of traditional aesthetics rejects the nineteenth-century Romantic conception of popular poetry. He sums up his position, both in 1932 and in 1935, with the words of Juan Ramón Jiménez: "No hay arte popular sino tradición popular del arte." The influence of Giner and the Institucionistas is clear in his statement that "lo popular que hoy conocemos repite, copia, sin saberlo, en sus coplas, romances, bordados, cerámicas, estos viejos modelos de autores ya perdidos."[20]

As an example of a poem whose literary origin is of no consequence, he plays a recording of "Las tres morillas de Jaén," performed by Federico García Lorca and La Argentinita (a song originally included in the *Cancionero musical de Palacio* of the late fifteenth century).[21] His comments following the song make clear that he rejects the romantic "Das Volk dichtet" theory of popular poetic creation:

> Otras muchas canciones como éstas fueron divulgadas y cantadas por aldeas y pueblos durante siglos, lo que hizo creer a algunos que eran productos espontáneos de la inspiración popular, no siendo, como antes dijimos, sino repeticiones de una gran tradición poética, que, con los romances, ha sido conservada en la memoria del pueblo.[22]

Thus Alberti does not see the origin of these songs as a spontaneous outburst of an anonymous *pueblo*, but would seem to accept, rather, the idea that the *pueblo* adopts and retains poetic material from learned sources.[23]

However, Alberti is careful to stress that the role of the *pueblo* in keeping alive poetry received from other sources is active, not passive. He insists that the *pueblo* is not a mere repository for a forgotten poetic tradition, but, on the contrary, that the *pueblo* regenerates and revitalizes the poetry of invention. "Claro que al copiar o repetir, unas veces los embellecen, recreándolos, y otras, por el contrario, los estropean. Residiendo en esos retoques y añadidos la gracia y la fuerza viva de esta *memoria en movimiento*."[24] By "memoria en movimiento" Alberti wants to bring attention to the dynamic, creative aspects of "la tradición popular del arte." In his view, the popular memory is neither static nor faithful. "Los grandes poetas, los individuos, inventan, y el pueblo recoge lo inventado y lo transforma, a veces haciéndolo ir más lejos."[25] The "gracia" and the "fuerza viva" of this poetry, its creative capacity to "ir más lejos," is what Alberti wants to convey to his audience. Again, he does not try to define or analyze these terms, but to illustrate them, to convince his audience through the phenomena of the songs themselves.

By having the audience listen to the songs and experience them directly, he helps them to participate in his enthusiasm. He thus circumvents the step of intellectual definition, which would constitute a barrier to his purpose, and resorts instead to another metaphor, "los aires vivos de la poesía popular."[26] For Alberti, the impact of this "poesía popular" is ineffable. The problem is how to describe this impact. One solution of how to communicate "los aires vivos" is resolved by letting the texts speak (or sing) for themselves. His only other solution is to use the self-referential terms of popular poetry and folklore situations. For instance, the song he cites from Lope's *Peribáñez*, Act II,

> Trébole, ¡ay Jesús, cómo huele!
> Trébole, ¡ay Jesús, qué olor!

refers to the circle of customs surrounding the eve of St. John's Day, when young lovers seek each other through the symbolic search for the "trébol," or clover, which blooms in mid-June. Alberti uses this tradition as an analogy to describe the poet "que también saliese a buscar su trébol al campo de la poesía popular."[27] Thus the qualities of this poetry that he attempts to communicate can only be delineated through the terminology of the poetry itself. What he wants to convey in the use of "el toro," "los aires vivos," and "a coger el trébol," are the qualities of strength, vitality, force, grace, and a naturalness, seemingly free of artifice.

Lorca, too, was affected by these qualities, by the artistry of a poetic tradition which is in the hands of the "anónimo poeta de pueblo."

> Las metáforas que pueblan nuestro cancionero andaluz están casi siempre dentro de su órbita; no hay desproporción entre los miembros espirituales de los versos y consiguen adueñarse de nuestro corazón de una manera definitiva. Causa extrañeza y maravilla cómo el anónimo poeta de pueblo extracta en tres o cuatro versos toda la rara complejidad de los más altos momentos sentimentales en la vida del hombre. Hay coplas en que el temblor lírico llega a un punto donde no pueden llegar sino contadísimos poetas.[28]

Both poets feel the rare power—"el temblor lírico"—of this apparently simple poetry as constituting a recognizable aesthetic, an aesthetic they would like to make their own.

The Lyric Exchange between the *Pueblo* and the *Poeta culto*

Through his illustrations and commentary, Alberti makes his concept of his role as a learned poet in relationship to the art of the *pueblo* perfectly clear. In view of the energetic attraction he claims this poetry holds for him and other contemporary poets, and departing from the base idea of the *pueblo* as *receptor* of the products of the high art tradition, he maintains that the work of a poet such as himself "vuelve a enriquecer la memoria popular, a encandilarla con nueva lumbre."[29]   However, since this "memoria popular" is "memoria en movimiento," the *pueblo*, in the act of appropriating the materials from learned or exterior sources, transforms and enriches them, making it its own. The products of this process, subjected to the variations and enrichment of oral tradition, become the resource for learned poets. The role Alberti envisions for the poet, then, is to take from and return to the *pueblo*, "reinventado," the poetry of tradition. He

names this function "el intercambio lírico entre el pueblo y nosotros,"[30] and
describes it as a dialectic: "ese ir y venir, ese dar y devolver que sube de la calle
a lo alto de la casa, bajando la escalera con un nuevo traje."[31] The role left to
the poet, then, is to participate in "ese ir y venir, ese dar y devolver."

In fact, Alberti posits this dialectic as the cornerstone of his manifesto. He
presents himself and García Lorca as primary participants in this mutual give and
take, which he also terms "el canje de la poesía culta y la popular."[32] Lorca's
contribution, he claims, is and will be realized both through his poems and his
theater:

> La trayectoria de Federico hacia el futuro, sintiéndose también
> palpitante de inquietud con su tiempo, augura a su teatro y a sus
> poemas larga vida en los oídos tradicionales, que ya le repiten casi
> anónimo, por aldeíllas y plazuelas.[33]

On his own behalf, Alberti relates how he once heard some of his own poetry sung
by an anonymous "cantaor" in the Triana district of Sevilla:

> En general, estos *cantaores*...apoyan casi todas sus canciones en el
> verso castellano más sencillo: el octosílabo de los romances. Tienen
> la memoria, los oídos tan llenos de este ritmo, fácil de retener, que
> yo mismo, una noche, oí cantar en una taberna de Triana cuatro
> versos míos, separados de una elegía que escribí a la muerte del
> matador de toros 'Joselito' y que habían publicado un año antes los
> periódicos de Sevilla.[34]

In this way he presents himself and other contemporary poets as living proof ("la
muestra viva") of the collaboration between the *autores* and the *pueblo*.

> Como esta copla mía, muchas de Manuel Machado, Federico García
> Lorca y otros poetas antiguos y actuales, unidas ya a sus compañeros
> anónimos, andan, incorporados al repetorio de los *cantaores*, llevando
> así una vida errante....[35]

According to Alberti, this ongoing lyric exchange is not particular to modern times but stretches throughout Spanish history, "desde hace siglos."[36]

Gil Vicente and Lope de Vega: Primary Models of the Link between *Poesía popular* and *Poesía culta*

In the condensed critical survey of Spanish literary history traced by Alberti in order to situate himself and García Lorca in an historical continuum, Lope de Vega and Gil Vicente are seen as the earliest and unsurpassed models of this "canje lírico," and their theater is seen as the medium of exchange.

> Vamos a coger los aires, sus aires, los que Lope, como un Gil Vicente un siglo antes, supo cazar en los aires vivos de la poesía popular, y no para matarlos, sino para soltarlos otra vez, llenos de sangre nueva; para devolverlos otra vez al mismo aire que se los había entregado.[37]

The Lope that captures Alberti's imagination and that he elects to portray for his audience is not the "católico, apostólico, romano, llegando, en momentos, hasta el empacho y la pesadez más fatigosa,"[38] but a vital, creative, sensuous Lope, a writer who is engaged and thoroughly integrated in

> toda esa alegría renacentista, que en Lope es popular, de pueblo español, de romería donde se baila, se bebe, se canta y, entre matorrales, se les da zancadillas a las mozas. Pues bien, es a este Lope jaranero, juerguista, atolondrado como pudiera ser un señorito del siglo XVII, al que vamos a dedicar un homenaje....[39]

And where among Lope's prodigious literary production does Alberti find "ese Lope de aire, esos aires de Lope que buscamos, que queremos para nosotros?" Precisely in "los romancillos, letrillas y cantares esparcidos en su millonaria labor de hombre de teatro."[40]

In the mutual love of this popular traditional poetry and song, Alberti draws a connection (and establishes a continuity) between the Generation of 1927 and the Renaissance:

> Algunos poetas españoles de ahora estamos ligados a Lope íntimamente, continuando esa tradición que recrea lo 'popular,' que lo toma, para devolverlo reinventado. Él y Gil Vicente, dijimos, son, al menos para mí, los más grandes maestros en esta trayectoria. Ellos la impulsan: su embestida llega hasta nosotros, nos alcanza, cogiéndonos, volteándonos.[41]

Although Alberti's claim to an intimate link between poets of his generation and Lope is certainly self-serving within the context of the lecture, he is not alone in seeing this connection. Rather, it is a shared and generational point of view. Years later Dámaso Alonso reiterates this view as a now established precept of literary criticism.

> Allí, en los albores del tercer decenio del siglo, ocurre el hecho de que dos muchachos que han de ser grandes poetas, Rafael Alberti y Federico García Lorca, no "vuelven los ojos a lo popular," sino se meten en la entraña de lo popular, lo intuyen y crean, con un tino y una hondura, no de imitación, de voz auténtica que se había perdido desde la época de Lope.[42]

Remembering that on both occasions of his lectures, Alberti is very conscious of being the ambassador of his literary generation to audiences abroad, he appends a list of its members for whom Gil Vicente and Lope serve as "puntos de partida." The list (Moreno Villa, Jorge Guillén, Pedro Salinas, García Lorca, Fernando Villalón, Luis Cernuda, Emilio Prados, and Manuel Altolaguirre) comprises, in Alberti's words, "la generación que mejor conoce y ha estudiado a Lope." He is careful to point out that the list includes not just poets but scholars ("poetas-catedráticos").

However, lest his audience mistakenly believe that his approach to Lope be purely academic, he is also careful to distinguish himself, Lorca, and Villalón as belonging to a separate category, as poets who are related not through intellect, but through a common endeavor: "Pero Federico García Lorca, Villalón y yo, tres poetas que no hemos sufrido nunca las aulas de una Universidad, somos los más contagiados, los más ahijados de Lope."[43] Thus the line he draws stresses a vitalistic, intuitive grasp of Lope's art. It is the creative, aesthetic response to "los aires vivos" of popular poetry which links them all: Gil Vicente and Lope, Alberti and Lorca. "Y es Lope, primero, el que con más abundancia y maestría vuelve a enriquecer la memoria popular."[44] In that common response, Alberti sees what he thinks of as a family bond. Singling out Lorca's relationship to Lope,

> ¡Qué contento estaría Lope con este hijo lopesco, semi gitano de Granada! Con su mismo desenfado, arrebata la copla de la guitarra de los cantaores, romancillos de las criadas que cantan en los patios y los intercala en su teatro y en sus poemas.[45]

But Alberti does not want to convey to his audience that Lorca simply appropriates material from the popular tradition. He is careful to stress at the same time that Lorca's borrowing from the popular tradition is balanced, on the other side of the exchange, by his individual creativity. "Pero, con la misma aguda gracia que un Lope, inventa también...."[46]

The "Línea llanista" in Spanish Literature and the Reevaluation of Spanish Literature as a Whole

Although Alberti considers Gil Vicente and Lope as "los más grandes maestros," or models, to be followed, he sees tham not as isolated instances of interest in popular traditional poetry, but as part of an essential trajectory running throughout the literary history of his country.

According to Alberti, the Renaissance in Spain produced a line of great literary models (Garcilaso de la Vega, Pedro de Espinosa, and Góngora, whom he designates as "limite, meta, maravilla"[47])—but in spite of their innovations and formal achievements, he claims, "la línea llanista, hablada,[48] sencilla, nacional, fluida," inherited from the Middle Ages (from the Arcipreste de Hita and Santillana, through Jorge Manrique, Gil Vicente, and Cristóbal de Castillejo), is never lost.[49]   Its pulse continues throughout the sixteenth and seventeenth centuries ("tan cargado está el aire de las viejas músicas y cantos sigue latiendo su sangre al compás de los antiguos ritmos").[50]   Especially in the seventeenth century, amidst an explosion of technical discoveries and cultural influences, the "viejos aires" continue to surface in the works of sophisticated poets.   "Hay que reposar, que descansar de los largos y difíciles endecasílabos, hay que coger nuevamente del aire, para soltarlos otra vez, los versillos menores, llenos de gracia, desvergüenza o ternura."[51]   Thus Alberti describes the phenomenon in the seventeenth century.

Later, however, the "pedantería" of the eighteenth century and the "grandilocuencia" of the nineteenth-century Romantics (who, with two exceptions, Alberti claims, "no pueden comprender la transcendencia, la gracia de esta poesía") obscure "la línea llana" in literature, blotting it out under an ornate façade of works reflecting the tastes of a growing bourgeoisie.   The stream of simple poetry, according to Alberti, goes underground, surfacing only in the works of anonymous poets and musicians, in the "cafés cantantes," and in the common theatrical farce of the "sainetistas."   But it remains untouched by the poets who receive the public accolade (Alberti names Núñez de Arce, Campoamor, and Balart): "una burguesía disminuída por los acontecimientos nacionales exalta y corona con laureles de hojalata a los poetas de este período mamarrachesco."[52]

The only two poets Alberti salvages from this general disqualification of nineteenth-century Romantic writers, and their public, are Bécquer ("por su gran simpatía hacia lo popular"), and Rosalía de Castro ("con una percepción y finura extraordinarias, vuelve...a expresarse en el tono...de los primitivos cancioneros galaico-portugueses").   The "período mamarrachesco" comes to an end during the last decade of the century with the appearance of Ruben Darío and Walt Whitman, whose impact on Spanish poetry transforms the scene.

When he comes to the period of the Generation of 1898, the generation of his immediate "fathers," Alberti saves almost the entire group (Unamuno, Valle

Inclán, etc.), recognizing among them two final "super-fathers," Antonio Machado and Juan Ramón Jiménez, "libres ya de su primer arranque francés y rubeniano." He claims these two as the "verdaderos maestros" for the Generation of 1927: "son en este momento los poetas más respetados por las últimas generaciones españolas. Ambos vuelven a hallar las raíces, demasiado enterradas, de la poesía tradicional, poniéndolos al aire."[53]   In Machado he finds the "gravedad y llaneza" of Jorge Manrique, the profound anguish of the *cante jondo*, and, at times, the monotone of the blind man who recites his ballads in the public square. In Jiménez he finds "el verdadero creador del romance moderno," although unlike Machado, he dilutes the narrative component of the ballad in favor of its musical qualities.[54]   With these two poets, he maintains, the double line, which had characterized Spain's literature from its earliest days—that of the great works of official poets and that of the minor tradition of popular and unknown origin—is finally restored.

From this we see what is in essence the "program" of 1927, based on a fundamentally coherent vision: first, a defense of the "doble línea" of poetry throughout Spain's classic literature: that which stretches between Garcilaso and Góngora, and that exemplified by Gil Vicente and Lope as the "maestros" in the trajectory which makes the continual exchange between *poesía popular* and *poesía culta* possible; and second, the acceptance, in the part of the contemporary learned poets, of the role so admirably realized by Lope (and Gil Vicente before him): to capture from the *pueblo* "los aires vivos" of popular poetry, and to enrich the "memoria popular" with new and reinvented material, which in turn will be the "aires" repeated anonymously in public plazas and villages in an ongoing, vital tradition.

The Recovery of the *Pueblo* and its Poetry by the Poets of 1927: The Historical Context

A major question raised by a perusal of Alberti's two lectures is why he rejects the cultured literature of the eighteenth and nineteenth centuries, but not that of his immediate "fathers." An avant-garde generation, by definition disposed to break with old forms, to shock into awareness, to experiment and invent, nevertheless respects the generation of its immediate teachers and accepts a major part of its system of values. This peculiarity finds an explanation in the fact that the Generation of 1927 is the first generation in Spain to be fully integrated into Europe. The poets, painters, composers, scholars, and educators of this new generation feel themselves to be at the forefront of developments in Europe. They consider themselves plenary members, with full rights and privileges, of the leading European movements of the day, without the doubts and conflicts that characterized the previous generation. While defending the values inherited from their fathers, who were, at best, marginal in turn-of-the-century Europe, members of the Generation of 1927 present themselves to Europe and America as part of a new Spain, heralding a new cultural Golden Age. Amid a plethora of revolutionary "isms" and manifestos, they define themselves as continuing the legacy of 1898, not opposing it. The difference, as they see it, is that they are better equipped to join Europe and to convey Spain's particular and unusual heritage to countries abroad.

In the process of shifting through inherited ideas, it is important for us to look at what they cull and retain from that heritage, and what they choose to present abroad. In defense of a Spanish culture that is *not* the culture of the bourgeoisie (be it liberal or conservative), they take recourse to the affirmation that they are the inheritors of what Unamuno had termed Spain's "intrahistoria," that they are qualified interpreters of the authentic essence of Spain, embodied still in the *pueblo*. Unamuno's 1895 essay, *En torno al casticismo*, had called upon future generations to delve into "la tradición eterna" of Spain, not the "superficie que se hiela y cristaliza en los libros y registros," but the inner substance of history, "porque hay algo que sirve de sustento al perpetuo flujo de las cosas... inmensamente más hondo que la capa que ondula."[55] In an attempt to overcome the trivializing connotations of the word *folklore* ("¡hasta tiene nombre extranjero para mayor ignominia!"), Unamuno terms the linguistic manifestation of Spain's inner history "lenguaje soto-literario o intra-literario."[56] The literature of the *pueblo*, he claimed, was the true literature of Spain, although long ignored and deprecated by official historians and scholars:

> Se ignora hasta la existencia de una literatura plebeya, y nadie para
> su atención en las coplas de ciego, en los pliegos de cordel y en los
> novelones de a cuartillo de real la entrega, que sirven de pasto aun
> a los que no saben leer y los oyen.... Y mientras unos importan
> bizantinismos de cascarilla y otros cultivan casticimos librescos,
> alimenta el pueblo su fantasía con las viejas leyendas europeas de los
> ciclos bretón y carolingios, con héroes que han corrido el mundo
> entero, y mezcla a las hazañas de los doce Pares, de Valdovinos o
> Tirante el Blanco, guapezas de José María y heroicidades de nuestras
> guerras civiles.[57]

Throughout his essay, Unamuno stressed the need for looking inward, to the
roots of Spanish culture, simultaneously with the need to look out and abroad, at
the main currents of European culture. "España está por descubrir y sólo la
descubrirán españoles europeizados.... Tenemos que europeizarnos y chapuzarnos
en el pueblo."[58] The double direction he indicates for any investigation of
Spanish reality becomes, by the end of the essay, an impassioned plea for reform
and renovation among the younger generation:

> ¡Ojalá una verdadera juventud, animosa y libre, rompiendo la malla
> que nos ahoga y la monotonía uniforme en que estamos alineados, se
> vuelva con amor a estudiar el pueblo que nos sustenta a todos, y
> abriendo el pecho y los ojos a las corrientes ultrapirenaicas y sin
> encerrarse en capullos casticistas...ni en diferencias nacionales
> excluyentes, avive con la ducha reconfortante de los jóvenes ideales
> cosmopolitas el espíritu colectivo intracastizo que duerme esperando
> un redentor![59]

Members of the Generation of 1927, from a stance firmly situated within
Europe, respond to Unamuno's call for a close examination of the culture of the
"pueblo desconocido" as if they had written it themselves. In selecting out what
is representative of that culture they coincide in good measure with the aesthetic
program of the Institucionistas (Giner de los Ríos, Cossío, and especially Menéndez

Pidal), the scholars and educators whose admiration for the authentic traditional culture of the *pueblo* permeates and determines much of their work.

In general we find a widely disseminated influence of the Institución's recuperation and promotion of traditional popular culture: their discovery of "lo tradicional"—in *pueblo* architecture, the lace-making of Lagartera, Talavera ceramics, and so on—provides an essential environment for much of the activity at the Residencia de Estudiantes and the Instituto Escuela.[60] In identifying "lo tradicional" in the realm of popular traditional poetry, Ramón Menéndez Pidal's inaugural lecture at the Ateneo in 1919 proved to be a pioneering first step, and paved the way for the younger generation's understanding of the hitherto unknown lyrical tradition of the *pueblo*. Entitled *La primitiva poesía lírica española*, the lecture opened the door onto an entirely new field of investigation, stimulating the research interests of linguists and literary scholars for generations to come.[61] In it, Menéndez Pidal traces the origin of lyrical poetry in the Castilian language not to the refined poetry of the medieval aristocracy, but to its roots in poetry of the oral tradition.

Respectfully refuting the opinion of Menéndez Pelayo, who had said "categóricamente que una lírica popular no había existido nunca en España,"[62] he introduces his audience to examples of brief, simple verses, antithetical both in form and content to the studied techniques of the *poetas cultos*: "serranillas," "cánticas del velador o de centinela," "villancicos," "mayas," "canciones de San Juan," "canciones de romería," etc. Among other sources, Menéndez Pidal credits Lope with having preserved the greatest volume of these traditional songs. In Lope's theater, he claims, "hallaremos el más copioso florilegio de lírica popular que jamás fue recogido. Sin el opulento teatro de Lope no conoceríamos la lírica tradicional en toda aquella extensión que le hemos señalado como característica..."[63]

The boldest and most significant aspect of Menéndez Pidal's presentation was his demonstration of an indigenous poetic tradition, in no way influenced by the Italian and Provenzal schools of court poetry. Reversing the direction most often taken by previous scholars (for whom popular poetry was a vestige of *poesía culta*, degenerated through imperfect oral repetition), he argues that a popular lyrical tradition underlies and nourishes the learned tradition:

> No es fácil admitir un completo exotismo en el arte lírico primitivo de un pueblo que tiene muy desarrollado otros órdenes de poesía, y entonces hay que pensar que todo género literario que no sea una mera importación extraña, surge de un fondo nacional cultivado popularmente antes de ser tratado por los más cultos. Algo así como sucede con el lenguaje mismo; empieza por ser meramente oral y vulgar antes de llegar a escribirse y a hacerse instrumento de cultura; en su origen puede sufrir grandes influencias exteriores, pero siempre es una creación propia del pueblo que lo maneja. De igual modo, lo indígena popular está siempre como base de toda la producción literaria de un país.... La sutileza de un estudio penetrante hallará lo popular casi siempre, aun en el fondo de las obras de arte más personal y refinado.[64]

As though in response to Unamuno's charge that the literature of the *pueblo* has been entirely overlooked, Menéndez Pidal calls attention to this body of popular poetry as deserving of a new chapter in literary history:

> En cambio, las formas líricas anteriores, están del todo desatendidas...pues que los eruditos, en general, apenas las mencionan sino alguna vez de pasada. Y, sin embargo, ellas debieran constituir un capítulo en toda historia literaria, y que acabamos de ver cómo en nuestros orígenes poéticos, al lado de la lírica culta de los cancioneros medievales existió una abundante lírica popular.[65]

And, finally, he unknowingly anticipates the role of popular and traditional poetry in the Generation of 1927:

> ¿Y quién sabe si el estudio de esta poesía, tantas veces sentida en común, podría hacer que entre nuestros eximios poetas españoles, más que ningunos encastillados en su magnífica morada interior,

surgiese la meditación fecunda que lanzase alguna vez su inspiración
a guiar los sentimientos colectivos, con audacia renovadora de lo
viejo?[66]

The Ateneo lecture effectively corraborates what Menéndez Pidal had
postulated in an earlier article: that the popular verse forms, of eight and six
syllables or irregular measure, and assonant rhyme, had a deeper and more
enduring influence in Spain than in other European literature.[67] Thus, in his
view, the "línea llanista" is what distinguishes Spain's literary history as a *national*
literature.   Menéndez Pidal's view could have been rejected or ignored by a
generation in the process of leaping the barriers created by nationalistic interests,
but interestingly enough, his view is accepted by the younger scholars. Dámaso
Alonso, for instance, in his lecture at the Ateneo in 1927, retains the concept of
what Menéndez Pidal had termed "la tendencia extremamente popular" in Spanish
literature.[68] But he also amends it by placing equal emphasis on the line of
literary production represented by Góngora, Garcilaso, and Quevedo. The "doble
línea," he insists, is what is truly characteristic of his country's literature, from the
Middle Ages down to his own generation.[69]

The interest in the popular tradition initiated in the late nineteenth century
and defined by the Institucionistas was promoted and handed down through a chain
of institutional relationships during the early years of this century.[70] In 1907,
Giner organized the Junta para Ampliación de Estudios e Investigaciones
Científicas for the purpose of funding young scholars to do research abroad. At
the same time educational reform was planned at home: in 1910 the Residencia
de Estudiantes was founded, modelled after the residential colleges of Oxford
University, to promote a closer exchange of ideas between students and recognized
scholars in a more informal atmosphere than that of the traditional lecture hall.[71]
Shortly thereafter, the Instituto Escuela was established, providing a climate of
progressive secular education at the secondary and elementary levels.[72] Also in
1910 the Centro de Estudios Históricos was founded as a branch of the Junta para
Ampliación de Estudios, initiating a new period of innovative investigation among
scholars in areas as diverse as music, archaeology, philosophy, and history.[73]

As director of the Centro, Menéndez Pidal's theories influenced a wide circle of colleagues, including Américo Castro, Eduardo Martínez Torner, Solalinde, Federico de Onís and Tomás Navarro Tomás. This group, in turn, attracted and shaped the interests of the younger generation of scholars: among them, Jesús Bal, Rafael Lapesa, Dámaso Alonso, Amado Alonso, and José F. Montesinos. The Centro also attracted a number of Hispanists from abroad, such as Karl Vossler, Leo Spitzer, Fritz Krüger, and Marcel Bataillon. In fact, an entire new school grew out of the Centro which is largely responsible for the shape of Hispanic studies today.[74]

The Generation of 1927 thus inherits the rediscovery of Spanish cultural history from the activities of the Institución Libre and the Generation of 1898, by way of the Centro de Estudios Históricos, the Junta para Ampliación de Estudios, and the Residencia de Estudiantes. Américo Castro, for instance, introduced Montesinos to the study of Lope de Vega, and Montesinos, through his contacts at the Residencia de Estudiantes, revolutionized the Generation of 1927's view of their national prodigy. Both Lorca's and Alberti's knowledge of Lope can be traced directly to Montesinos, who later modestly acknowledges his role:

> Tres años después caía en el Centro de Estudios Históricos, donde me enseñaron los métodos rigurosos de la filología moderna, y donde Américo Castro fue mi segundo padre. Andaba él entonces entregado al menester de fomentar la empresa del *Teatro Antiguo Español* y de rehacer la *Vida de Lope de Vega* de Rennert. Castro me lanzó al estudio de Lope, y Lope era uno de los ídolos de mi generación, aunque apenas lo conocía. Lo conoció, en parte, gracias a mí—Dios me perdone la inmodestia. Las *Letras para cantar* de mi edición de Clásicos Castellanos fueron una revelación para muchos.[75]

Although in Havana Alberti does not acknowledge his debt to Montesinos, it is clear he used the *Letras para cantar* as a source for several of the songs illustrating his talk on Lope and contemporary poets. The "Canción de velador" of Alberti's lecture appears, according to Montesinos, in Lope's *Las almenas de Toro*, Part XIV, and in *El nacimiento de Cristo*, Act III:

> Velador que el castillo velas
> vélale bien y mira por ti,
> que velando en él me perdí.
> . . . .

Similarly, Alberti correctly attributes the "Cantar de siega," which Lope uses in Part VII of *El gran duque de Moscovia*,

> Blanca me era yo
> cuando entré en la siega:
> dióme el sol y ya soy morena.
> . . . . [76]

as well as the song of the "Trébol" cited earlier, not to Lope's authorship but to the anonymous authorship of the *pueblo*. "Oid este chorro de agua clara que él, generoso, devuelve, engrandecido, a su pueblo."[77] The "Canción de velador" and the "Canción de siega" were both originally included in Menéndez Pidal's Ateneo lecture as examples of the earliest authentically Castilian lyric.[78]

In the case of the "Trébol," Alberti even repeats the wording of the information Montesinos gives in *Letras para cantar*: "Aun hoy se conservan en Asturias canciones lejanamente relacionados con este tema."[79] Yet here Montesinos did not use Menéndez Pidal's lecture as his source; undoubtedly he had seen Martínez Torner's collection of "Tréboles" from both oral and printed sources.[80] For Alberti, these songs are perfect examples of the adoption of popular lyrics by the *poeta culto*, and of their return to the *pueblo*. In this capacity he also presents a string of "Sevillanas" Montesinos had culled from Lope's theater, but which Alberti prefers to situate in the Madrid of Goya's time, "al mismo tiempo que en la corte se baila el minué."[81]

The points of contact between members of the Generation of 1927 and "Institucionismo" occur throughout a diffuse network of relations at both institutional and personal levels. Lorca's relationship to "Institucionismo" is primarily through his family's friendship with the family of Giner in Granada, as well as indirectly through his association with members of the Centro de Estudios Históricos and his colleagues at the Residencia de Estudiantes. His prolonged stay at the Residencia meant prolonged contact with the ideals and the philosophy of "Institucionismo" as realized through the efforts of Jiménez Fraud. His friendship with Montesinos, both in Granada and in Madrid, is especially important: through Montesinos, Lorca was introduced to Lope's creative artistry in the manipulation of popular, oral material.[82]

Alberti's acquaintance with the Menéndez Pidal family is reinforced by his relationship with María Teresa León, whose mother was a member of María Goyri's family. Like Lorca, however, the more penetrating influences on Alberti came through close peer relationships; for instance, his friendship with Dámaso Alonso, who introduced Alberti to the works of Gil Vicente. "Le tomé mucho cariño. A él le debo muchas cosas. Una, fundamental, sobre todas: me dio a conocer a Gil Vicente, quien todavía refresca mis canciones de estos últimos años."[83] Professionally, Alberti benefited from a travel grant from the Junta para Ampliación de Estudios, which took him to Berlin and to the Soviet Union in 1931–32, so that he could study the latest developments in European theater.[84]

Thus, the nineteenth-century attempts at educational and intellectual reform came to fruition in the Generation of 1927. The spirit of cooperation and creativity that surrounded the Residencia de Estudiantes, for instance, was something entirely new. The coexistence of scholars, poets, painters, educators, archaeologists, musicians, and physicists resulted in a rich exchange and continual intercrossing not only of knowledge, but of ideas and values. These institutional bridges between the Institución Libre and the Residencia explain the continuity between 1898 and 1927. But a discontinuity between these generations is to be found in the younger generation's dissolution of the barriers between learning and art, between scholar and performer, and between professor and poet. And the merging of these distinctions permitted the explosion of creativity that characterizes the years before the Civil War.

The Concept of "lo Popular" in the
Generation of 1927: Points of Departure

The shared continuity in the appreciation of traditional popular culture—in the *romancero* and the lyric as well as in other aspects of the artisan mode of production—spans the Generations of 1898 and 1927. The generation of Alberti and García Lorca, Montesinos and Dámaso Alonso inherits the Generation of 1898's attempt to discover a different Spain, to bring to light the hidden roots of an authentically Spanish culture. With a difference, however: they bring a new emphasis and a different point of departure to the inheritance from their "fathers." Whereas Menéndez Pidal moved toward a reconstruction of the popular lyrical tradition, demonstrating the enduring strength of "lo popular" in Lope's work, a younger scholar such as Montesinos discovers "el Lope artista popular." What interested Menéndez Pidal was the undiluted purity and continuity of the oral tradition as it is preserved in Lope's work. Montesinos sees in "lo popular" the capacity for artistic creativity that the poet Lope displayed in his "recreación" of popular poetry for the stage. Menéndez Pidal uncovered and brought to light the presence of "lo popular en lo culto." Montesinos points to the creative initiative of the "poeta culto" within "el campo de la poesía popular."

Also, unlike their predecessors, members of the Generation of 1927 do not reject, within their concept of "lo popular," what had previously been considered "lo vulgar" in the sober and puritanical aesthetic framework of 1898. Neither do they reject "lo andaluz," which members of the Generation of 1898 had recoiled from as part of their attempt to adopt a more Europeanized (or more Anglicized) standard. As Alberti's lectures show, the new generational program makes room for the bullfight, the gypsy, all the "majeza" of the eighteenth century, and, within the *Romancero tradicional*, the *Romancero vulgar* of common street oratory. They reject the puritan ethic of their fathers and embrace in its stead a playful love of fun and an open sensuality.

Evidence of the more ample and inclusive concept of "lo popular" among Lorca's and Alberti's generation is the "Festival del Cante Jondo," organized by Lorca and Manuel de Falla in 1922. Held in Granada and attended by singers such as Manuel Torre and Pastora Pavón ("La Niña de los Peines"), the Festival demonstrated a new attitude of acceptance of the fusion of the *cante gitano* with folkloric Andalusian song, and thereby dignified an element of popular culture which had been scorned and deprecated by members of 1898. Antonio Mairena describes the exclusion of "lo andaluz" from the Generation of 1898's definition of the popular lyrical tradition:

> Como todo pasa, también pasó la época de los cafés cantantes, y entonces se extendió un inmenso manto negro por encima del cante gitano-andaluz, condenándose su recuerdo con las frases más duras por muchos intelectuales de aquella época, ignorantes por supuesto del cante gitano. Tambíen salió mal parado lo flamenco, que empezó a considerarse como cosa panderetesca. Nadie quería saber nada de ese mundo, que era sinónimo de ambiente más bien encanallado. El silencio se hizo casi total....[85]

The enthusiasm for "los toros," for the song of the gypsy and the blind beggar, for the popular culture of their own day, opens dimensions to the Generation of 1927 that are inconceivable to members of 1898. Especially the challenge, or "embestida," of "el torillo suelto de la poesía popular" was confronted by both Alberti and García Lorca in two entirely new ways: aesthetically as artists, and as part of a joyful affirmation of self. As Alberti confesses in 1935, their initial position vis-à-vis the *pueblo* included the distance of a subject/object relationship ("ese pueblo que antes sólo utilizábamos como tema").[86] Yet their attitude corresponds to an important stage in Spanish history in that an exceptionally prepared group, endowed with educators, scholars, and artists, concur in the task of constructing a new Spain, free of the mediocrity and fettered values imposed by the dominant class. They believe in the Spanish *pueblo*, still "virgin," bearer of a strong and extremely personal cultural tradition. And they believe that this *pueblo*, illuminated ("encandilado") by them, will be the protagonists in the adventure they see unfolding before Spain: to enter fully into the modern world, without the need of having to mould themselves to fit the societies and the literary traditions around them.

Notes

1. In *Prosas encontradas (1924–1942)*, ed. Robert Marrast (Madrid: Ayuso, 1970), pp. 87–103. (In the notes that follow, citations from this lecture are designated 'Berlin.')

2. There is no information about the contents of this lecture, only notice that it took place. See Carlos Morla Lynch, *En España con Federico García Lorca* (Madrid: Aguilar, 1958), pp. 347–348. Also see Marie Laffranque's key study, "Bases cronológicas para el estudio de Federico García Lorca," in *Federico García Lorca*, ed. Ildefonso-Manuel Gil (Madrid: Taurus, 1973), p. 437.

3. *Lope de Vega y la poesía contemporánea, seguido de La pájara pinta*, prologue by Robert Marrast (Paris: Centre de Recherches de l'Institut d'Etudes Hispaniques, 1964), pp. 3–36. (Citations from this lecture are designated 'Havana.')

4. Federico García Lorca, *Obras completas*, III (Madrid: Aguilar, 1986, 22nd edition), pp. 282–300. This work is hereafter cited as *OC*. Information on Lorca's reading at the Residencia can be found in Jorge Guillén's prologue to the *OC*, I, "Federico en persona," p. xliv. For the presentations of this lecture abroad, see Laffranque, "Bases," pp. 429–430, and Daniel Eisenberg, "Dos conferencias lorquianas (Nueva York y La Habana, 1930)" in *Papeles de Son Armadans*, vol. 79, no. 236–237 (1975), pp. 196–212.

5. See Laffranque, "Bases," p. 440 and p. 443. The text of this lecture, including the songs, has been published in Francisco García Lorca's *Federico y su mundo*, ed. Mario Hernández (Madrid: Alianza Editorial, 1980), pp. 471–485.

6. *OC*, III, pp. 306–318. This talk was apparently given only to audiences abroad, first in Havana during the spring of 1930. In Buenos Aires it was given on October 20 and again on November 14, 1933; in Montevideo on February 5, 1934. Laffranque, "Bases," pp. 430, 439, 440, and 443.

7. *OC*, III, pp. 195–216 and 217–222. "El cante jondo" was read in Granada on February 19, 1922.

8. The "Arquitectura del cante jondo" revives the substance of the earlier lecture but is entirely reformulated. According to Eisenberg, p. 199, it was first given in Havana on April 6, 1930. Laffranque's study does not agree. She gives March 30, 1932 as the

date of the first presentation of the lecture in Seville, under the title "Cantos populares andaluces, Arquitectura del cante jondo." See "Bases," p. 433.

9. See Marrast's prologue to *Lope de Vega y la poesía contemporánea*, p. x.

10. According to Carlos Blanco Aguinaga, Julio Rodríguez Puértolas, and Iris M. Zavala, *Historia social de la Literatura española*, II (Madrid: Castalia, 1978), p. 286. In a personal interview (July, 1983), Carlos Blanco added that Alberti's membership in the Communist Party did not become formally official until 1936, the year he started paying dues.

11. María Teresa León, *Memoria de la melancolía* (Buenos Aires: Losada, 1970), pp. 46–47.

12. Jerónimo Pablo González Martín, *Rafael Alberti* (Madrid: Júcar, 1978), p. 106.

13. Marrast's prologue, p. x.

14. The changes Alberti does make to his 1932 lecture are important, however, and will be discussed later.

15. Havana, p. 5.

16. Rafael Alberti, *La arboleda perdida* (Barcelona: Bruguera, 1980), p. 275.

17. Alberti's enthusiasm for the "corrida" was not merely literary. At the invitation of his friend Ignacio Sánchez Mejías, he participated in the "paseíllo" of a "corrida" in Pontevedra. See *La arboleda perdida*, p. 235.

18. Havana, pp. 5–6.

19. Alberti's choice of metaphor is neither capricious nor unique. García Lorca had already used the same analogy to describe his theory of the "duende," the mysterious power that is the culmination of art, not only in the arena where the Andalusian "cante jondo" is sung and danced, but in the arena of the bullfight as well:

> En los toros [el duende] adquiere sus acentos más impresionantes....
> El toro tiene su órbita; el torero, la suya, y entre órbita y órbita un
> punto de peligro donde está el vértice del terrible juego. Se puede
> tener musa con la muleta y ángel con las banderillas y pasar por buen
> torero, pero en la faena de capa, con el toro limpio todavía de
> heridas, y en el momento de matar, se necesita la ayuda del duende
> para dar en el clavo de la verdad artística.

Lorca also warns against the art that is no more than imitation of the authentic:

> El torero que asusta al público en la plaza con su temeridad no torea,
> sino que está en ese plano ridículo, al alcance de cualquier hombre,
> de *jugarse la vida*; en cambio, el torero mordido por el duende da
> una lección de música pitagórica y hace olvidar que tira
> constantamente el corazón sobre los cuernos.

"Juego y teoría del duende," *OC*, III, pp. 316–317.

20. Berlin, p. 87; Havana, p. 6.

21. Alberti apparently had with him a record by Lorca and La Argentinita for his presentation in Berlin. This is clear from passages in his lecture, for example: "La versión que van a oír está acompañada al piano por el poeta granadino Federico García Lorca, del que hablaré dentro de unos momentos, y cantada por una conocida bailadora: 'La Argentinita'," Berlin, p. 88. In Havana he appears to have recited the texts of the song himself.

22. Berlin, p. 89.

23. This was the basic premise of John Meier's *Rezeptiontheorie*, which attempted to discredit the Romantics' notion of the spontaneous origin of "Naturpoesie." However, the idea that the *pueblo* only receives and does not create art was rejected, in turn, by Ramón Menéndez Pidal, *Romancero hispánico (Hispano-portugués, americano y sefardí)*, I (Madrid: Espasa-Calpe, 1968), pp. 28–30. The problem with Meier's theory was also noted by Gordon H. Gerould: "Sensible, too, as far as it went, was his [Meier's] remark that the development of a song in oral circulation determines its character as a folk-song; but unfortunately he made no effort to distinguish between the casual malformation of current songs by people without a homogeneous tradition, and ballads or other genuine folk-songs as moulded by a traditional art. His purpose was wholly destructive, indeed—to show that popular poetry and melody were but warmed-over dishes from the table of the aristocracy, which blinded him to the real significance of the variants he studied with so much zeal." *The Ballad of Tradition* (New York: Oxford University Press, 1957), pp. 166–167.

24. Berlin, p. 87; Havana, p. 7. Emphasis mine.

25. Havana, p. 7.

26. Havana, p. 4. Alberti's use of "aires" here recalls the traditional popular lyrics included in the *Villancicos...y Recopilacíon* of Juan Vásquez in 1560;

> De los álamos vengo, madre,
> de ver cómo los menea el aire.

Included in José María Alín's, *El Cancionero español de tipo tradicional* (Madrid: Taurus, 1968), p. 522. Margit Frenk notes the persistence of these verses in the works of modern poets, citing Blas de Otero's "Canción de amigo":

> De los álamos tengo envidia,
> de ver cómo los menea al aire.

Entre folklore y literatura (México: El Colegio de México, 1971), p. 48.

27. Havana, p. 11.

28. "El cante jondo," *OC*, III, p. 205.

29. Berlin, p. 91; Havana, p. 9.

30. Havana, p. 8.

31. Havana, p. 15.

32. Havana, p. 35.

33. Havana, p. 32. It has often been observed that verses from Lorca's *Romancero gitano* were circulated orally by people who had never heard of the poet.

34. Berlin, p. 90.

35. Berlin, p. 90; Havana, p. 8.

36. Havana, p. 8.

37. Havana, p. 4. Margit Frenk also draws attention to the omnipresent "aire" of traditional lyrics: "el aire, obsesión de esa poesía," in *Entre folklore y literatura*, p. 52.

38. Havana, pp. 4–5.

39. Havana, p. 5.

40. Havana, p. 5.

41. Havana, pp. 5–6.

42. "Federico García Lorca y la expresión de lo español," *Ensayos sobre poesía española* (Madrid: Revista de Occidente, 1944), p. 344.

43. Havana, p. 29.

44. Havana, p. 9.

45. Havana, p. 30.

46. Havana, p. 30.

47. Havana, p. 9.

48. "Labrada" in 1935, probably *per errata*.

49. Berlin, p. 91.

50. Berlin, p. 91.

51. Havana, p. 9.

52. Berlin, p. 95; Havana, p. 25.

53. Berlin, p. 95; Havana, p. 26. García Lorca echoes Alberti during an interview he gave in 1936: "Hay dos maestros: Antonio Machado y Juan Ramón Jiménez." *OC*, III, p. 685.

54. Berlin, p. 96; Havana, p. 27.

55. *En torno al casticismo* (Barcelona: Antonio López, 1902), pp. 55–56.

56. *En torno*, pp. 28–29.

57. *En torno*, p. 204.

58. *En torno*, pp. 204, 206.

59. *En torno*, p. 212.

60. Richard Herr, *An Historical Essay on Modern Spain* (Berkeley: University of California Press, 1971), pp. 124–125.

61. All quotations are from the first edition published by the Ateneo in Madrid, 1919. Also included in Menéndez Pidal's *Estudios literarios* (Madrid: 1920), pp. 255–344.

62. *La primitiva poesía*, p. 9.

63. *La primitiva poesía*, p. 82. Since Menéndez Pidal's signal speech, major collections and studies have appeared, most notably Antonio Sánchez Romeralo's *El villancico. Estudios sobre la lírica popular en los siglos XV y XVI* (Madrid: Gredos, 1969); and Margit Frenk's *Corpus de la antigua lírica popular hispánica (Siglo XV a XVII)* (Madrid: Castalia, 1987).

64. *La primitiva poesía*, pp. 8–9.

65. *La primitiva poesía*, p. 83.

66. *La primitiva poesía*, pp. 84–85.

67. "Algunos carácteres primordiales de la literatura española," *Bulletin Hispanique*, XX, no. 4 (1918), pp. 205–232.

68. "Algunos carácteres primordiales," p. 211.

69. "Escila y Caribdis de la literatura española," *Ensayos sobre poesía española*, pp. 9–27.

70. Manuel Tuñón de Lara, *Medio siglo de cultura española* (Barcelona: Bruguera, 1982), pp. 52–53.

71. The success of the Residencia was due mostly to the work of Jiménez Fraud, a student of Giner, who was married to a daughter of Cossío. A history of the Residencia and its educational philosophy can be found in Alberto Jiménez Fraud, *La Residencia de Estudiantes* (Barcelona: Ariel, 1972). See also the short but highly informative article by William F. Fichter, "A Great Spanish Educational Institution: The Residencia de Estudiantes (1910–1936)," in *Homenaje a Juan López-Morillas*, eds. J. Amor y Vázquez and David A. Kossoff (Madrid: Castalia, 1982), pp. 209–220.

72. For the relationship between the Junta and the Residencia and the Instituto Escuela, see José Castillejo, *Wars of Ideas in Spain* (London: John Murray, 1937), pp. 113–131.

73. José-Carlos Mainer, *La Edad de Plata (1902–1939)*, 2nd ed. (Madrid: Catédra, 1981), pp. 88–89.

74. This intricate network of scholarly relationships deserves a separate study unto itself. For an introduction, see Rafael Lapesa, "Menéndez Pidal, creador de escuela: el Centro de Estudios Históricos," in *¡Alça la voz, pregonero! Homenaje a Don Ramón Menéndez Pidal* (Madrid: Catédra Seminario Menéndez Pidal y la Corporación de Antiguos Alumnos de la Institución Libre de Enseñanza, 1979), pp. 43–79.

75. In a letter to Joseph Silverman, published in José F. Montesinos, *Ensayos y estudios de literatura española*, ed. Joseph H. Silverman (México: Ediciones de Andrea, 1959), pp. 5–6.

76. Havana, pp. 10–11. The *Letras para cantar* are included in Lope de Vega, *Poesías líricas*, I, ed. José F. Montesinos (Madrid: Clásicos Castellanos, 1925), pp. 133–134.

77. Havana, p. 10.

78. *La primitiva poesía*, pp. 53—54.

79. *Letras para cantar*, p. 39.

80. See Eduardo Martínez Torner, *Lírica hispánica: Relaciones entre lo popular y lo culto* (Madrid: Editorial Castalia, 1966), pp. 19—22.

81. Cf. Havana, p. 23, and *Letras para cantar*, pp. 160—162. In the Berlin lecture, Alberti played a variation of these "Sevillanas" as recorded by Lorca and La Argentinita.

82. Lorca's "Baladilla de los tres ríos," which opens the *Poema del cante jondo* (*OC*, I, pp. 153—154), was directly inspired by Lope's enthusiastic use of "¡Ay, río de Sevilla, / cuán bien pareces, / con galeras blancas / y ramos verdes!" See Montesinos, *Letras para cantar*, p. 160, and his commentary, pp. 40—42. Alberti also attributes the poem's gestation to Lope in *Imagen primera de...* (Madrid: Ediciones Turner, 1975), p. 23.

83. *La arboleda perdida*, p. 141.

84. According to a personal interview with Gonzalo Menéndez Pidal (August, 1982), the purpose of the grant was to study the dramatic theories and works of contemporary playwrights such as Brecht, Pirandello, and Piscator. The idea was to establish a travelling theater group, under the direction of Alberti and María Teresa León, to perform these works of the European avant-garde theater throughout Spain. Conceived as an adjunct to "La Barraca," which performed works of the classical theater under Lorca's direction, the project was never realized, unfortunately.

85. *Las confesiones de Antonio Mairena*, ed. Alberto García Ulecia (Sevilla: Universidad de Sevilla, 1976), p. 29. In 1980 Antonio Mairena received an award from the Cátedra Seminario Menéndez Pidal for his life-long dedication to the preservation of the authentic *gitano-andaluz* tradition.

86. Havana, p. 36. It is clear that by 1935 Alberti begins to envision himself and the other writers of his generation as subjects.

2

The Experience of Traditional Poetry
between Author and Audience

Concurrent with the Generation of 1927's discovery of Lope and Gil Vicente as masters of traditional lyricism is their discovery of this poetry's dramatic use. The theater of Gil Vicente and Lope not only provides a "field" for the collection of "romancillos, letrillas y cantares" (which is to regard them as individual poems or an assortment of aesthetic objects), it also offers a potential model for the exploitation of the plastic qualities inherent in this type of poetry for the stage. For members of the Generation of 1927 the lesson of Gil Vicente and Lope is the discovery of the innate "dramaticity" of traditional poetry. From an initial aesthetic appreciation of lyricism, shared by members of 1898, they move progressively towards uncovering its dramatic possibilities.

The Dramatic Potential of Popular
Lyric and Narrative Poetry

The dramatic force of traditional poetry springs from its particular method of representation. Perhaps the most distinctive quality of the poetry of oral tradition that we are beginning to understand is the inherent dramatism of the word itself, thanks not just to the constant participation of dialogue in both the *romance* and the lyric, but to the ability to envelop the listener in concrete representation.

Among the various lyric and narrative modes, the method of popular poetry is to select those which actualize. In the case of the Romancero, the ballad's capacity for dramatizing an event depends to some extent on a high proportion of direct dialogue, which suppresses the exterior and possibly intrusive presence of a narrator, and leaves the listener directly exposed to the words of the characters themselves.[1] An even more basic feature is its propensity for visualization of the event. The *romance* brings the events of the narration into the present, and represents them. Diego Catalán has noted the innate dramaticity of the ballad method of representation:

> El primer nivel de articulación lingüistica con que tropezamos es, claro está, la estructura verbal actualizadora.... En el siguiente nivel, quizá el más definitorio a la hora de describir "poéticamente" el Romancero, los romances manifiestan un contenido narrativo, una "historia", a través de un "discurso" doblemente articulado: a. métricamente; b. dramáticamente.... Creo preciso subrayar la importancia de la articulación dramática: el discurso romancístico, aunque no pueda ser definido como mimético, utiliza preferentemente un modo de representación escencialmente dramático. Los relatos pretenden hacernos asistir a la transformación de un antes en un después; reproducen, reactualizándolo, el discurrir del tiempo.[2]

By visualizing the event, we—as listeners—are made to attend the scene, to participate as actual witnesses. The *romance* technique is not so much to narrate the events as to verbally stage them, to portray them as taking place. In this regard the *romance* operates selectively. Its method is not to "tell" but to "show," not to represent the whole spectrum of events in a logical and chronological sequence (although in the mind of the listener, this logical chain of events can be reconstructed), but to select out certain scenes capable of carrying intense symbolized meaning, and, within them even, to focus on particular detail. This close-up permits the representation of a generalized value through the portrayal of a concrete one. Concretization can be seen, for instance, in "Los mozos de

Monleón," a ballad included in the *Cancionero salmantino* of Dámaso Ledesma, which García Lorca put to harmony and performed with the dancer, La Agentinita:

> Compañeros, yo me muero;
> amigos, yo estoy muy malo;
> tres pañuelos tengo dentro
> y éste que meto son cuatro.[3]

Instead of narrating the scene in which the bull has gored him, the *romance* concretizes the meaning of "mortally wounded" into a ritualized description of the size and severity of the wound. This visualized description of the wound (or its equivalent) can be found in a number of different ballads. Linguistically it will vary widely (the wound can be large enough to let a bird fly through, or for the sun or moon to shine through, etc.), but the level of signification remains the same. The ballad's method of representation is to single out a series of actions and to concretize the narrative in them, deemphasizing the explicative tissue between.[4]

On the other hand, the lyric of oral tradition concerns itself, by definition, not with the development of a story through a series of scenes, but with the representation of emotional and psychological events. Its methods largely parallel those of the narrative, however, in that it seeks out a plastic realization of these events. It seeks to portray inner realities through the terms of exterior landscapes and visualizable acts. Metaphor is generally eschewed in favor of that which is lived and perceived directly. With regard to the early traditional lyrics, Margit Frenk has observed:

> Varían los temas, cambia el tono. Lo permanente es esa expresión directa y clara, sin segundas intenciones, aunque no siempre sin misterio. Por eso la imagen, si se da, suele ser evocación de una realidad tangible, directamente percibida por los sentidos....[5]

This power of concrete, visual representation is inherent in the word itself. Yet what I choose to call the innate "dramaticity" of this poetry consists of two aspects: first, as we have seen, its method of narration—presenting lived experience, and bringing it into the present—which is dramatic in itself; second, its orality, performance, and distinct mode of communication in the relation author/ audience as mediated by the dramatic work. This double capacity is what interested Lope and Gil Vicente, and explains why their theatrical work is not merely a box of random possibilities, but a model of how to use this poetry dramatically, in all its four dimensions—voice, volume, color and movement.

The poetry of oral tradition lends itself particularly well to theatrical exploitation due to its potential plasticity. *Poesía culta* has historically depended on print (or manuscript, until the late fifteenth century) for its propagation, and through the print medium both the acts of emission and reception of the literary text become progressively isolated phenomena.[6] But popular and traditional poetry has depended primarily on the oral/audial mode of transmission. First, and most obviously, popular poetry is song, and is meant to be sung. In addition to the spatial dimension of melody, it brings with it a rhythmical dimension written poetry cannot achieve. Sung, recited, even danced at times,[7] it thus possesses a voice, volume, color and action unknown to poetry destined to private reading.

It cannot be overstressed that the popular poetry of oral transmission shares with theater their common nature of collective art—they are meant to be performed and received collectively. Since the inherent qualities of sound, movement, and color are capable of being theatrically expressed, the magnification of these qualities on stage transforms the poetry into "espectáculo," into public three-dimensional display appealing to the eye and ear simultaneously. From the beginning, theater has recognized this potential of popular, traditional song, and has claimed it as a rightful part of the theatrical experience.

The Integration of Popular Poetry in the Theatrical Representation of the Siglo de Oro

When Gil Vicente and Lope are composing for the public, whether at court or in the open-air "corrales," theater is still celebrative. The distinction between "autor" and "actor" and "auto/acto" is barely visible. The performance and the attendance of a theatrical act is a type of celebration in J. L. Styan's sense of the term, and the barriers between the act of emission and reception of a text have only barely been raised.[8]

The affinity between theater, popular festivals, and folklore goes back to early medieval theatrical representations, when the enactment of religious scenes moved from the steps of the Church out to the street. During the sixteenth century, the theater of Spain develops a combination of elements, in varying proportions, which are not in themselves strictly dramatic but which belong rather to the popular tradition of festivals and *espectáculos* of the times: songs, dances, and folkloric rituals. As theater developed and met with increasing success, these popular extra elements became vitally important.

The extent to which dramatic works, as such, integrated the ingredients of popular tradition varied greatly. Certainly the nonexistence of the stage as we now know it greatly facilitated the incorporation of external elements, whether the work was destined for the private chambers at court or the platforms in public squares and "corrales." The musicians who played and sang behind a blanket hung on a cord (which served as a backdrop to define the stage space) could just as easily come out in front and join in the scene being represented.[9] The absence of heavy sets and props allowed a different scene to take place immediately, or even the representation of something totally unrelated to the previous scene, such as the performance of a dance and song then currently in favor. The absence of walls and a roof permitted a plastic expansion into the surrounding space, and a softening of the divisions between the stage and the audience. The internal dramatic structure of a work was correspondingly much more flexible and the script itself more porous. And it is important to remember that the theater of popular poetry is open-air theater: its borders are not rigidly fixed at any level. Even when represented indoors in the private residences of the nobility or the royalty, members of the audience would, on occasion, participate in the play. The utilization of popular lyrics and ballads was the way to inject song into a spoken work and thus maintain the fundamentally festive nature of theater.

As the public appetite for theater increased during the late sixteenth and early seventeenth centuries, the utilization of popular poetry and song bifurcated into separate branches. One branch relegated the elements of folklore and song to positions outside and in between the acts of the more serious *comedia*. The other branch allowed the popular material to penetrate the dramatic text and there to absorb a dramatic function. From the first branch grew the *teatro menor*, which outlived the *comedia* and survived as the *sainete* of the eighteenth century, and the *género chico* of the nineteenth and early twentieth centuries.

The *teatro menor* thrived in the interstices of the *comedia*, giving rise to an impressive array of genres and subgenres which took place in the "parenthesis" of the principal play.[10] Whereas the term *comedia* was used for almost any work of substantial length, the briefer pieces received a rich and varied nomenclature: *entremés, loa, baile, representación graciosa, sainete, jácara, mojiganga, fin de fiesta,* etc. The distinction between one and the other was often vague, as songs, dances, humor, popular sayings, games and celebrations pervaded them all. They could be performed before, during, and at the conclusion of the *comedia* proper, which was itself only one of the components of the total performance function. The commonality of these brief eruptions of sound and color and collective movement derives from their value as "espectáculo," and "fiesta," as the reciprocal celebration of a cultural heritage through performance.

Of all the ways in which the *entremés* and its related forms enrich the *comedia* of the Siglo de Oro, I wish only to emphasize its recourse to the ingredients of traditional folklore, whether narrative, lyric, choreographic, or musical. The briefest of stage directions ("Salen cantando," "Bailan todos," "Saca cada uno su trompeta," "Salen los músicos cantando y todos los más que pudieren acompañando"), followed by the texts of simple songs, preserve for us some notion of the wealth and liveliness of that traditional, ephemeral heritage.

Though the *entremés, romance representado,* etc., developed a strict autonomy in relation to the *comedia*, the second branch of the theater of popular poetry sees the incorporation of this material into the dramatic work itself. The theater of the Siglo de Oro is forever bursting into song. Its varied metric and also nonmetric capacities allowed for the inclusion of songs and dance, at times as mere adornment, at times as interludes to the dramatic action. As the century progresses we see a greater integration of popular material into the fabric of the *comedia*. The songs begin to complement a character; the ballads begin to reveal information important to our understanding of the plot.

It is well known that both Gil Vicente and Lope were masters at integrating popular material into the dramatic actions of their plays. What appears to modern readers of printed versions of their plays as short lines of simple verse is, in the actual staging, an explosion into sound, color, volume, and movement, as the verses are sung (and usually danced as well) throughout numerous weddings, baptisms and feast scenes. Yet it should be emphasized that their techniques involved much more than the simple presentation of a song or dance at appropriate intervals. At moments they arrive at the construction of a play *out* of the songs and poetry so familiar to their audience. For a focussed demonstration of just how Lope and Gil Vicente appropriated traditional poetry for the stage, "The Lesson of the Theater of Gil Vicente and Lope de Vega" in the Appendix.

Both García Lorca and Alberti admired Gil Vicente's and Lope's ability to squeeze out the inherent dramaticity of popular songs and to establish a special communication, alive and direct, with their audiences. Yet their admiration in no way precludes their attraction to "lo popular" of their own immediate milieu, nor does it mean that without the model represented by these masters they would be unable to experiment with the possibilities of communicating directly with an audience through personal performance. However, as we shall see, the theatrical art of Gil Vicente and Lope helped them to comprehend more accurately the distinctive artistry of popular, or artisan, literature.

Lorca: From Song to Performance

The renewed interest in traditional popular poetry, commencing with the pioneer research of scholars such as Menéndez Pidal, Montesinos, and Henríquez Ureña, has tended to reinforce the concept of this material as literary text. But for Lorca, this poetry is first and foremost *canción*, as it was for the early compilers of *cancioneros* in the late fifteenth and early sixteenth centuries. Lorca's natural love of traditional popular song antedates his literary expression, and explains the development of a major part of his mature artistic production. From his earliest contacts with popular song derive his private performances of these songs on the piano, which give rise, in time, to the "canto en público" and theatrical performance.

Lorca's early gift for music has been noted by many of his commentators. According to his brother Francisco, the poet could sing before he could speak. "Aunque fue precoz en el hablar, la música precedió en él a la palabra. Entonaba canciones con singular afinación antes de poder articular sonidos....podía repetir, antes de poder hablar, cualquier melodía que se le cantase."[11] Francisco further relates how his brother learned "canciones, romances y melodías populares" from different women who served in the García Lorca family when Federico and Francisco were children.[12] Today, as then and probably always, women, from *pueblos* and *aldeas*, at times illiterate or uneducated, are usually the active bearers of the oral tradition. Lorca noticed the predominant role of women in the chain of oral transmission, and in his lecture, "Las nanas infantiles," he described it thus:

> El niño rico tiene la nana de la mujer pobre, que le da al mismo tiempo, en su cándida leche silvestre, la médula del país. Estas nodrizas, juntamente con las criadas y otras sirvientas más humildes, están realizando hace mucho tiempo la importantísima labor de llevar el romance, la canción y el cuento a las casas de los aristócratas y los burgueses. Los niños ricos saben de Gerineldo, de don Bernardo, de Tamar, de los amantes de Teruel, gracias a estas admirables criadas y nodrizas....[13]

At home Lorca learned to play the guitar from his aunt, and later at school, the piano. In 1920 he met and became friends with Manuel de Falla, who exerted a strong influence on his musical education. We have noted that in 1922 he collaborated with Falla in organizing the "Festival del Cante Jondo" in Granada. But whereas Falla's interest in popular music was placed in the service of his interests as a learned composer, for Lorca the attraction of popular music *sui generis* was primary.

> Al ya citado interés por la canción infantil, fondo de su propia
> infancia, se va a añadir, con importancia creciente, la afición por la
> música folklórica.... Llega un momento, que sería necesario fijar
> cronológicamente, en que la inspiración de tipo popular es lo que le
> interesa predominantemente, casi con exclusión de la música
> culta....[14]

Lorca's numerous performances of popular song developed out of his custom of playing and singing for his family at home in Granada. These private recitals widened to include a circle of friends during his stays at the Residencia de Estudiantes, from 1919 to 1928. During this period his repertoire of songs widened, too, from the Andalusian songs learned directly to songs taken from printed collections, most notably the *Cancionero popular de Burgos* (1903) of Federico Olmeda, the *Cancionero salmantino* (1907) of Dámaso Ledesma, the *Cancionero musical popular español* (1919 ss.) of Felipe Pedrell, and Eduardo Martínez Torner's *Cancionero musical de la lírica popular asturiana* (1920). The exact number of songs Lorca knew by heart has never been determined. According to his brother, "La extraordinaria retentiva de Federico llegó a hacer de él un depositario incalculable de canciones populares."[15] Unfortunately, only a few of the songs he knew, including traditional songs of his own arrangement, have been included in what posterity has come to consider the *obra* of García Lorca.[16]

Lorca's enthusiasm for popular song was shared by a number of people at the Residencia, who identified in these nameless songs something akin to a national treasure. Eventually the renewed appreciation for this art became a hallmark for the entire generation. Alberti's recall of Lorca's performances, for instance, transcends mere anecdote:

> En todas partes García Lorca encontraba un piano. Uno grande, de
> cola, estuvo siempre abierto para el poeta en la sala de cursos y
> conferencias de aquella casa madrileña de los estudiantes. Si existe
> aún, y hoy levantáramos su tapa, veríamos que guarda años enteros
> de melodías romancescas y canciones de España. La voz, las manos
> de Federico están enterradas en su caja sonora. Porque Federico era
> el cante (poesía de su pueblo) y el canto (poesía culta); es decir,

Andalucía de lo *jondo*, popular, y la tradición sabia de nuestros viejos cancioneros. Aunque en casi todos los poetas contemporáneos del Sur, con Antonio Machado y Juan Ramón Jiménez a la cabeza, pueda encontrarse esta misma veta, este recuperado hilillo de agua transparente, es García Lorca quien con más fuerza y continuidad representa esta línea.... Federico cantaba y se acompañaba, en ese piano que para él se abría en todas partes, con un gusto y una gracia muy suyos, reinventando las melodías y palabras semiolvidadas de esos cantos y cantes, sustituyendo las fallas de su memoria con añadidos de su invención. Es decir, era una fuente de poesía popular, que manaba con el mismo chorro, lleno de torceduras, ausencias e interrupciones, que el verdadero que alimenta la memoria del pueblo. Aquel piano de cola, en aquel íntimo rincón de la Residencia... recordará mejor que nadie la capacidad asombrosa de transformación, de recreación, de adueñamiento de lo de nadie y lo de todos, haciéndolo materia propia, que, como un Lope de Vega, poseía Federico...[17]

Although still informal, the song fests at the Residencia provided Lorca with a larger notion of audience than he had known before, and gave him his first experiences of performing in public.

At the Residencia Lorca also put his talent into the performance of classical works, but his demeanor underwent a profound change when he played the music he loved best. José Moreno Villa's detailed description of Lorca's informal recitals makes note of the energy engendered through the direct, immediate contact of the "autor/actor" with his "público" through the medium of traditional song.

Nos reuníamos el en salón de conferencias de la Residencia de Estudiantes o en alguno de nuestros cuartos; en el de [Emilio] Prados, en el de Federico y en el de [Pepín] Bello, más comunmente.... En el salón estaba el piano; en los cuartos, la guitarra.... Después de tocar Chopin, o Schubert o Mozart, Debussy, Ravel o Falla, este viejo amigo que hoy lo recuerda le pedía que se metiese de lleno con las tonadillas del XVIII, que iba coleccionando en sus viajes por Andalucía. ¡Qué maravillosa transfiguración se operaba en él y repercutía en nosotros! Ya no miraba las teclas. Levantaba la cabeza, cambiada la mirada, de perdida en picante, de divagada en precisa, quebraba hacia atrás la cintura, alargaba los brazos, sonreía con su gran boca iluminada y cantaba aquello de "Corre que te pillo, corre que te alcanzo, corre que te lleno, la cara de barro." Y después, todas esas que arregló para la Argentinita y corren en discos por el mundo.[18]

Most striking in this description is Lorca's deep, physical engagement with the songs and his obvious enjoyment in performing them for and with his friends. Indeed, Lorca continued to carve out and captivate new audiences throughout this period. In Sitges, in 1927, he included Catalan popular songs among the rest. A member of the gathering recalls:

Evidentemente, el poeta andaluz tenía gusto, cultura e inteligencia.... Pero lo que constituyó el colofón de mi deslumbramiento fue su erudición excepcional de música y folklore.... Nuestra admiración se desbordó cuando nos habló del folklore popular de nuestro país. Tocaba una tonadilla y, girando sobre la banqueta, se volvía hacia el auditorio y nos explicaba sus orígenes con toda clase de detalles.... Después pasó a ilustrarnos sobre el cancionero castellano.... Pasó revista también al folklore gallego, pero la sorpresa fue cuando empezó a hablarnos del nuestro, del catalán.... Para asombro y vergüenza nuestra, ninguno de nosotros conocía enteras las letras de las canciones catalanas. Nos arrancábamos todos, coreando las primeras estrofas, pero al final Federico se quedaba solo.[19]

Along with his vast knowledge of popular song, we see here another instance of the celebrative and participatory aspects of Lorca's art, which later so largely shapes his dramatic production.

These testimonies also document the next stage in Lorca's growing experience with the innate dramatism of popular song and its performance before an ever-widening audience. His friends at the Residencia urged him to "cantar todo eso en público,"[20] which well may have contributed to his collaboration with the renowned actress-dancer, La Argentinita, whom Lorca had first met at a small "pensión" when he arrived in Madrid in 1918. La Argentinita danced the role of the "mariposa blanca" in the first play Lorca staged in Madrid, *El maleficio de la mariposa*, which opened at the Teatro Eslava in March, 1920.[21]

Lorca's Collaboration with La Argentinita

Out of the impromptu recitals and general ambience of enthusiasm for "lo popular" at the Residencia de Estudiantes, the idea emerged for a recording of traditional popular songs. The three records, entitled *Colección de canciones populares antiguas*, included in notes that the songs were "transcritas y armonizadas por Federico García Lorca," and sung by La Argentinita "con acompañamiento de piano de Federico García Lorca."[22] According to Mario Hernández, the recording was made in 1931,[23] as a corollary to Lorca's increasing collaboration with La Argentinita following his stay in New York during the fall and winter of 1929–30.

Although New York surrounded Lorca with a radically different environment, alien to his senses and temperament, it does not seem to have altered his customary spontaneous performance of popular song. Wherever he was, if there was a piano, he was at home:

> Pero estamos ahora en Nueva York, en una *wild party*, por el capricho de un millonario americano: dispersión total por los amplios salones en pequeños grupos gesticulantes, donde los brebajes empiezan a producir su efecto. De repente, aquella masa alocada y disgregada se polariza hacia un piano. ¿Qué ha ocurrido? Federico se ha puesto a tocar y cantar canciones españolas. Aquella gente no sabe español ni tiene la menor idea de España. Pero es tal la fuerza de su expresión, que en aquellos cerebros tan lejanos se abre la luz que no han visto nunca y en sus corazones muerde el suave amargo que no han conocido.[24]

While living at Columbia University, Lorca enjoyed the company of a group of Spaniards, including Angel del Río, Federico de Onís, León Felipe, and Dámaso

Alonso, who was a visiting professor at Hunter College that year. Andrés Segovia and other artists also passed through New York at that time. But for my purpose, the most important friendship was the one that developed between Lorca and La Argentinita. "Intimó mucho aquel año con La Argentinita y con Ignacio Sánchez Mejías, que pasaron una larga temporada en Nueva York. Ayudando a la Argentinita a armonizar alguna canción para su repetorio, surgió la idea de una colaboración más estrecha."[25]

The title of the recordings, *Colección de canciones populares antiguas*, is somewhat misleading, since the majority of the songs included were collected from the modern oral tradition. The series includes ten songs. Four of these *canciones* Lorca learned as a boy from "gente del campo" in rural Granada: "Los cuatro muleros," "Las tres hojas," the "Romance de los pelegrinitos," and "El café de Chinitas." These, according to Federico de Onís, are among those

> que había aprendido de niño en Granada y que eran allí conocidas por todo el mundo...todas ellas son auténticamente populares y proceden del fondo común de la tradición popular granadina. Muchas de ellas son canciones del corro que cantaban las niñas en la misma ciudad de Granada. Las hemos podido recoger en discos fonográficos, de personas ancianas que no podían tener conocimiento de la labor musical de Lorca.[26]

The origin of these songs in the oral tradition of Granada can be demonstrated in the case of the "Romance de los pelegrinitos." Furthermore, in regard to this ballad, the fidelity of García Lorca's text to the one he heard can be studied in detail, since several versions of the *romance*, proceeding from diverse regions in Spain, are conserved in the Menéndez Pidal Archives.[27]

Traditional versions of the "Romance de los pelegrinos" tend to be spicier than Lorca's versions. Compare, for example, this version from Vierdes, Riaño (León), recited by Mónica Grande, and copied down by Menéndez Pidal himself in 1909,

Para Roma caminan   dos peregrinos,
hijos de dos hermanos   carnales primos.
De plumaje muy fino   lleva el sombrero
y el peregrino hermoso   de terciopelo.
Por las calles de Roma   van preguntando
donde estaba la silla   del Padre Santo.
Llegaron a la silla,   se arrodillaron:
—Como primos carnales,   señor, pecamos.
El Padre Santo dice: —No es maravilla,
que es hermosa en extremo   la pelegrina.
El peregrino hermoso,   desque oyó eso,
por cima del costazo   le tiró un beso.
El Padre Santo dice,   aunque es un santo:
—Quién tuviera licencia   para otro tanto.
El Padre Santo dice: —Váigase a acostar,
que a la peregrinita   quiero confesar.
El peregrino dice: —No estoy cansado,
que a la peregrinita   quiero a mi lado.
Les echó de penitencia   a los dos amantes
que fueran a Palencia   ensin hablarse.
Llegaron a Palencia,   nació una niña
y de nombre le ponen   Rosa María.[28]

with the text popularized by Lorca:

Hacia Roma caminan   dos pelegrinos,
a que los case el Papa   porque son primos.
Sombrerito de hule   lleva el mozuelo,
y la pelegrinita,   de terciopelo.
Al pasar por el puente   de la Victoria,
tropezó la madrina,   cayó la novia.
Al llegar a palacio   suben arriba,
y en la sala del Papa   los desaminan.
Le ha preguntado el Papa   cómo se llaman.
El le dice que Pedro   y ella que Ana.
Le ha preguntado el Papa   que qué edad tienen.

> Ella dice que quince   y él diecisiete.
> Le ha preguntado el Papa   de dónde eran.
> Ella dice de Cabra   y él de Antequera.
> Le ha preguntado el Papa   que si han pecado.
> Ella dice que un beso   que él le había dado.
> Y la pelegrinita   que es vergonzosa,
> se le ha puesto la cara   como una rosa.
> Y ha respondido el Papa   desde su cuarto:
> —¡Quién fuera pelegrino   para otro tanto!
> Las campanas de Roma   ya repicaron
> porque los pelegrinos   ya se han casado.[29]

The contrast between these two texts cannot be traced to the poet's intervention. If we look at a multiplicity of texts from different regions, we see that versions from the South of the peninsula differ remarkably from the narrative's dominant form in the North and East of Spain. In the latter, there is no emphasis on either the age or the homeland of the pilgrims. Rather the motive for the pilgrimage is clearly the incestuous relationship between the two cousins. For example, in a version from Salamanca published by Ledesma, the pilgrims confess, saying, "Padre Santo, pecamos, / primos hermanos."[30] But in the South, typically, we find:

> Ha preguntado el Papa   la edad que tienen.
> —Yo tengo quince años   y él diez y siete.[31]

Also, versions from the South stress the innocence of the young girl. For instance, this one from Málaga:

> En medio del camino   dice el mozuelo:
> —¡Peregrina del alma,   cuánto te quiero!
> Y a la peregrinita,   de vergonzosa,
> se le puso la cara   como una rosa.

In Sevilla the "sin" which they confess is expressed euphemistically, while at the same time the family relationship is emphasized:

> Ha preguntado el Papa   que si han pecado.
> —Al pasar el arroyo   le di la mano.[32]

In a revision from Antequera, the meaning of the "slip" in the stream is interpreted further:

> —Al pasar el arroyo   le di la mano.
> —Dile a tu madre   que haga la cama
> que la pelegrinita   ya está casada.[33]

In general, traditional versions from the South do differ from Lorca's text in two important details: the birth of a child (on the pilgrims' arrival, or even "en medio de la sala"), and the shameless corruption of the Papal court. For example, in the version from Sevilla we find:

> El sobrino del Papa   hacía señas
> a la peregrinita   que no se fuera.
> El demonio 'el muchacho,   como es travieso,
> en medio de la sala   le ha dado un beso.
> Ha respondido el Papa   desde lo alto:
> —¡Quién tuviera esa dicha   para otro tanto!
> —Peregrinita mía,   vámonos de aquí,
> que, por lo que yo veo,   me quedo sin ti.
> Si no me casa usía,   me casa el cielo,
> estos ojitos negros   son pa su dueño.[34]

The absence of these motifs in Lorca's version could be attributed to an attempt by the poet to "purify" the traditional text and thereby render it more exquisite. However, it is very likely that the version Lorca knew was similar to this one, collected by J. Marqués Merchán from a nineteen-year-old girl in Málaga:

Hacia Roma caminan   dos peregrinos,
a que los case el Papa   porque son primos.
Sombrerito de hule   lleva el romero
y la peregrinita   de terciopelo.
En medio del camino   dice el mozuelo:
—¡Peregrina del alma,   cuánto te quiero!
Y a la peregrinita,   de vergonzosa,
se le puso la cara   como una rosa.
Ya la peregrinita   no bebe vino,
porque le da vergüenza   del peregrino.
Llegan, al fin, a Roma,   suben arriba,
y en la sala del medio   los examinan.
El Papa les pregunta   que qué edad tienen.
Ella dice que quince   y él diez y nueve.
El Papa les pregunta   que de qué tierra.
Ella dice de Cabra   y él de Lucena.
Les echa el Padre Santo   de penitencia,
que no se den el habla   hasta Venecia.
Las campanas de Roma   suenan cascadas,
porque la peregrina   ya está casada.

Nevertheless, other versions from the South retain the more serious notion of the sin. For example, a version from Granada, which begins, "Hacia Belén caminan dos peregrinos," describes the young girl's shame:

Al pasar un arroyo   le dio la mano
y la peregrinita   se ha avergonzado.
Y el peregrinito   le nota a la moza
que se le ha puesto   la cara como una rosa.

Once the text is fixed by Lorca, however, the normal variations created through oral circulation cease. But the song still continues to be susceptible to minor changes.[35]

Lorca's fidelity to the oral tradition (as we have seen in the text of "Los pelegrinitos") does not presuppose that he would always, systematically reject any opportunity to intervene in the process of popular creation. The case of "El Café de Chinitas" reveals the other facet of the artist's collaboration with the *pueblo*.

The title of this song refers to a "café cantante" in Málaga which was very popular in the mid-nineteenth century. According to Francisco García Lorca, a great-uncle, also named Federico, performed at the Café de Chinitas as a professional *bandurrista*.[36] An uncle from the next generation taught the song to Lorca:

> En el Café de Chinitas
> dijo Paquiro a su hermano:
> soy más valiente que tú,
> más torero y más gitano.
>
> En el Café de Chinitas
> dijo Paquiro a Frascuelo:
> soy más valiente que tú,
> más gitano y más torero.
>
> Sacó Paquiro el reló
> y dijo de esta manera:
> Este toro ha de morir
> antes de las cuatro y media.
>
> Al dar las cuatro en la torre
> se salieron del Café
> y era Paquiro en la calle
> un torero de cartel.[37]

Actually the last strophe, which is now perhaps the best known, is an example of the creative side of the traditional process. The entire strophe was added spontaneously during the recording session by Ignacio Sánchez Mejías, in order to fill the remaining time on the record.[38]

According to Onís, these and other songs on the record seem to have derived from an old strain of Andalusian song that, at the end of the eighteenth and beginning of the nineteenth centuries, takes on new life and complexity due, in part, to the influence of Latin American imports. Such is the case with the "Zorongo gitano," and "Anda jaleo" (also known as "El contrabandista"), both of which Lorca introduced in his theater.[39] The "Sevillanas del siglo XVIII" also reflect the new fusion of the old tradition with exterior influences.[40]

Two of the recorded *canciones* Lorca doubtlessly learned from printed song books: "Los mozos de Monleón" from Ledesma's collection from the province of Salamanca, published in 1907,[41] and "Las tres morillas" from Barbieri's 1890 edition of the *Cancionero musical [de Palacio] de los siglos XV y XVI*,[42] a late fifteenth-century collection of works performed in the court of the Catholic Kings. La Argentinita's rendition of "Los mozos de Monleón" is half sung and half recited, to break up the monotony of the same melody repeated throughout the long narratuve chain, even though this repetition is distinctive of traditional folk performance.

As noted earlier, Alberti carried the record made by Lorca and La Argentinita to Berlin in order to illustrate his talk on contemporary Spanish poets in 1932. Five of the ten recorded songs are cited in the text of Alberti's lecture/demonstration. As an example of a "canción maravillosa, perfecta...escrita indudablemente por un poeta culto, es decir, por un hombre que tiene conciencia de su arte," Alberti has his audience listen first to "Las tres morillas":

> Tres morillas me enamoran
> en Jaén,
> Axa, Fátima y Marién,
> Tres morillas tan garridas
> iban a coger olivas
> y hallábanlas cogidas
> en Jaén,
> Axa, Fátima y Marién.
> . . . .[43]

To illustrate the continuing but underground existence of "lo popular" during the late eighteenth century, he plays Lorca and La Argentinita's lively rendition of the

"Sevillanas," emphasizing the contrast between them and the music accepted at court. "A la par que en la corte se baila el minué, por las plazuelas de los barrios bajos saltan las zarabandas, las chaconas, los buleros, las tonadillas, y...estas sevillanas."

> ¡Qué bien pareces,
> ay río de Sevilla,
> qué bien pareces,
> lleno de velas blancas
> y ramos verdes!
> ¡Viva Sevilla,
> viva Sevilla!
> . . . .[44]

Although in 1935 in Havana Alberti did not have the record with him for his presentation, he reconstructs this section of his original talk by citing a string of similar verses culled from Lope's theater by José F. Montesinos.[45] Thus although Alberti knew the "sevillanas" originated from a much earlier period, he continues to cite them to support his view of the resurfacing of "lo popular" from Lope's time, to that of Goya, to the present.[46]

He then goes on to play "El Café de Chinitas" as an example of "toda la majeza, la bravuconería de la torería romántica," which he also finds reflected in the *Romances del 800* by Fernando Villalón.[47] Here again, Alberti draws a comparison in service of his basic paradigm: "para volver a lo popular, a este intercambio, a este flujo y reflujo de la tradición conservada, oral, con la recreada por el poeta."[48] In a parallel manner he links "La Tierra de Alvar González" by Antonio Machado (who, he claims, "continúa el romance narrativo, muy semejante al conservado en la memoria del pueblo") with the "Romance de los pelegrinitos," which he introduces as "uno popular tradicional, narrativo, bastante extendido hoy, con distintas variantes, por toda la Península."[49]

The remaining song on the record Alberti uses is the lullaby, "Nana de Sevilla." The haunting beauty of this cradle song, with its elongated syllables,

extensive repetition, and rolling rhythmic structure, is impossible to convey in
words:

> Este galapaguito
> no tiene mare,
> a, a, a, a.
> No tiene mare, sí,
> no tiene mare, no,
> no tiene mare,
> a, a, a.
>
> Lo parió una gitana,
> lo echó a la calle,
> a, a, a, a.
> Lo echó a la calle, sí,
> lo echó a la calle, no,
> lo echó a la calle,
> a, a, a.
>
> Este niño chiquito
> no tiene cuna,
> a, a, a, a.
> No tiene cuna, sí,
> no tiene cuna, no,
> no tiene cuna,
> a, a, a.
>
> Su padre es carpintero
> y le hará una,
> a, a, a, a.
> Y le hará una, sí,
> y le hará una, no,
> y le hará una,
> a, a, a.[50]

Here is no doubt that Lorca's version comes from the oral tradition, and that he heard it directly. Some of the verses appear, with variants, in lullabies from the late nineteenth century.[51] For Alberti this type of song provides another link in the chain binding the poets of his generation to poets of previous periods of history. As evidence he recites *nanas* by Gil Vicente, Lope de Vega, and even one by Unamuno, in addition to Lorca's.[52]

On the other hand, what struck Lorca most about this particular *nana* was its peculiar mixture of terror and tenderness. He had included it, among others, in his earlier lecture/demonstration on "Canciones de cuna españolas," given first at the Residencia in 1928, at which time he sang the songs himself: "Es particularmente triste la nana con que duermen a sus hijos las gitanas de Sevilla." The lullaby of the "galapaguito," he says, "es una nana de ese tipo triste en que se deja sólo al niño, aun en medio de la mayor ternura."[53] Lorca also defends the capacity of traditional popular song to bridge centuries, to create what Margit Frenk terms a directly perceptible "realidad tangible."[54] In García Lorca's own words:

> Mientras una catedral permanece clavada en su época, dando una expresión continua del ayer al paisaje siempre movedizo, una canción salta de pronto de ese ayer a nuestro instante, viva y llena de latidos como una rana, incorporada al panorama como arbusto reciente, trayendo la luz viva de las horas viejas, gracias al soplo de la melodía.[55]

The immediacy of living song, its ability to jump the frame of historical reference and to take shape in the present, is what draws Lorca to the *nana* and to other forms of oral tradition. He was proud of his knowledge of popular song. When asked, during an interview in 1933, if he had studied "el cancionero español," he replied:

> Sí; he ido a él con la misma curiosidad con que han ido otros, a estudiarlo científicamente, y me he enamorado de las canciones. Durante diez años he penetrado en el folklore, pero con sentido de poeta, no solo de estudioso. Por eso me jacto de conocer mucho y

de ser capaz de lo que no han sido capaces todavía en España: de poner en escena y hacer gustar este cancionero de la misma manera que lo han conseguido los rusos. Rusia y España tienen en la rica vena de su folklore enorme e idénticas posibilidades, que no son las mismas, por cierto, en otros pueblos del mundo.[56]

Alberti's 1932 and 1935 lectures intend to demonstrate the very same qualities Lorca describes, but he takes a further step and argues, at a more objective level, that the immediacy of popular song for the present generation of poets is precisely the same as it was for poets such as Gil Vicente and Lope. This is what Alberti means by "los aires vivos de la poesía popular," and what Lorca describes as "los elementos vivos, perdurables, donde no se hiela el minuto, que viven un tembloroso presente."[57]

The ten recorded songs described here represent only a small fraction of Lorca's total knowledge of popular and traditional song.[58] More than any other, García Lorca was responsible for introducing popular and traditional song to members of his generation:

En España, al piano, con unos cuantos amigos, dos, cuatro horas, incansablemente, canciones y canciones. Nunca mejor para ver su sentido total hispánico: canciones andaluzas, gitanas, castellanas, leonesas, portuguesas, gallegas, asturianas, con la sardana y el zortzico. Todo lo antiguo de los cancioneros, todo lo moderno de los campos de hoy, todo lo español en tesoro inacabable....[59]

From Lorca's apparently casual performances at the piano of the Residencia, there emerged an entire generational attitude of enthusiastic appreciation for the art of the *pueblo*:

¡Tardes y noches de primavera o comienzos de estío pasados alrededor de su teclado, oyéndole subir de su río profundo toda la millonaria riqueza oculta, toda la voz diversa, honda, triste, ágil y alegre de España! ¡Época de entusiasmo, de apasionada reafirmación

nacional de nuestra poesía, de recuperación, de entronque con su
viejo y puro árbol sonoro...[60]

The tremendous success of Lorca's recording with La Argentinita resulted in the widespread diffusion of these songs within an urban context during the following months.[61]

By the advent of the Second Republic in April of 1931, these traditional songs were being heard throughout Spain, forming a close association with the jubilant atmosphere which characterized the early days of the Republic. Even today, in the minds of many people, the songs bring instant recall of the optimistic enthusiasm of that period in Spanish history. As the political climate changed in the early 1930's, especially during the period just prior to and including the outbreak of the Civil War, some of these songs continued to be heard, though now adapted to entirely different circumstances. "Los cuatro muleros," for instance, was adopted by ranks of Republican soldiers to sing in the battlefield.

In New York, García Lorca's and La Argentinita's decision to collaborate on the recording was probably simultaneous with their decision to form a small company for the performance of popular song onstage. The undertaking was financed by their friend, the bullfighter Ignacio Sánchez Mejías. According to Alberti, he was the "animador y empresario de una compañía de bailes españoles encabezada por su amiga Encarnación López, 'La Argentinita'."[62]

A series of stage performances with La Argentinita followed Lorca's return from New York and Latin America in the summer of 1930. The chronology of their collaboration is difficult to reconstruct. Newspapers of the time would document these performances more fully; we have already noted one article, describing a performance in the Teatro Español, that appeared in the *Crónica* of Madrid on March 20, 1932, entitled "Federico García Lorca y el Romancillo popular y La Argentinita." The article prints Lorca's version of "Los pelegrinitos," with minor variants.[63]

Some of the songs performed onstage by La Argentinita and García Lorca passed into the repertory of other contemporary artists. In Madrid's Teatro de la Comedia, complete with costumes and sets, González Marín staged "Los mozos de

Monleón" and "Romance de los pelegrinitos," along with some of Lorca's own compositions: "Canción" and the "Romance de la luna, luna" (from the *Romancero gitano*).[64] This performance is particularly interesting, due to its mixture of popular songs of the oral tradition with poems by known, contemporary poets. The lack of distinction between two such disparate texts as "Romance de la luna, luna" and the "Romance de los pelegrinitos" creates a general parity (and confusion) between the poetry of the *pueblo* and Lorca's individual creation. Performances such as this one no doubt contributed to the labelling of Lorca as a "poeta popular." In addition to García Lorca, González Marín selected works by two other poets of the Generation of 1927 for that evening's performance: the "Chuflillas" and "Nanas" by Rafael Alberti, and "Saltas" and "Seguiriyas gitanas" by Fernando Villalón.

Still another example of "herencia culta" in the designated two-way process of lyric exchange between artist and *pueblo* is recalled by Antonio Mairena. During the late 1940's, in Madrid's Teatro Fuencarral, Mairena collaborated with the dancer, Carmen Amaya, in performing Lorca's "Romance de la luna, luna":

> Sin embargo, el éxito era muy grande cada día, sobre todo con el número de la fragua, que se había montado escenificando con cante y baile un poema del *Romancero gitano* de García Lorca: El *Romance de la luna, luna*. En el escenario aparecía yo en una fragua, y el recitador Juan José empezaba a decir los versos:
>
> > La luna vino a la fragua con su polisón de nardos. El niño la mira, mira. El niño la está mirando...
>
> Seguía el romance hasta llegar a la parte que dice:
>
> > Huye, luna, luna, luna. Si vinieran los gitanos, harían con tu corazón collares y anillos blancos.

> Y en ese momento, simbolizando a la luna, aparecía Carmen Amaya
> con bata blanca de cola, y yo le cantaba por soleá, mientras ella
> bailaba.[65]

The audience loved it. According to Mairena, "Este número de la fragua era el número bomba.... El teatro se venía abajo."[66]

The collaboration between García Lorca and La Argentinita did not preclude their own independent performances of popular song. Lorca continued his impromptu performances offstage, although in front of new audiences. In the spring of 1932 he visited Santiago de Compostela, at the invitation of the Comité de Cooperación Intelectual, to give his lecture on the "cante jondo." At the piano of the Hotel Compostela, he won over a group of Galician poets through his "recitales íntimos de canciones populares andaluzas y castellanas."[67] Some nine months later he repeated the performance in Santiago, although this time in conjunction with a reading of work of a radically different focus, the *Poeta en Nueva York.*[68]

The synchronicity of such widely different aspects of his art—the intense, surrealistic images of despair juxtaposed with the liveliness and simplicity of traditional popular song—presents a seeming contradiction, but only if we forget that the simultaneous appreciation of the traditional and the avant-garde was a constant, defining characteristic of the Generation of 1927 as a whole. Lorca's love of "lo popular" never left him, even while breaking with all his earlier work and venturing into experimental and revolutionary new forms. As we shall see, Alberti, too, proceeded to make his early love of the traditional lyrics of the old *Cancioneros* the basis of new directions for his art, both in poetry and in the theater.

Notes

1. Dialogue has always been a principal stylistic recourse of the Romancero, but Suzanne Petersen's statistical study of this feature shows a significant increase of direct discourse in ballads of the modern tradition. See her "Cambios estructurales en el Romancero tradicional," in *El Romancero en la tradición oral moderna*, eds. Diego Catalán, Samuel G. Armistead, Antonio Sánchez Romeralo (Madrid: Cátedra Seminario Menéndez Pidal, 1972), pp. 168–169.

2. "Análisis semiótico de estructruas abiertas: El modelo 'Romancero'," *El Romancero hoy: Poética*, eds. D. Catalán, S. G. Armistead, A. Sánchez Romeralo, et al. (Madrid: Gredos, 1979), pp. 232–234.

3. The *romance* is much more extensive than these few lines cited, but the power of this particular figure did not escape Lorca. In his 1930 talk on the "Juego y teoría del duende," he selects these lines to illustrate his idea that "Un muerto en España está más vivo como muerto que en ningún sitio del mundo." *OC*, III, p. 312.

4. "El lenguaje poético del romancero ha descubierto que la representación de actos o sucesos vicarios fácilmente vizualizables constituye la forma más eficaz de vivificar los relatos, de actualizar, como ocurriendo ante los ojos del auditorio las fábulas narradas." Diego Catalán, in collaboration with J. Antonio Cid, Beatriz Mariscal, Flor Salazar, Ana Valenciano, and Sandra Robertson, *Teoría general y metodología del Romancero*, vol. 1.A of the *Catálogo General del Romancero Pan-Hispánico (CGR)* (Madrid: Seminario Menéndez Pidal and Gredos, 1984), p. 189. See also pp. 170–172.

5. *Entre folklore y literatura*, p. 52.

6. In the sixteenth and seventeenth centuries, according to Margit Frenk, the verb *leer* is used predominantly to mean the act of reading out loud (a meaning conserved, for example, in the English "lecture"). Keeping this in mind, much of our thinking about the literature of the Golden Age is subject to revision. Printed texts at that time were often circulated orally and audibly, and were not destined to single or solitary acts of consumption. The episodic structure of *Don Quijote*, for example, would allow each episode to be read aloud at one sitting. Certainly the number of *pliegos sueltos* sold in

that period could not be taken as an accurate reflection of the literacy rate. See "'Lectores y Oidores.' La difusión oral de la literatura en el Siglo de Oro," *Actas del Séptimo Congreso de la Asociación Internacional de Hispanistas*. August 1980 (Rome: Bulzoni, n.d.), pp. 101–123.

7. Ramón Menéndez Pidal notes: "El baile acompañado de canto es la manifestación de arte popular más compleja y acabada, concurriendo a ellas los instrumentos, la voz, la rítmica coreográfica y la poesía. Bajo esta forma en los siglos XVI y XVII eran muy cantados también los romances, lo mismo en la aldea que en la ciudad." In "Cómo vivió y cómo vive el Romancero," *Estudios sobre el Romancero*, Vol. XI of the *Obras completas de R. Menéndez Pidal* (Madrid: Espasa-Calpe, 1973), pp. 422–423. In some places the custom has continued into the twentieth century. See his detailed description of "El baile de tres," a version of the ballad "Gerineldo," danced by one man with two women alternatively, in Las Navas del Marqués (Ávila), pp. 432–435.

8. *Drama, Stage and Audience* (London: Cambridge University Press, 1975).

9. When young Cervantes saw a performance by Lope de Rueda, around 1560, "todo el adorno del teatro era una manta vieja tendida sobre unos cordeles, detrás de la cual estaban los músicos cantando 'algún romance antiguo'," according to Menéndez Pidal, *Romancero hispánico*, II, p. 106.

10. Hannah E. Bergman, ed., *Ramillete de entremeses y bailes (Siglo XVII)* (Madrid: Castalia, 1970). I refer here to her excellent introduction, pp. 9–46.

11. *Federico y su mundo*, p. 61. Rafael Martínez Nadal gives a somewhat distorted version of the same information: "Hasta los tres años no podía hablar, pero al año podía seguir el ritmo de una canción y a los dos años ya tarareaba los aires populares...." Quoted by Angel del Río in "Vida y obra," *Federico García Lorca (1899–1936)* (New York: Hispanic Institute, 1941), p. 8.

12. *Federico y su mundo*, p. 71.

13. *OC*, III, p. 286.

14. *Federico y su mundo*, p. 425.

15. *Federico y su mundo*, p. 426.

16. See the "canciones populares" in *OC*, vol. II, pp. 1153–1184.

17. *Imagen primera*, pp. 19–20.

18. *Los autores como actores* (México: El Colegio de México, 1951), pp. 64–65.

19. From interviews with Joan V. Foix and Josep Carbonell, recorded by Antonina Rodrigo in *García Lorca el amigo de Cataluña* (Barcelona: Edhasa, 1984), pp. 161–163.

20. *Los autores como actores*, p. 66.

21. Laffranque, "Evocación lejana," p. 462.

22. I am indebted to Gonzalo Menéndez Pidal who kindly allowed me to listen to his tape of the records and to see the record jacket. The recordings have since been reissued on cassette, *Colección de canciones populares españolas*, recogidas, armonizadas e interpretadas por Federico García Lorca (piano) y La Argentinita (voz), produced by Pedro Vaquero Sánchez, for the Casa-Museo Federico García Lorca (Madrid: Sonifolk, 1990), no. J–105

23. See his note on p. 471 of *Federico y su mundo*. The date is verified, moreover, by a note Ramón Menéndez Pidal wrote across the top of a review describing La Argentinita's stage performance of "Los pelegrinitos": "el romancillo se puso en discos en 1931." (The review, "Federico García Lorca, el romancillo popular y La Argentinita," appeared March 20, 1932, in *Crónica* in Madrid.) Lorca himself refers to the recording in a letter to La Argentinita written during the summer of 1931. See vol. II of his *Epistolario*, ed. Christopher Maurer (Madrid: Alianza, 1983), pp. 139–140.

24. Dámaso Alonso, "García Lorca y la expresión de lo español," pp. 345–346.

25. Angel del Río, "Vida y obra," p. 20.

26. In "Lorca, folklorista," the important introductory essay to "Cantares populares recogidos por Federico García Lorca," included in *Federico García Lorca (1899–1936)* (New York: Hispanic Institute), p. 113. Onís' knowledge of the modern oral tradition is extremely reliable, since it is based on actual experience in the field. Along with Tomás Navarro Tomás, Américo Castro, Eduardo Martínez Torner, and other members of the Centro de Estudios Históricos, Onís participated in several field trips under the direction of Ramón Menéndez Pidal. See Antonio Sánchez Romeralo, "El Romancero oral ayer y hoy: Breve historia de la recolección moderna (1782–1970)," in *El Romancero hoy: Nuevas fronteras* (Madrid: Cátedra Seminario Menéndez Pidal and Gredos, 1979), pp. 31–32.

27. As a "romancillo" of six syllables, as opposed to the more common eight-syllable hemistique, the ballad interested Menéndez Pidal, who opened a separate file for it in his collection. All the unpublished versions cited here are from the Archives of Menéndez Pidal.

28. Analogous to this version is the one published by Dámaso Ledesma in his *Folklore o Cancionero salmantino* (Madrid: Imprenta Alemana, 1907), pp. 161–162, which offers the following variant in lines 15–18:

> El Padre Santo dice: —Vaya a cenar, que la pelegrinita aquí cenará.
> —No la dejo yo sola con Su Santidad, porque es de carne humana
> como los demás.

29. The music of Lorca's version is not the music published by Felipe Pedrell in *Cancionero popular español*, p. 28, no. 32. The text I show here is as it appears on the record. Published texts offer the following variants: 7 han llegado FGL; 8 desaniman FO, FGL, MH; 13–14 omitted FO; 16 El le dice que un beso / que le había dado FO, y él dice que un beso / que ella le ha dado FGL, ella dice que un beso / que le había dado MH; 19 respondo (*errata*) FGL; 22 ya se casaron FGL. [FO = Federico Onís, "Cantares populares recogidos por Federico García Lorca," pp. 132–136; FGL = Francisco García Lorca, *Federico y su mundo*, pp. 476–477; MH = Mario Hernández, ed. *Obras de Federico García Lorca*, vol. 5 (Madrid: Alianza, 1981), pp. 171–173.]

30. The same can be seen in a version from Riaza (Segovia), copied in María Goyri's hand: "Padre Santo de Roma / aquí venimos // a que usted nos perdone / que somos primos." In another from Sarroca: "Señor, havem pecat, / primos hermanos."

31. Similar to this is the version sent by a sixteen-year-old girl, Filomena Caballero Melgarejo, of Granada: "También le ha preguntado / cuánta edad tienen: // Ella dice que quince / y él diez y nueve."

32. The same euphemism can be seen in the version from Granada, in which, aside from the confession, the "sin" appears earlier in the scene: "Al pasar el arroyo / le dio la mano // y la peregrinita / se ha avergonzado. // Y el peregrinito / le nota a la moza // que se le ha puesto la cara / como una rosa." Compare this scene with the one cited above from Málaga.

33. Francisco López Estrada, "El romance de 'Don Bueso' y la canción de 'La peregrinita' en el cancionero folklórico de Antequera," *De los romances-villancico a la poesía de Claudio Rodríguez*, ed. J. M. López de Abiada and A. López Bernasocchi (Madrid: Gráficas Sol, 1984), p. 258.

34. Compare this with the version from Algeciras, sung by Natividad Patricio at age 14, and collected by Manrique de Lara: "El Padre Santo andaba / de silla en silla // para verle la cara / a la peregrina: // —¡Peregrinita hermosa, / cuánto te quiero! // —Esta carita

hermosa / es de mi dueño. // —Peregrinita hermosa, / de buen parecer, // dáme tu mano blanca, / yo te salvaré."

35. See the variants already cited in note 29.

36. *Federico y su mundo*, pp. 32–33. "Me cuenta mi tía Isabel, testigo presencial, que el Café de Chinitas, conocido en toda Andalucía como café cantante, no se dedicaba únicamente al cante y baile flamenco...era, por el contrario, un lugar de espectáculos variados." The *bandurria* is a type of small guitar.

37. This is the text given by Francisco García Lorca, *Federico y su mundo*, p. 33. Variants: 9 Frascuelo FO, MH; 13–16 omitted FO, MH. Alberti's Berlin lecture omits the second strophe but includes the last one.

38. In a personal interview with Gonzalo Menéndez Pidal (August, 1982). Whether Sánchez Mejías knew these verses from memory or whether he improvised them, G. Menéndez Pidal was unable to say. In either case they are now indelible in the memory of those who know the recorded version of the song. We see the strophe retained, for instance, by Francisco García Lorca, though it is missing in the versions published by Onís, pp. 127–128, and by M. Hernández, p. 163.

39. Onís: "Lorca, folklorista," pp. 113–114.

40. The surfacing of gypsy song into a more public arena after 1860, and its transformation into "cante flamenco" under the pressures of the "café cantante," is described in *Las confesiones de Antonio Mairena*, pp. 17–28.

41. *Cancionero salmantino*, p. 183; melody, p. 18.

42. See p. 62; melody, pp. 254–255.

43. Berlin, p. 89.

44. Berlin, p. 93; Havana, p. 23.

45. See his edition of Lope's *Letras para cantar* in *Poesías líricas*, I (Madrid: Clásicos Castellanos, 1925), pp. 160–161.

46. "¿Qué milagro sucede? Estas seguidillas, populares aún en el siglo XVIII, son de Lope de Vega. Todavía hoy, la primera sobre todo—*¡ay río de Sevilla, qué bien pareces!*—alternada con otras sevillanas posteriores, ha reaparecido en los tablados, en las calles y en discos de gramófono, con gran éxito, ayudada por Federico García Lorca y la gran bailadora 'La Argentinita'." Havana, p. 24.

47. Included in José María de Cossío's edition of Villalón's *Poesías* (Madrid: Hispánica, 1944).

48. Berlin, pp. 99–100.

49. Berlin, pp. 95–96. Probably Alberti knew of the existence of these "distintas variantes" through his relationship with Ramón Menéndez Pidal.

50. Text, with music, in Onís, "Cantares populares recogidos por Federico García Lorca," pp. 129–131. See also Berlin, p. 92. In Havana Alberti adds verses at the end from another traditional *nana*, p. 17.

51. In Francisco Rodríguez Marín's collection, *Cantos populares españoles*, I (Sevilla: Francisco Álvarez, 1882), pp. 3–4, among other "Nanas o coplas de cuna": (3) "Este niño chiquito / no tiene cuna; // su padre es carpintero / y le hará una." (6) "Este niño chiquito / no tiene madre: // lo parió una gitana / lo echó a la calle."

52. Berlin, p. 92; Havana, pp. 15–17. Alberti's comments on the traditional *nana* are quoted in the *Appendix*, "The Lesson of the Theater of Gil Vicente and Lope de Vega."

53. *OC*, III, p. 295.

54. *Entre folklore y literatura*, p. 2.

55. *OC*, III, pp. 282–283.

56. *OC*, III, pp. 579–580.

57. *OC*, III, p. 282.

58. The study of "Lorca, folklorista" by Federico de Onís contains the fullest description of his repertoire, but is nonetheless incomplete. See also Roger D. Tinnel, *Federico García Lorca: Catálogo-Discografía de las "Canciones populares antiguas" y de música basada en los textos lorquianos* (Plymouth, NH: Plymouth State College of the University of New Hampshire, 1986).

59. Dámaso Alonso, "García Lorca y la expresión de lo español," p. 346.

60. Alberti, *Imágen primera*, p. 20.

61. In an article dedicated to La Argentinita after her death in New York, Onís observed that these "canciones que aprendió Federico cuando era niño, de las criadas y campesinos de Granada...eran totalmente desconocidas del resto de los españoles, que las aprendieron de él y de la Argentinita. Lo que ha ocurrido con estas canciones, que todo el mundo cree haber oído toda la vida, es un ejemplo significativo de cómo lo folklórico conservado en la tradición campesina local puede, por la vía culta, volver a ser popular en un sentido amplio y general." See "La Argentinita," *Revista Hispánica Moderna*, 13, nos. 1–2 (January-April, 1946), p. 183.

62. *La arboleda perdida*, p. 223. In a more recent interview, Alberti again described the dance company formed by Lorca and La Argentinita. After their deaths in 1936 and 1946, respectively, the performances were carried on by Pilar López, sister of La Argentinita. Eventually, Antonio Gades joined the troupe, which then became the base of his present-day company. Alberti observes this relation when he describes Gades: "a quien he tomado mucho cariño porque es como un miembro de una familia larga que empezó hacia el año 31 o por ahí y todavía existe." See José Miguel Velloso, *Conversaciones con Rafael Alberti* (Madrid: Sedmay, 1977), p. 256. Not coincidentally, Gades has choreographed and danced in a ballet version of Lorca's *Bodas de sangre*, filmed by Carlos Saura.

63. Verses 9–10 are omitted in the review article. In the Archives of Menéndez Pidal. See also Laffranque, "Bases," p. 433.

64. The program of "Recitales González Marín," dated December 5, 1930, is in the Archives of Menéndez Pidal.

65. *Las confesiones de Antonio Mairena*, pp. 123–124.

66. *Las confesiones*, pp. 124–125.

67. Laffranque, p. 434.

68. Laffranque, p. 436.

3

At the Frontier:
Traditional Poetry and the *Teatro menor*

The discovery of a "público" was an important stimulus in the development of experiments for the stage by both García Lorca and Alberti in the period during the last days of the monarchy and the establishment of the Republic. Their experiences with the immediacy of popular traditional art lead both poets to attempt to renovate the theater—to awaken audiences to the fresh possibilities, already latent in the cultural tradition, for an authentically Spanish dramatic expression. As part of their attempt, they turned to both lyric and narrative forms of traditional poetic expression. Though characteristic of the generation in general, it is Lorca, especially, who looks at past traditions as an opening into the future.

Lorca and the "Teatro de guiñolillo"

Lorca's piano performances both on and off stage broaden his experience of communicating with an audience. Yet another, much earlier, demonstration of his interest in the live relationship between author and audience through the medium of popular literature is to be found in Lorca's puppet theater. Like so much of his art, his interest in theater develops in childhood. His brother Francisco recalls: "For me, Federico's theatre begins with my first childhood memories. The first toy that Federico bought with his own money, by breaking open his savings bank, was a miniature theatre.... No plays came with this little theatre, so they had to be made up."[1]

Lorca's first theatrical representations were imitations of religious ceremonies. Later, his childhood fascination with a travelling group of gypsies staging a traditional puppet farce led to his first attempts to put on a puppet show at home:

> Para sus "representaciones" infantiles Federico...representaba muy seriamente funciones religiosas, como las que había presenciado en la iglesia del pueblo.... Mas un día—tendría Federico siete u ocho años—llegó al pueblo una pequeña *troupe* de gitanos, que hizo representar durante unos días su modesto teatrito de marionetas, con las aventuras de Cachiporra y otros populares personajes. Aunque ya puede suponerse lo rudimentario de aquel teatrito errante, el espectáculo de las marionetas entusiasmó al niño Federico, que no se perdió una sola función. Al día siguiente de marchar los gitanos, la habitual representación religiosa era substituída por el primer teatro de marionetas creado por el futuro autor de *Bodas de sangre*.[2]

The itinerant puppet theater introduced him to the traditional cuckold figure, Don Cristóbal, and to an entire panorama of stock characters and situations which abound in Andalusian folklore, and which later form the basis for most of Lorca's mature theatrical work. Indeed, the extent to which all of Lorca's theater is related, thematically or structurally, to the puppet farce of popular tradition, has been only partially assessed.[3]

For Lorca's interest in the traditional puppet plays was not circumscribed to his childhood years. On January 5, 1923, to celebrate the "Día de los Reyes Magos," he staged an elaborate puppet show, "Los Títeres de Cachiporra," for over 100 children and some 20 adults at the family home in Granada.[4] Falla directed the chamber music for the program, which consisted of the anonymous medieval mystery play, the *Auto de los Reyes Magos*; the comical one act *entremés*, *Los habladores*, attributed to Cervantes (set to music by Stravinsky); and Lorca's verse rendering of an old Andalusian folktale, which he composed for the occasion, *La niña que riega la albahaca y el príncipe preguntón.* This work is considered to be Lorca's first "fully developed puppet play."[5]

In the staging of *La niña que riega la albahaca*, Lorca moved and spoke the puppet representing the Prince, while his sister Concha performed the part of La Niña. Following the custom of the classic *comedia*, where the formal division of the play into acts was marked by the performance of an *entremés*, Lorca allowed room for comic diversion during *La niña* by having the traditional puppet Don Cristóbal come on stage and address the children in the audience, calling them by name and engaging them in dialogue, much to their delight. The poet's brother recalls that the lively exchange made a deep impression on Lorca. "Este momento de comunicación espontánea con un público infantil, o infantilizado por el espectáculo, quedó grabado en el ánimo del poeta."[6]

The play itself is a lyric version of the old story that love overcomes all obstacles, even those of social rank. The Príncipe courts the Niña at her window:

> Niña que riegas la albahaca,
> ¿cuántas hojitas tiene la mata?

She responds to his impertinence with a riddle in kind:

> Dime, rey zaragartero,
> ¿cuántas estrellitas tiene el cielo?

These and other verses, according to Francisco García Lorca, "tienen un tan marcado sabor tradicional" that there is little doubt they originate in oral tradition.[7]

The performance in the García Lorca home is also significant in that it was a rehearsal for Falla's *El retablo de Maese Pedro*, presented in Paris the following summer, with the collaboration of the same artists who had designed the sets and costumes for Lorca's puppet stage.[8]

In 1922, a few months prior to the puppet festival for the children, Lorca was at work on another puppet farce, the *Tragicomedia de don Cristóbal y la señá*

Rosita, also known as *Los títeres de Cachiporra*. In 1932 he apparently revised this work for a live performance by actors of Margarita Xirgu's company, with dances by La Argentinita. Lorca's friend, Carlos Morla Lynch, expressed his reservations about the revision:

> Me habría gustado más que esta representación se efectuara conforme a su idea: *Títeres*, y, si no fuera posible, con personajes que hicieran de tales, esto es, de fantoches con hilos estirados hacia el techo atados en los pies, en la cabeza y en las manos. Que los actores se movieran como marionetas.[9]

Apparently Lorca saw the same possibility, for in 1935 he was at work on a third version, "una versión musical, enriqueciendo el texto con canciónes y bailes."[10] Since this last version is lost, an intriguing ambiguity remains: whether Lorca meant the work to be performed as a traditional puppet play, with puppets representing people, or whether he intended to invert the roles and have actors take the role of puppets. Later plays develop and even exploit the same ambiguity and play on roles, especially in the relationship of the author to his audience and to the characters onstage.[11]

In any case, the *Tragicomedia* presents the next step in Lorca's evolving strategy in the use of popular and traditional art. As before, the puppet play provides a showcase for the display of the popular song he loved so well. In the opening scene, Lorca introduces Rosita with this traditional song:

> Por el aire van
> los suspiros de mi amante,
> por el aire van,
> van por el aire.[12]

But it also provides him with stock characters and situations which thereafter never quite leave his theatrical imagination.

Rosita is the young girl promised by her tyrannical father to be married to "don Cristobita el de la porra," a wealthy and repulsive old man, who speaks of her only in terms of lechery: "Es una hembrita suculenta. ¡Y para mí solo! ¡Para mí solo!"[13] Quite naturally, she is in love with someone her own age who shares her poetical innocence, and whose expression for her therefore is equally lyrical:

> Mi amante siempre se baña
> en el río Guadalquivir,
> mi amante borda pañuelos
> con la seda carmesí.

Lorca's obvious enjoyment here is in delineating the contrast between the characters by means of the songs he puts in their mouths. Like Irene in *La niña que riega la albahaca*, Rosita sings the well-known

> Con el vito, vito, vito,
> con el vito, que me muero;
> cada hora, niño mío,
> estoy más metida en fuego.

Cristobita's song in response underlines his perverted, vulgar character, devoid of all poetic sensibility:

> La rana hace cuac, cuac,
> cuac, cuac, cuac.[14]

The use of popular lyrics to identify character is a natural step in a puppet farce where the major figures are already known. The situation of the unhappy May-December marriage is also a stock item of folklore, and one that Lorca will use again in *Retablillo de don Cristóbal*, *La zapatera prodigiosa*, and *Amor de don Perlimplín con Belisa en su jardín*. But in 1922, Lorca's attention is primarily focused on creating a play for puppets illustrated with popular songs.

Alberti and the Performances at the Instituto Escuela

Rafael Alberti did not restrict his interest and knowledge of traditional popular poetry to the realm of purely theoretical observations. Like Lorca, though in his own manner, he was a practitioner of popular and traditional forms, especially in the early period of his art. His first three books of poems, *Marinero en tierra, La Amante*, and *El Alba del Alhelí* (composed between 1924 and 1927), are excellent examples of the "recreación de lo popular" he was later to describe in his lectures.

By the author's own testimony, the overriding influence on *Marinero en tierra* (awarded the Premio Nacional de Literatura in 1924–25 by a committee comprised of Ramón Menéndez Pidal and Antonio Machado, among others) was his reading of Gil Vicente and the anonymous "lírica antigua" of the fifteenth and sixteenth centuries.

> Iniciado no hacía mucho en Gil Vicente por Dámaso Alonso y en el *Cancionero musical de los siglos XV y XVI*, de Barbieri, escribí entre los pinos de San Rafael mi primera canción de corte tradicional: "La corza blanca," en la que casi seguía el mismo ritmo melódico de una de las más breves y misteriosas que figuran entre las anónimas de aquel cancionero y que comienza: "En Ávila, mis ojos..."[15]

In the two books of poetry that followed, Alberti consciously moved beyond his first purely imitative tendencies, when he was striving to reproduce the air of antiquity found in the old *cancioneros*, to make his poems at once more direct and more reflective of the current popular tradition. "La esencia dramática de mis nuevos poemas: algunos, con verdadero aire de coplas, más para la guitarra que para la culta vihuela de los cancioneros."[16] Alberti was not alone in recognizing the new vigor of his verse. One of the poems of *El Alba del Alhelí*, for instance, was selected for performance by La Argentinita:

> Aceitunero que estás,
> vareando los olivos,

> ¿me das tres aceitunitas
> para que juegue mi niño?

Alberti was obviously pleased with the poem's diffusion in this manner, and even more so with its resulting anonymity: "Años más tarde la hizo famosa, con ligeras variantes, la compañía de bailes y cantos populares de 'la Argentinita,' repitiéndose por toda España como de autor anónimo."[17] As in the case of the *coplas* he composed on the death of Joselito, the anonymous circulation of the song was for him the real sign of its success. The experience made a lasting impression on Alberti. In 1977 he reiterates it thus:

> Luego, cuando se formó la compañía, en la que Federico intervino tanto, Ignacio, para halagarnos y darnos importancia a los poétas de nuestra generación, a los que tanto quiso y a la que estuvo tan ligado, hizo que en unos villancicos que se cantaban por las calles de Cádiz se cantara una canción mía: "Aceitunero que estás—vareando los olivos." Ahora todo el mundo cree que es una canción popular, porque ha pasado al cante jondo y se canta como villancico aflamencado desde entonces.[18]

Indeed, Alberti's boast appears to be supported: Jimena Menéndez Pidal, in her *Auto de Navidad*, includes, along with a melody, the following text,

> Aceitunero que vas
> vareando los olivos,
> ¿me das una aceitunita
> para que juegue mi Niño?

accompanied by a religious refrain:

> ¡Gloria!
> Y a su bendita Madre
> ¡Victoria!

¡Gloria al Rey de los Cielos,
Gloria![19]

As stated in *Auto*'s "Guía de melodías," the music proceeds from the oral tradition and was collected by Magdalena Rodríguez Mata in Granada. Rodríguez Mata made her collection during 1945–46.[20] Did she also collect the text? Or did Jimena Menéndez Pidal appropriate Alberti's poem and combine it with the traditional Granada melody? Whatever the answer may be, the result is a perfect example of the tradition—"ese ir y venir"—of anonymous popular song.

The idea of representing his poetry dramatically had already occurred to Alberti by the time *Marinero en tierra* was published. A list of "Obras en preparación" included at the end of the volume announced two forthcoming works for the theater: "Ardiente-y-fría (madrigal dramático)" and "La novia del marinero." The first was never written (though a staged version is easily imagined on reading the poem of the same title included in the collection). The second work, according to Alberti, was "un pequeño auto a la manera de los de Gil Vicente, que fue terminado, pero que perdí también antes de la guerra."[21]

From his apprenticeship with the dramatic works of Gil Vicente in the early 1920's, Alberti's theatrical interests moved steadily towards the stage utilization of elements of the modern oral tradition, especially children's folklore. By the early years of the Republic, the forms and materials of popular tradition dominate his theatrical production. Of course the theatrical strategies in the recourse to popular poetry of the Renaissance theater are never lost to him; he simply applies them within a wider understanding of what constitutes the oral tradition in more immediate surroundings.

In *Santa Casilda* Alberti dramatizes an old legend about the daughter of the Moorish king of Toledo, who falls in love with a captive Christian count and runs away with him to Burgos. When the count dies, she founds a monastery, still standing, in Briviesca. Another version of this legend inspired a play of the same name by Lope, as well as *Los lagos de San Vicente* by Tirso de Molina, both works of purely hagiographic intent. Unfortunately, Alberti's play was never staged and has since been lost,[22] but Marrast accounts for at least four separate

readings of the work, accompanied by Alberti's drawings—one at the home of
Pedro Salinas, and one at the home of the Menéndez Pidal family in San
Rafael.[23] Carlos Morla Lynch also describes a private reading of the work in
his home.[24] The only public reading of *Santa Casilda* took place in January of
1931, at the Residencia de Señoritas, and received the following review:

> *Santa Casilda* está destinada al teatro y es perfectamente
> representable, aunque habrá de vencer, quizá, en la escena, aquello
> con que suele chocar en la realidad toda producción de elevado
> lirismo. Su autor ha escrito tres actos con los elementos sencillos,
> primitivos, claros, del romancero. Figuras del romance son el Conde
> cautivo, el Rey moro, su hija renegada; la esclava, el coro de los
> soldados de Alí—uno blanco y el otro negro—el frailecillo de las
> barbas blancas....las estampas se preceden con la sugestión de los
> tonos de oro de los retablos del siglo XV, de cuya época suenan en
> el relato letras de canciones ingenuas y otras, transmitidas por labios
> infantiles de generación en generación....un misticismo sencillísimo
> ...en que el poeta suele respetar la construcción y las formas clásicas
> del romance, pero sin temor a graciosos anacronismos.... El espíritu
> infantil, que es conducido de la mano por su autor a través de la
> narración poética, fue uno de los valores más tiernos, y de mayor
> éxito de público.[25]

During this period, the traditional ballad enjoyed a new vogue among the
intellectual and artistic elite, much as it had among the "cortesanos" during the
early sixteenth century. No doubt, the publication of Ramón Menéndez Pidal's
Flor nueva de romances viejos, in 1928, did much to stimulate a new appreciation
of the old form among a reading public much wider than the scholarly circles of
the Ateneo. Whereas his 1919 lecture on the early Castilian lyric and his discovery
of the relationship between the ballad and the epic had touched off a series of new
investigations among his colleagues, it was not until the late 1920's and early
1930's that the circle widened to include poets, artists, actors, and a general public
receptive to the artistry of their own and hitherto largely unknown traditional
literature.

Traditional ballads even came to be included in poetry readings, and, as we have seen, in performances of popular song. Menéndez Pidal makes note of this new development when describing "medios de difusión erudita" of the *romance tradicional*:

> Una manera de exponer los romances en público, desconocida en lo antiguo, es su inclusión como parte de los recitales poéticos. Esta recitación prescindiendo del canto fue práctica en que sobre salió la declamadora ruso-argentina Berta Singerman, que estuvo en España en 1926 y 1932. También se los presenta en público bajo su forma auténtica, cantados; pero entonces, el espectáculo moderno rechazaba la repetición prolongada de la misma melodía, y la Argentinita interrumpía a trozos el canto para sustituirlo por la recitación simple, como puede verse en *Los mozos de Monleón*, grabado en disco gramofónico dirigido por García Lorca. La misma alternancia de canto y recitación hacía González Marín en sus programas teatrales.[26]

Another key source of "difusión erudita" Menéndez Pidal neglects to mention here is the publication and subsequent reissues of his own *Flor nueva de romances viejos*. Over twenty editions of *Flor nueva* had sold out by the late 1960's.

Alberti's interest in early traditional poetry intersected with another previously unknown means of diffusion of the ballad: the "escenificación del romance." In 1932 the Instituto Escuela, grandchild of the Institución Libre de Enseñanza, introduced the staging of traditional ballads as part of the school's theatrical activities. The first ballad of oral tradition staged by the Instituto Escuela was *La boda estorbada*. Through his contact with the Menéndez Pidal family, Alberti had the chance to collaborate on several of the school productions.

The performances at the Instituto Escuela were mixed media events, often highly experimental, involving costume and set design, dramatic readings, singing, and dance choreography. Alberti's talents as a painter (a career he never abandoned completely) were put to the service of the purely visual aspects of the "escenificación" on more than one occasion. For the production of the *Romance del Conde Sol* (also known as "La condesita"), there exists a drawing by Alberti, in the Archives of Menéndez Pidal, of the character of El Conde. First staged in June, 1932, the Instituto Escuela put on a second performance of the *El Conde Sol* nearly a year later, which was attended by Alcalá Zamora, then President of the Republic, and other government officials. Individual *pliegos* were specially printed for distribution to the audience, containing not just the text and the music of the ballad, but also the standard *grabado*, in this case depicting the set, costumes and characters of the play. On one of these *pliegos sueltos*, María Goyri de Menéndez Pidal wrote the following notes:

> El 24 de Abril de 1933 se representó este romance en el Campo del Moro con motivo de la fiesta que el Presidente de la República D. Niceto Alcalá Zamora ofreció a los niños de las Escuelas gratuitas de Madrid. Fue interpretado por un grupo de niños del Instituto Escuela para quienes se había hecho la escenificación en Junio de 1932. El mismo día 24 de Abril se representó por los mismos niños en la Fiesta del Libro que se celebró en el Teatro Español. El pliego se repartió a los 3000 niños de las Escuelas. Pocos días después la Directora del grupo escolar Menéndez Pelayo proyectaba hacerlo interpretar por sus alumnos, y en la calle de Torrijos lo cantaban algunos niños.[27]

That the ballad was taken up by children playing in the streets would indicate that this "medio de difusión" was extraordinarily effective, but it is also possible that the *romance* was known to them through oral transmission.

Another project for a production by the Instituto Escuela was Alberti's dramatization of *La dama y el pastor*, based on the text published in *Flor nueva*, "Canción de una gentil dama y un rústico pastor."[28] Although the project was never carried to completion, a series of drawings remain in which Alberti illustrated the movements of La Dama on singing specific verses; for example, "Tres viñas de tierra buena / te daría en casamiento" and "Oh, malhaya el vil pastor / que dama gentil la ame." Apart from the captivating grace of these sketches, they are valuable graphic testimony to Alberti's imaginative response to the capacity for visualization inherent in the song.

In 1933 or 1934, the Instituto Escuela also staged a poem written by Lorca for Jorge Guillén's young daughter, Teresa: "El Lagarto está llorando." The exquisite pathos of the scene was acted out on the stage by "lagartos viejos y setas vivas que comentan":

> El lagarto está llorando,
> la lagarta está llorando,
> el lagarto y la lagarta
> con delantalitos blancos.
> ¡Míralos, qué viejos son,
> qué viejos son los lagartos!
> Han perdido sin querer
> su anillo de desposados.
> ¡Ay su anillito de plomo,
> ay su anillito plomado!
> El lagarto y la lagarta
> con delantalitos blancos.[29]

The Instituto Escuela staged even the difficult metaphoric descriptions of the sun and sky, which would seem to be Lorca's poetic invention in the manner of Góngora:

> Un cielo grande y sin gente
> monta en su globo a los pájaros.
> El sol, capitán redondo,
> lleva un chaleco de raso.[30]

For the children watching, the plight of the defenseless "largatos viejos" and their lost wedding ring, symbol of the bond that had held them together throughout the years, must have constituted one of their earliest experiences of tragedy.

In this case there is no doubt that Lorca's poem derived from a circle game he probably played as a child in Granada, and which we find preserved in folklore collections of the late nineteenth century. Compare, for instance:

> La niña
> que vino de Sevilla
> y trajo
> un delantal muy majo,
> ahora
> como se le ha perdido
> la niña llora.[31]

Alberti's Dramatization of
El Enamorado y la Muerte

Alberti's plans for the "escenificación" of the ballad, "El Enamorado y la Muerte," were carried to completion during this same period.[32] According to the author, the *romance* was staged on various occasions by experimental theatrical groups; he recalls having seen it put on at the Instituto Francés.[33] Here, too, the immediate source for Alberti's dramatization of the traditional *romance* is the composite "versión facticia" from Menéndez Pidal's *Flor nueva de romances viejos.*

Alberti's staged rendition of *El Enamorado y la Muerte* is a perfect example in miniature of the effective exploitation of the pictorial and dramatic elements of the ballad. He organizes the narrative into levels: the exterior lines, in the mouth of El Lector, are read at the front of the stage; the other lines, handled as dialogue, are distributed between El Enamorado, his beloved La Enamorada, and La Muerte, who first appears as La Doncella, dressed in white. El Lector begins the scene by reading from a book in his hand:

> Durmiendo estaba el amante,
> durmiendo y sin compañía,

soñando con sus amores,
que en sus brazos los tenía.

From this foreground plane, we enter the young man's dream, which opens up behind El Lector in the interior of the stage. While the action takes place there, El Lector's voice continues to punctuate the dialogue at intervals:

EL ENAMORADO (Como sonámbulo.)
   ¿Por dondé has entrado, amor? ¿Cómo has podido, mi vida? Las puertas están cerradas, ventanas y celosías.

LA DONCELLA
   Yo entro sin abrir las puertas, ventanas y celosías.

EL ENAMORADO
   Ven que te abrace, mi amor, y duerma en tu compañía.

EL LECTOR
   Galán el enamorado, brazos y manos abría.

LA DONCELLA
   A tientas te busco, amante: la alcoba no está encendida.

EL ENAMORADO
   También a tientas mis manos te buscan a ti, mi vida.

EL LECTOR
   Mientras sus manos la buscan, ella sus manos esquiva. Al borde de la almohada una vela le encendía.

The ghostly illumination by candlelight, and the stage movements accompanying the dialogue, contribute to show the increasing anxiety of El Enamorado. These elements are all products of Alberti's imagination. At the culminating moment, when Death reveals herself, the poet's intervention in the original text is minimal:

LA DONCELLA (De pie, quitándose la careta y abriéndose la
túnica, muestra la calavera y el esqueleto de LA MUERTE.)
  No soy tu amor, soy la muerte, la muerte que Dios te envía.

EL ENAMORADO (De súbito, suplicante, arrodillándose otra vez
sobre el lecho.)
  ¡Ay muerte, si eres mi muerte, déjame vivir un día!

LA MUERTE
  Un día no puede ser, un hora tienes de vida. Pasada una hora,
  amante, tu vida será cumplida.

In fact, if we compare Alberti's dramatization overall to Menéndez Pidal's text, we
have a good demonstration of how the ballad's capacity for visualization takes
shape in Alberti's mind.   What the audience sees onstage are imaginative
magnifications expressed out of the *romance*'s compressed and rapid narrative.

> Un sueño soñaba anoche,
> soñito del alma mía,
> soñaba con mis amores,
> que en mis brazos los tenía.
> Vi entrar señora tan blanca,
> muy más que la nieve fría.
> —¿Por dónde has entrado, amor?
> ¿Cómo has entrado, mi vida?
> las puertas están cerradas,
> ventanas y celosías.
> —No soy el amor, amante:
> la Muerte que Dios te envía.
> —¡Ay, Muerte tan rigurosa,
> déjame vivir un día!
> —Un día no puede ser,
> un hora tienes de vida.[34]

Alberti's "escenificación" of *El Enamorado y la Muerte* offers a practical illustration of how the innate dramatic strategy of the traditional *romance* can be utilized for the stage. It is also a clear and tangible example of what Alberti meant by the process of "dar y devolver, ir y venir" between *poesía culta* and the *poesía del pueblo.* In this case, as in so many others, it is difficult to separate the tangled strands resulting from the fertile mixing of the learned, conscious mode of literary production and the products of the unformalized, oral chain of transmission.

There is no doubt that the versions of "El Enamorado y la Muerte" existing in the modern oral tradition derived from the "composición culta" of Juan del Encina, c. 1496 ("Yo estava reposando / durmiendo como solia").[35] However, the source for Alberti's dramatized version is not the text by Encina, as Marrast has stated,[36] but rather the version in *Flor nueva*, "composed" by Menéndez Pidal out of several versions collected from the modern oral tradition. Encina's composition elaborates the theme of the lover's desperation and the insensitivity of his beloved, by taking recourse to the personification of an emotional state ("el ciudado"), along the lines of troubadoresque poetry. From this "artificioso" poem, the oral tradition had created a narrative *romance* which develops the conflict in a dramatic way. According to Diego Catalán, the oral tradition

> alteró profundamente el sentido de ambas escenas: en el 'romance' de Enzina, el poeta se debate con su propia pasión, analizada de acuerdo con la técnica introspectiva entonces en moda, y la Muerte que tiene en su compañía es sólo un estado de conciencia, al que llega con naturalidad desde el amor desesperado; el estar muriéndo de amor es una situación tan común para el poeta, que al acercarse el día, buscará descanso saliendo de su posada y yendo a calmar sus ansias con la vista de su Señora. En el romance tradicional todas las disquisiciones introspectivas desaparecen y el Enamorado se encuentra frente a frente con la Muerte, cuya visita, imprevista e inexorable, viene a truncar su ventura amorosa.[37]

Evidence of the dependence of Alberti's dramatized version on Menéndez Pidal's factitious text can be found in Alberti's retention of the lines, "La muerte me está buscando, / junto a tí vida sería," in the dying young man's petition to his beloved. Apparently Menéndez Pidal found the version from oral tradition poetically lacking at this point ("la muerte me está buscando, / puede que no me hallaría"), and thus added a second hemistich of his own invention.[38] This is a case in which the *romance tradicional* clearly derives from the "poema culto." Then, out of several field versions of the *romance tradicional* comes the "versión facticia." Finally, from this composite version, comes Alberti's theatrical piece, perfectly exemplifying the process of "herencia" and "creación" which Alberti described in his lecture.

La pájara pinta: Popular Poetry as "Espectáculo"

Following his talk in Havana, in 1935, Alberti read the prologue and first act of his "guirigay lírico-bufo-bailable," entitled *La pájara pinta*. Conceived as a three-act play with a prologue, only the prologue and first act have been conserved.[39] Written in 1925 (according to Marrast), *La pájara pinta* shows an evident relationship with Lorca's *Los títeres de Cachiporra*. Alberti first planned the work "para las marionetas de Podrecca, con música de Oscar Esplá."[40] Instead the roles were taken by actors, and the play was first performed in 1932, at the Salle Gaveau in Paris. The music was composed by Federico Elizalde, who also collaborated with Lorca on a musical and danced version of *Los títeres de Cachiporra*.[41] Elizalde seems to have understood better than Esplá the playful sense of celebration underlying both these works. Subsequent productions of *La pájara pinta* in Madrid also included the collaboration of Esplá, whose more formal music was perhaps better suited to a concert than to a "guirigay lírico-bufo-bailable." In Madrid the play was presented twice by the Instituto Escuela at the Campo del Moro (on the same dates as the *Romance de la Condesita*), and thus was also attended by Don Niceto Alcalá Zamora and other government representatives.[42]

La pájara pinta can only be read by imagining a stage full of colorful figures costumed in feathers and bells resembling birds and flowers, swirling in dance formation and singing in chorus verses such as:

El colorín colorado
va del jardín al tejado;
colorado y colorín,
va del tejado al jardín.
Colorín colorado.[43]

The greatest value of the work stems from the ebullient rhythm and rhyme of the lyrics, some of them Alberti's invention, and others transcribed directly from children's songs and street games. Alberti described it thus:

Obra escrita con los pies más que con la cabeza, pero pensando en lo descoyuntado que son las marionetas. Pero siempre en coincidencia con la palabra; así es que si había un salto, las palabras coincidían con los saltos.[44]

The names of the characters are all lifted from popular sources. The central figure, La Pájara, is taken from the song previously used by Lorca in the *Tragicomedia de don Cristóbal*:

Estando una pájara pinta
sentadita en el verde limón...
con el pico movía la hoja,
con la cola movía la flor.
¡Ay! ¡Ay!
¿Cuándo veré a mi amor?[45]

Rodríguez Marín included this children's song in his folklore collection, published in 1882:

Estaba la pájara pinta
Sentadita en el verde limón;
Con el pico recoge la hoja,
Con la hoja recoge la flor.
¡Ay, mi amor!
M'arrodillo a los pies de María,

M'arrodillo porqu' es madre mía.
M'arrodillo a los pies de mi hermana,
M'arrodillo porque me da gana.
Dé usté media vuelta.
Dé usté la vuelta entera.
Pero nó, pero nó, pero nó,
Pero nó, que me da vergüenza.
Pero sí, pero sí, pero sí,
Amiguita, te quiero yo a tí.[46]

The lyrics accompany a game in which the actions described in the song are acted out by a child who finishes by selecting an "amiga." The game's origins are remote, since we find it already cited at the beginnings of the seventeenth century by Alonso de Ledesma in his *Juegos de Noches Buenas* (1605):[47]

¿Dónde pica la pájara pinta?
¿Dónde pica?

It is also cited as a song by Luis de Briceno, *Methodo mui facilissimo para aprender a tañer la guitarra a lo español* (Paris, 1626):[48]

Bolava la palomita
por encima del verde limon
con las alas aparta las ramas
con el pico lleva la flor.

After nearly 400 years, it is remarkable that the game/song remains alive in the tradition, even up to the end of the twentieth century.[49]

Although Alberti builds the entire "guirigay" around this central figure, the song as such does not appear in the published fragmentary version of his play. Rather, Alberti incorporates the following version, bringing the first act to a close as a chorus of voices sings:

Ochavito a la Pájara Pinta
pinta, pinta en el verde limón.
Con el pico picaba la hoja,
con la hoja picaba la flor
¡ay!
¿cuándo vendrá mi amor?
¡ay!
¿cuándo lo veré yo?

Me arrodillo a los pies
de mi amante
fiel y constante.
Dame una mano,
dame la otra;
toma un besito
para tu boca.

Daremos la media vuelta,
daremos la vuelta entera.
Daremos un paso atrás...
pero no, pero no, pero no...
pero no, que me da vergüenza;
pero sí, pero sí, pero sí...[50]

Alberti places La Pájara center stage, as "una señora casamentera...que tenía un jardín donde ella proporcionaba bodas en el pueblo."[51]   The other characters dance around her, bringing her gifts and paying their respects.   La Carbonerita, Antón Perulero, La Viudita del Conde Laurel, El Conde de Cabra, Juan de las Viñas, Bigotes, and Don Diego Contreras ("que corta narices con sus tijeras," as Alberti explains) can all be traced to children's games, rhymes, proverbs and familiar sayings of the oral tradition.   Many sources have been uncovered by Marrast in his excellent study of Alberti's theater.   Especially interesting are the relationships he finds to characters in Quevedo's *La visita de los chistes*, and to lyrics that serve as *estribillos*, or refrains, in two *entremeses* by Quiñones de Benavente, *El entremés del tiempo* and *La visita de la cárcel*.[52]

La Viudita, El Conde de Cabra, and La Carbonerita figure prominently in many children's songs. In addition to the sources cited by Marrast, the following game introduces us to all three characters at once. An uneven number of players join hands and circle around one girl (the "widow"), who sings:

> Soy viudita,
> lo manda la ley,
> quiero casarme,
> no encuentro con quién.

Or, according to another variant:

> ¿Quién dirá de la carbonerita,
> quién dirá de la del carbón,
> quién dirá que yo soy casada,
> quién dirá que yo tengo amor?

The ones in the circle answer:

> La viudita, viudita,
> [la viudita] se quiere casar
> con el conde, conde de Cabra,
> conde de Cabra de esta ciudad.

The girl in the center then responds:

> Yo no quiero al conde de Cabra,
> conde de Cabra triste de mí!
> yo no quiero al conde de Cabra,
> conde de Cabra si no es a ti.

She then embraces one of the girls from the circle, the others all hug a partner, and the one who is left out then takes her place in the center, and the game is repeated.[53]

The structure of *La pájara pinta* is difficult to perceive if the existence of this game and its structure are not held foremost in mind. To judge the play in terms of the conventional dramatic structure of bourgeois psychological theater is to miss the point entirely.[54] Alberti's play *is* the game, burst open and exploded onstage with familiar characters coming to life and folklore situations amplified into dance, color and rhythm. The circle of characters around La Pájara duplicates the form of the game. By the final scene all the characters are onstage and, as the last character is introduced, the action is crowned with an enactment of the game itself. The Viudita enters, singing another popular children's song:

> Yo soy la viudita
> del Conde Laurel
> que quiere casarse
> y no encuentra con quién.

The other characters respond in chorus:

> La viudita, la viudita,
> la viudita se quiere casar
> con el Conde, Conde de Cabra,
> Conde de Cabra se le dará.

The following verses are alternated between La Viudita and La Pájara, with the chorus chiming in:

> LA VIUDITA, a la Pájara.
> Yo no quiero al Conde de Cabra,
> Conde de Cabra ¡triste de mí!
> Yo no quiero al Conde de Cabra,
> Conde de Cabra, sino a ti.

In spite of the similarity between Alberti's text and those published at the end of the nineteenth century, it is important to note that he did not take his version directly from the printed texts. In the Archives of Menéndez Pidal, various versions exist in which the "Widow" is called, agreeing with Alberti, "la viudita del conde Laurel." For example, a version from Colmenar, Málaga, sung by Teresa Llorente Selva at the age of 12, begins:

> Yo soy la viudita
> del conde Laurel,
> que quiero casarme
> y no tengo con quién.
> Pues siendo tan bella
> no tienes con quién,
> escoge a tu gusto,
> que aquí tienes cien.

And a Sephardic version from Tetuán, sung by Simi Chocrón, 37 years of age:

> Mocitas del prado,   del prado salí,
> a coger las flores   del mayo y abril.
> Yo soy la viudita   del conde Laurel,
> que quiero casarme,   no encuentro con quién.[55]

In Alberti's play, the lyrics are extended in conjunction with choreographed movement:

> LA PAJARA.
>   Yo sí quiero al Conde Cabra
>   Conde de Cabra, sí, sí, sí.
>   Yo sí quiero al Conde de Cabra.
>   Conde de Cabra, para ti.

> LA VIUDITA.
>   ¿Quién es el Conde Cabra, Conde Cabra?
>   ¿Quién es el Conde, triste de mí?

LA PAJARA.
> Un caballero de espada y dinero,
> y un buen marido para ti.

LA VIUDITA, consultando el retrato que lleva colgado al cuello.
> ¿Que haré yo, lindo amor,
> que haré yo?
> ¿Casaré
> con el Conde de Cabra?
> ¿Casaré, lindo amor
> o qué haré?

CORRO.
> Casarás con el Conde de Cabra
> casarás, almendrito en flor.

LA VIUDITA.
> ¿Casaré con el Conde de Cabra?

LA PAJARA.
> Casarás, que lo quiero yo.[56]

The repetition may seem tedious on reading but is quintessential to the play's performance. The rhythm of the popular lyrics demarcates the space for Alberti's intervention, as we see in the verses above. He merely extends the game's given vocabulary to round out the scene. The procedure has more to do with the composition of music than with the writing of a play in the ordinary sense. The sonority of the lyrics and their expansion into movement add another dimension to the meaning of the words by themselves. The words carry sense, but set within a total rhythmical structure, they accrue a different sense that escapes the act of reading. Thus the sound of alarm uttered by La Pájara

> ¡Paralelepípedo!
> ¡Paralelepípedo!
> ¡Paralelepípedo!

> ¡Paralelepípedo!
> ¡Paralelepípedo![57]

is pure onomatopoeia; at the same time it suggests the verbal experiments of the *creacionistas.*

For the Paris performance, the author took the role of actor, and recited the prologue to the play himself.[58] The prologue creates a special relationship between the spectators outside and the play's interior action by interposing a third plane between the two. The distantiation thus achieved reminds the audience of the original nature of theater as spectacle, never to be confused with reality. (We saw how, in *El Enamorado y la Muerte*, Alberti established the same intermediary plane through the use of El Lector at the exterior edge of the play.)

In *La pájara pinta*, the equivalent function is fulfilled by Pipirigallo,[59] a fantastic crested cock, who points to a large curtain drawn across the front of the stage. On the curtain all the figures are represented, dancing in a circle around La Pájara:

> Telón pintado. En el centro, sentada en la rama de un limonero, la
> Pájara Pinta. Alrededor de ella, todos los personajes de la obra,
> jugando al corro.[60]

The stage directions are explicit: the "guirigay" the audience is about to see is an imaginative amplification of the children's game. At a later date, Alberti specified that the effect he wanted to create on the painted curtain was that of "una aleluya popular."[61]

Alberti's description of the play's introduction helps to restore some of the original three-dimensionality inevitably lost in reading:

> Entonces, el personaje que dirigía esta compañía popular, llamada de
> la Pájara Pinta también, Pipirigallo, que era una especie de bululú
> que iba por los pueblos presentando la obra o, mejor dicho, el
> guirigay, aparece delante del telón. Suenan unas campanillas y
> Pipirigallo, todo calvo, con una esclavina llena de campanillas y

cascabeles, con un puntero en la mano, delante del telón donde están
pintados todos esos personajes que te he dicho antes, cada uno con
su letrero en la cabeza, dice lo siguiente. Bueno, él, como es un
director muy listo, piensa que si cuentas el argumento de la obra la
gente no va a interesarse por ella, entonces cuenta un argumento de
la siguiente manera, con todos los gestos y las inflexiones de voz
como si está contando un crimen que luego sucedía en la obra. Una
voz, detrás del telón, dice: ¡Atención, atención, el gran don
Pipirigallo, danzarín, titiritero, farsante y farandulero, va a explicar
con su puntero la función!   Entonces, pega un salto mortal y
dice....[62]

What immediately follows is a dazzling display of verbal pyrotechnics. Alberti
manages to suggest the jubilant crowing of a cock, while at the same time
reproducing the sonorous cadences and exaggerated rhetoric that characterize the
ballad style of the *cartelón de ciego*.[63] The prologue is too long to include here,
but ideally it should be heard in its entirety in order to capture the sense conveyed
by the gesticulating Pipirigallo:

>¡Pío-pío,
>pío-pic!
>¡Verdo-lari-lari-río,
>río-ric!
>¡Kikirikiiií!
>
>¡Ladón
>landera,
>deralón
>dinera,
>nedirlín
>nedirlón
>nedirlera,
>ronda, rondalín, randul,
>faró, faralay,
>guirí, guirigay,
>bul!

. . . .

¡Mórali ton, motón lira,
dalo dela vidovera!
¡Lendo diranda durindo,
dora dora virolindo!
¡Lumbrádol timbra darales,
moré toré loredales!
¡Uuuh,
ru,
bi,
buuu![64]

The difference is that while Alberti conserves the format of the *romance de cartelón*, the content is entirely invented. He empties the form of meaning in its conventional sense, in hopes that the form itself suggests meaning. Like the language of music, the total sense is conveyed through the conservation of the rhyme and rhythmical structure, which have the associative capacities of pure sound.

Alberti's sense of fun and spectacle must preclude any attempt to judge *La pájara pinta* as serious drama, but there is no reason to therefore conclude that he was not serious about the intentions behind the play. In fact, he considers it, even today, "realmente un estudio de las posibilidades rítmicas para una representación que fuera 'un guirigay lírico-bufo-bailable'":

> La palabra, aunque no hubiese música, tenía un valor expresivo a la vez que de movimiento. Fue una cosa que no he vuelto a hacer más y de la que sigo creyendo que tiene posibilidades si uno encontrara un músico con el que se entendiera de verdad y que llegara a hacer cierto tipo de obras. No estoy hablando del teatro corriente, sino de una combinación de música y otras artes.[65]

Lorca's *La zapatera prodigiosa*:
The Full Extension of the Traditional Farce

The composition of this two-act "farsa violenta," as García Lorca subtitled it (or "farsa común," as he later called it in an interview),[66] occurred in successive stages over more than a decade. As early as 1923 the body of the play and its principal characters had taken shape in his mind, as we see in a letter García Lorca wrote to his friend, Melchor Fernández Almagro, in July of that year:

> He trabajado bastante…. De teatro he terminado el primer acto de una comedia (por el estilo de Cristobicas) que se llama "La zapatera prodigiosa," donde no se dicen más que las palabras precisas y se *insinúa* todo lo demás.[67]

Included in the same letter is a "reparto" of the characters, most of which appear in the final version of the play ("La zapatera, La vecina vestida de rojo, La beata, El zapatero, Don Mirlo, El niño amargo, El niño alcalde, El tío del Tatachín, Vecinos y curas"), and indications for the music ("flauta y guitarra"). Years later, in an interview, Lorca said he finished the play in 1926,[68] though he had written Fernández Almagro, "He terminado la 'Zapatera Prodigiosa'," in January of 1928.[69]

For many years, the only published version of *La zapatera prodigiosa* was the one that opened a few months after the poet's return from New York, in Madrid's Teatro Español on December 24, 1930, with Margarita Xirgu in the lead role.[70]

Though García Lorca later rewrote the play, clearly from its initial conception he intended it as a celebration of the rich folkloric life of a small Andalusian *pueblo*, centered around the irrepressible shoemaker's wife. *La zapatera* shares with *Los títeres de Cachiporra* (or *Tragicomedia de don Cristóbal y la seña Rosita*) not just the traditional theme of the May-December marriage (resolved happily in *La zapatera*), but a common derivation from the traditional puppet farce. The same relation is conserved between the author (or puppeteer) and the audience that Lorca originally discovered in the *teatro de guiñol*. Lorca emphasizes this by means of a "Prólogo," in which El Autor appears before the curtain and addresses the audience directly, in order to remind them that what they are about to see is not conventional theater:

> Respetable público... (Pausa). No; respetable público, no; público solamente, y no es que el autor no considere al público respetable, todo lo contrario, sino que detrás de esta palabra hay como un delicado temblor de miedo y una especie de súplica para que el auditorio sea generoso con la mímica de los actores y el artificio del ingenio. El poeta no pide benevolencia sino atención, una vez que ha saltado hace mucho tiempo la barra espinosa de miedo que los autores tienen a la sala. Por este miedo absurdo, y por ser el teatro en muchas ocasiones una finanza, la poesía se retira de la escena en busca de otros ambientes....[71]

The Prologue reiterates the "Advertencia" of the *Tragicomedia*, in which El Mosquito addressed the audience:

> ¡Hombres y mujeres! Atención.... Yo y mi compañía venimos del teatro de los burgueses, del teatro de los condes y de los marqueses, un teatro de oro y cristales, donde los hombres van a dormirse y las señoras...a dormirse también. Yo y mi compañía estábamos encerrados. No os podéis imaginar qué pena teníamos....yo avisé a mis amigos, y huímos por esos campos en busca de la gente sencilla, para mostrarles las cosas, las cosillas y las cositillas del mundo....[72]

That Lorca perceived a need to alert his audience to the difference between his theater and the customary fare offered to urban audiences at that time is justifiable. The dialogue and dramatic action of *La zapatera* have more in common with the seventeenth-century *entremés* than the drawing-room comedy of the early twentieth century. Lorca was fully aware of this:

> Lo más característico de esta simple farsa es el ritmo de la escena,
> ligado y vivo, y la intervención de la música, que me sirve para
> desrealizar la escena y quitar a la gente la idea de que "aquello está
> pasando de veras", así como también para elevar el plano poético con
> el mismo sentido que lo hacían nuestros clásicos.[73]

Lorca's *re*creation of popular speech provides the major interest of the play. La Zapatera's opening diatribe against her neighbor sets the pace and flavor:

> Cállate, larga de lengua, penacho de catalineta, que si yo lo he
> hecho…, si lo yo he hecho, ha sido por mi propio gusto…. Si no te
> metes dentro de tu casa te hubiera arrastrado, viborilla empolvada; y
> esto lo digo para que me oigan todas las que están detrás de las
> ventanas. Que más vale estar casado con un viejo que con un tuerto,
> como tú estás. Y no quiero más conversación, ni contigo ni con
> nadie, ni con nadie, ni con nadie.
>
> (Entra dando un fuerte portazo.)[74]

The object of the invective is not important; what counts is its vivid imagery and the lively rhythm of its delivery. In this instance Lorca has drawn, in part, on the colorful lexicon of a Granada woman, who later reported how she scolded her *novio* at the window:

> Yo le decía a mi novio cuando estaba de "monos": "Que te vayas,
> que no vuelvas más, alcatufero, que aunque me dejes, prefiero vestir
> santos al penacho de tu catalineta diaria de todos los días,
> condenao."[75]

By using his ear for this popular speech and *re*creating it in his play, Lorca succeeds in interesting the followers of Menéndez Pidal as well.

> Tanto es así, que el lenguaje, el vocabulario puesto por mí en la
> pieza interesó vivamente a varios profesores del Centro de Estudios
> Históricos, discípulos de Menéndez Pidal en Filología.   Pedro

> Salinas, poeta y catedratico, analizó, precisamente, fragmentos del
> diálogo de *La zapatera.*[76]

Yet he derived inspiration from "fuentes cultas" as well. Another parallel
can be drawn between the speech rhythms of La Zapatera and those of Mariana in
El juez de los divorcios, an *entremés* written by Cervantes on the same subject (and
which well may have provided Lorca with the structural source for his play). In
the following scene, Mariana appears before the judge, clamoring for divorce from
her much older husband:

> Mariana: Señor, ¡divorcio, divorcio, y más
> divorcio, y otras mil veces divorcio!
>
> Juez: ¿De quién, o por qué, señora?
>
> Mariana: ¿De quién? Deste viejo, que está
> presente.
>
> Juez: ¿Por qué?
>
> . . . .
>
> Mariana: El ivierno de mi marido, y la
> primavera de mi edad....[77]

Again, Lorca was fully conscious of the artist's task of *re*creating the spontaneous
qualities of popular speech.

> El lenguaje es popular, hablado en castellano, pero de vocablos y
> sintaxis andaluzas, permitiéndome a veces, como cuando predica el
> zapatero, una breve caricatura cervantina.[78]

Cervantes brings his *entremés* to a close with a song celebrating the idea, "más vale el peor concierto / que no el divorcio mejor,"[79] also reflected in García Lorca's works.

The purely verbal level of popular idiom in this *comedia* is punctuated by songs and choreography which enrich the play's folkloric atmosphere. When El Zapatero complains to a Vecina that "mi casa no es casa. ¡Es un guirigay!,"[80] and similarly, to the Alcalde, "Yo no tengo edad para resistir este jaleo," his comments provoke a musical counterpoint, the Andalusian song "El contrabandista," which Lorca performed with La Argentinita and subsequently recorded:

> ZAPATERA. (Cantando dentro, fuerte.)
> ¡Ay, jaleo, jaleo,
> ya se acabó el alboroto
> y vamos al tiroteo![81]

Lorca also invents song for his comedy, which lends to it a style unmistakably his own. For instance, the Niño sings, near the end of the first act:

> Mariposa del aire,
> qué hermosa eres,
> mariposa del aire
> dorada y verde.
> . . . . [82]

And the choreographed movement Lorca creates for the close of Act I, when La Zapatera's husband has left her, is also highly stylized:

> (Por la puerta empiezan a entrar VECINAS vestidas con colores violentos y que llevan grandes vasos de refrescos. Giran, corren, entran y salen alrededor de la ZAPATERA, que está sentada gritando, con la prontitud y ritmo de baile. Las grandes faldas se abren a las vueltas que dan. Todos adoptan una actitud cómica de pena.)[83]

The Vecinas, dressed in red, yellow, black, green and purple, provide a colorful, comic version of the classic Greek chorus, chanting in turns, "Un refresco. Un refresquito. Para la sangre. De limón. De zarzaparrilla. La menta es mejor. Vecina. Vecinita. Zapatera. Zapaterita."

Just as Lope used the *canción* as the *vox populi* in *Peribáñez y el Comendador de Ocaña*, Lorca puts the news about La Zapatera in *coplas* sung by the townspeople.[84] In the second act, the song is first heard offstage at a distance and then is repeated *mise en scène*:

> La señora Zapatera
> al marchase su marido,
> Ha montado una taberna
> donde acude el señorio.
>
> ¿Quién te compra, Zapatera,
> el paño de tus vestidos
> y esas chambras de batista
> con encaje de bolillos?
>
> Ya la corteja el Alcalde,
> ye la corteja Don Mirlo.
> ¡Zapatera, Zapatera,
> Zapatera, te has lucido![85]

The insinuations of the song prove too much for La Zapatera, who reacts with characteristic defiance:

> La gente me canta coplas, los vecinos se ríen en sus puertas y como no tengo marido que vele por mí, salgo y a defenderme, ya que en este pueblo las autoridades son calabacines, ceros a la izquierda, estafermos.[86]

It also provokes a change in her attitude, so that the stage is set for her husband's return and the ultimately happy restoration of the status quo.

For this culminating moment in the dramatic action, Lorca appropriates two traditional figures of rural life, which were not long ago a common sight in Spain's towns and villages—the blind singer of ballads and the puppeteer. He meshes these two figures into one, and has El Zapatero return disguised as a *titiritero*, who announces his arrival with a flourish on the trumpet. But instead of *títeres*, Lorca has El Zapatero bring a *romance de ciego* and a large, rolled-up poster to illustrate the events of the ballad, the *cartelón de ciego*:

> Por la puerta aparece el ZAPATERO disfrazado. Trae una trompeta
> y un cartelón enrollado a la espalda; lo rodea la gente.[87]

It is clear from the detail of Lorca's stage directions that he himself has witnessed the performance of a *romance de cartelón*, probably as a young boy in rural Granada:

> EL ZAPATERO desenrolla el cartelón, en el que hay pintada una
> historia de ciego, dividida en pequeños cuadros, pintados con
> almazarrón y colores violentos.

He *re*creates the florid linguistic style of the *ciego*, who announces the subject of his narration with a typical moralizing preamble, or *exordium*:

> Respetable público: Oigan ustedes el romance verdadero y sustan-
> cioso de la mujer rubicunda y el hombrecito de la paciencia, para que
> sirva de escarmiento y ejemplaridad a todas las gentes de este
> mundo. (En tono lúgubre.) Agudizad vuestros oidos y enten-
> dimiento.[88]

The twofold identity of El Zapatero's disguise poses no problem since García Lorca's real purpose here is to use the *titiritero* to mount a "play within the play." In response to La Zapatera's question, "¿Y en qué consiste el trabajo de usted?," the disguised Zapatero describes his activities thus:

Es un trabajo de poca apariencia y de mucha ciencia. Enseño la vida por dentro. Aleluyas con los hechos del zapatero mansurrón y la Fierabrás de Alejandría, vida de don Diego Corrientes, aventuras del guapo Francisco Esteban y, sobre todo, arte de colocar el bocado a las mujeres parlanchinas y respondonas.[89]

His repertory could be that of any number of blind singers of ballads. The tale of the giant Fierabrás, the life of Diego Corrientes (a renowned eighteenth-century bandit), and the adventures of the outlaw Esteban were all conventional texts in the memory of the ambulant *ciego*. The themes added by Lorca are also plausible, although of course included for plot motives, in order to "catch the conscience" of La Zapatera.

The *romance* that El Zapatero recites, while pointing with a *varilla* to the scenes represented on the *cartelón*, offers a recapitulation of the play and invents a typically exaggerated outcome:

En un cortijo de Córdoba,
entre jarales y adelfas,
vivía un talabartero
con una talabartera.
Ella era mujer arisca,
él hombre de gran paciencia,
ella giraba en los veinte
y él pasaba de cincuenta.
¡Santo Dios, cómo reñian!
Miren ustedes la fiera,
burlando al débil marido
con los ojos y la lengua.
Cabellos de emperadora
tiene la talabartera
y una carne como el agua
cristalina de Lucena.
Cuando movía las faldas
en tiempos de primavera
olía toda su ropa

a limón y a yerbabuena.
¡Ay, qué limón, limón
de la limonera!
¡Qué apetitosa
talabartera!
Ved cómo la cortejaban
mocitos de gran presencia
en caballos relucientes
llenos de borlas de seda.
Gente cabal y garbosa
que pasaba por la puerta
haciendo brillar, adrede,
las onzas de sus cadenas.
La conversación a todos
daba la talabartera,
y ellos caracoleaban
sus jacas sobre las piedras.
Miradla hablando con uno
bien peinada y bien compuesta,
mientras el pobre marido
clava en el cuero la lezna.
Esposo viejo y decente
casado con joven tierna,
¡qué tunante caballista
roba tu amor en la puerta!
Un lunes por la mañana
a eso de las once y media,
cuando el sol deja sin sombra
los juncos y madreselvas,
cuando alegremente bailan
brisa y tomillo en la sierra
y van cayendo las verdes
hojas de las madroñeras,
regaba sus alhelíes
la arisca talabartera.
Llegó su amigo trotando
una jaca cordobesa

y le dijo entre suspiros:
"Niña, si tu lo quisieras,
cenaríamos mañana
los dos solos, en tu mesa."
"¿Y qué harás con mi marido?"
"Tu marido no se entera."
"¿Qué piensas hacer?" "Matarlo."
"Es ágil. Quizá no puedas.
¿Tienes revólver?" "¡Mejor,
tengo navaja barbera!"
"¿Corta mucho?" "Más que el frío.
Y no tiene ni una mella."
"¿No has mentido?" "Le daré
diez puñaladas certeras
en esta disposición,
que me parece estupenda:
cuatro en la región lumbar,
una en la tetilla izquierda,
otra en semejante sitio
y dos en cada cadera."
"¿Lo matarás en seguida?"
"Esta noche cuando vuelva
con el cuero y con las crines
por la curva de la acequia."[90]

The ballad narration is interrupted at this point by another plot development and is never completed. Yet it effectively demonstrates many of the stylistic features of the *romance de ciego*, including melodramatic exaggeration, lengthy exposition, and an emphatic sanguinary interest. (On the other hand, the segments of rapid dialogue are not characteristic of this type of ballad.) In addition, García Lorca shows that he also understands the process by which a *romance de ciego*, unlike the ballad whose variants signal a purely oral tradition, is memorized: word by word and line by line, in unvarying sequence. The interruption of any portion of the memorized recitation endangers its completion. He describes El Zapatero as "malhumorado" by the audience's reaction and intervention: "¡Hagan el favor de

no interrumpirme! ¡Cómo se conoce que no tienen que decirlo de memoria!"[91]
Lorca's knowledge of this rural figure is most certainly firsthand.

Lorca adds other short passages to reinforce the characterization of El
Zapatero as an active bearer of the tradition. In Act I El Zapatero sings the
traditional *coplas*:

> Si tu madre quiere un rey,
> la baraja tiene cuatro:
> rey de oros, rey de copas,
> rey de espadas, rey de bastos.[92]

In the second act La Zapatera recalls, in front of the "puppeteer," the extraordinary
lore stored in her absent husband's memory:

> ¿Ve usted todos esos romances y chupaletrinas que canta y cuenta
> por los pueblos? Pues todo eso es un ochavo comparado con lo que
> él sabía…, el sabía… ¡el triple!
> . . . .
> Y el cuadruple…. Me los decía todos a mí cuando nos acostábamos.
> Historietas antiguas que usted no habrá oído mentar siquira…y a mí
> me daba un susto…, pero él me decía: "¡Preciosa de mi alma, si esto
> ocurre de mentirijillas!"[93]

La zapatera prodigiosa is Lorca's attempt to *re*create the folkloric
environment of an anonymous Andalusian town for the stage. In the 1930 version
for Madrid's Teatro Español, he presents a sampler of popular verbal art, including
both the lyric *canción* and the narrative *romance de ciego*, as well as a variety of
popular speech forms.

> Las cartas inquietas que recibía de mis amigos de París en hermosa
> y amarga lucha con un arte abstracto me llevaron a componer, por
> reacción, esta fábula casi vulgar con su realidad directa, donde yo
> quise que fluyera un invisible hilo de poesía y donde el grito cómico

y el humor se levantan, claros y sin trampas, en los primeros términos.[94]

Yet Lorca was to create still another "versión musicalizada" of *La zapatera* during his stay in Buenos Aires and Montevideo in 1933—1934. His instincts in representing *La zapatera* were to increase the plastic elements of the work, to open it up to an even greater participation of volume, color, movement and music that characterize the *género chico*. On the eve of its première, he gave an interview for *La Nación*:

> La obra que yo monté en el teatro Español fue una versión de cámara donde esta farsa adquiere una mayor intimidad, pero perdía sus perspectivas rítmicas. En realidad, su verdadero estreno es en Buenos Aires, ligada con las canciones de XVIII y XIX y bailada por la gracia extraordinaria de Lola Membrives con el apoyo de su compañía.[95]

The "canciones del XVIII y XIX" Lorca refers to are his "escenificaciones" of three popular songs: the "Romance de los pelegrinitos" and "Los cuatro muleros," previously performed and recorded with La Argentinita, and the "Canción de otoño en Castilla":

> A los árboles altos
> los lleva el viento,
> y a los enamorados
> el pensamiento.[96]

Expounding on his love of this particular song for the Argentine press, Lorca added:

> Se canta en Burgos y es como la región misma: cosa de llanura con chopos dorados.... Digan ustedes si no es eso de una gran belleza. ¿Qué más poesía? Ya podemos callarnos todos los que escribimos

y pensamos poesía ante esa magnífica poesía que han "hecho" los campesinos.

In response to the objection of one of his interviewers who interrutped, "Es, sin embargo, de forma culta," Lorca was quick to explain:

> Culta, sí, en su origen desconocido. Pero luego ¿no les dije que las canciones viven? Pues esta ha vivido en los labios del pueblo y el pueblo la ha embellecido, la ha completado, la ha depurado hasta esa belleza que hoy tenemos ante nosotros. Porque esto lo cantan en Burgos los campesinos, ¡ni un señorito! En las casas de la ciudad no se canta esto.[97]

These three songs accompanied the main play as a "fin de fiesta," *re*creating the total theatrical function of the *comedia* during the Siglo de Oro. From another interview, we have Lorca's description of these performances:

> Este "fin de fiesta" es un entretenimiento que yo he planeado.... Durará alrededor de media hora, y se pasarán tres partes. La primera consistirá en la escenificación de *Los pelegrinitos*, así como suena, pues ésta es la pronunciación popular y andaluza. Se trata de una de las canciones más difundidas del siglo XVI [*sic*] español, un romance anónimo, que yo he arreglado para esta versión escénica. A continuación se pasará la conocida canción *Los cuatro muleros*, y, finalmente, Lola Membrives interpretará un romance del siglo XVI, algo modernizado, que titularemos *Canción castellana*. Yo considero que escenificar la canción, sobre todo estos romances, es una labor de más trascendencia que la que puede inferirse por su tono. La canción escenificada tiene sus personajes, que hablan con música, su coro, que juega el mismo papel que en la tragedia griega. Por tanto, es, dentro de un marco reducido, sobre todo tiempo, un espectáculo breve, pero completo, lleno de sugerencias y bellezas.[98]

In yet another interview, it is clear that the second version is closer to Lorca's intentions: "Esta versión que da Lola Membrives de mi farsa es la perfecta, la que yo quiero. En ella hay música y bailes que no me fue posible poner cuando el estreno en España."[99]   According to Francisco García Lorca, who possessed a copy of the original, the Buenos Aires version amplified the 1930 text with "abundantes adiciones musicales que, en algunos casos, comportan nuevas escenas." The added scenes apparently result from new musical interventions, "más algun intermedio de bailes." The incorporation of more songs and dances, and even more characters ("tres gitanillas," for example), does not seem to have altered the play's basic structure. Instead,

> estos añadidos acentuaban el vago aire de ballet, que ya tenía antes
> la obra, y la línea cuasi musical de su desarrollo, dentro de una
> estilización hacia la ópera cómica que extrema a veces el perfil de los
> personajes.[100]

García Lorca himself took the part of his Autor, and recited the prologue every night of the play's run in Buenos Aires. This musical version, with dance performances during the intermissions and the "canciones escenificadas" at the end, was repeated by Lola Membrives and her company in Madrid's Coliseum throughout the month of March, 1935.[101]

Clearly García Lorca never lost interest during these years in the traditional art forms that had captured his childhood imagination. Just as he took his private performance of popular song from his home to an increasingly wider public, he expanded his first toy theater to the full dimensions of theatrical expression in front of audiences at home and abroad. The *teatro de guiñolillo*, presented with the collaboration of Falla in the García Lorca home in 1923, was the basis for a performance of *Los títeres de Cachiporra* Lorca directed as a "función de despedida" before leaving Buenos Aires in March of 1934, as well as for his presentation of the *entremeses* of Cervantes and the *Retablillo de don Cristóbal* in the Hotel Florida on his homecoming celebration in Madrid that May.[102] He moved the puppets himself in a *teatro de guiñol* session given in the Lyceum Club the following February, which was repeated during the Feria del Libro on Paseo Recoletos in May, 1935.[103] Another performance of *Los títeres de Cachiporra*

---

was given for the students at the Residencia in early 1935, while at the same time he was directing Lope's *Peribáñez y el Comendador de Ocaña* for presentation in the Club Anfistora.[104]

From the spring of 1932 on, all of García Lorca's work with the forms of *teatro menor* was simultaneous with his direction of *comedias* and *entremeses* of the seventeenth century for the traveling theater group, "La Barraca." "La Barraca" was to provide him with still another arena for the development of his dramatic art.

Notes

1. In the "Prologue" to *Three Tragedies* by Federico García Lorca (New York: Directions, 1955), p. 1.

2. José Luis Cano, *García Lorca: Biografía ilustrada* (Barcelona: Ediciones Destino, 1962), p. 16. See also Claude Couffon, *Granada y García Lorca* (Buenos Aires: Losada, 1967), pp. 23–24. According to Carmen Ramos, who looked after Lorca as a child, "Cuando Federico, que volvía de la iglesia con su madre, vio a los comediantes levantando el teatrillo, no quiso retirarse de la plaza del pueblo. En la noche no cenó, y se desesperó por asistir al espectáculo. Volvió en un terrible estado de excitación. Al día siguiente el teatro de títres reemplazó al 'altar' en el muro del jardín."

3. For a preliminary study, see Suzanne Byrd, "The Puppet Theater as Genesis of Lorcan Drama," *García Lorca Review*, 6 (1978), pp. 139–149. I have not yet seen Isabel Vázquez de Castro's unpublished diss., "El títere y su proyección en la obra de Federico García Lorca" (Paris: Institute Iberique et Latino Americain, 1985). Piero Menarini's overview is important: "Federico y los títeres: Cronología y dos documentos," *Boletín de la Fundación Federico García Lorca*, III, no. 5 (June, 1989), pp. 103–128.

4. Laffranque, pp. 419–420. Also Ian Gibson, *Federico García Lorca*, vol. 1 (Barcelona: Grijalbo, 1985), pp. 334–339.

5. Byrd, p. 142. See also Luis T. González-del-Valle's "Perspectivas críticas: horizontes infinitos. *La Niña que riega la albahaca y el Príncipe preguntón* y las constantes dramaticas de Federico García Lorca," *Anales de la literatura española contemporánea*, v. 7 (1982), pp. 253–264.

6. *Federico y su mundo*, p. 273.

7. *Federico y su mundo*, p. 271. Lorca later repeats the riddle pattern in *La zapatera prodigiosa*, when the Mozo courts La Zapatera with the question, "¿Cuántas semillas tiene el girasol?"

8. Falla's *Retablo* is taken from the scene of the travelling puppeteer in *Don Quijote*, which was, in turn, a comical rendition of the traditional Carolingian ballad, "Gaiferos libera a Melisendra." See *Don Quijote*, Part II, chap. XXVI, ed. Riquer, pp. 729–738.

9. *En España con Federico García Lorca*, p. 175.

10. *Federico y su mundo*, p. 276.

11. In the article cited above, p. 114, P. Menarini notes the ambiguity in a letter Lorca wrote to Adolfo Salazar on January 1, 1922: "Yo estoy muy contento también porque si hacemos esto saldré contigo, Adolfito, en una obra que es la ilusión de mi juventud." For more correspondence on the *guiñol*, see the *Epistolario*, ed. C. Maurer, pp. 48–50. For the inversion of author and actor, see the Prologue to *La zapatera prodigiosa* and the Prologue of *Retablillo de don Cristóbal*. All of these recall Lorca addressing the children in the audience during his puppet show in Granada. In *El Público*, the "Director" goes on to participate as a principal character throughout the play.

12. *OC*, II, p. 110. The play is hereafter referred to as *TC*. Lorca no doubt learned this song from Torner's *Cancionero musical de la lírica popular asturiana*, no. 21. In *Lírica hispánica*, p. 294, Torner describes this song as one of the "cantos populares de hoy" intended for dance.

13. *TC*, p. 116.

14. *TC*, p. 122. Irene's version offers a well-known variant: "Yo no quiero que me miren, / que me pongo colorá." *OC*, II, p. 63.

15. *La arboleda perdida*, p. 153. Alberti's verses ("Mi corza, buen amigo, // mi corza blanca. // Los lobos la mataron // al pie del agua. // Los lobos, buen amigo, // que huyeron por el río. // Los lobos la mataron // dentro del agua."), along with two others of the same collection, were set to music by three young composers living at the Residencia de Estudiantes: Gustavo Durán, and Rodolfo and Ernesto Halffter. It became widely known, or, in Alberti's words, "consiguió, a poco de publicada, una resonancia mundial" (p. 196). The song from the *Cancionero musical de Palacio* which inspired Alberti is: "En Ávila, mis ojos, // dentro en Ávila. // En Ávila del Río // mataron mi amigo. // Dentro

en Ávila." Included in Alonso and Blecua's anthology, p. 21, and in Margit Frenk's *Lírica española de tipo popular* (Madrid: Cátedra, 1978), p. 156.

16. *La arboleda perdida*, p. 172.

17. *La arboleda perdida*, p. 214. Alberti echoes the sentiments of the nineteenth-century poet Augusto Ferrán, who wrote in the prologue to his book of poems, *La soledad* (1861): "En cuanto a mis pobres versos, si algún dia oigo salir uno solo de ellos de entre un corrillo de alegres muchachas, acompañado por los tristes tonos de la guitarra, daré por cumplida toda mi ambición de gloria y habré escuchado el mejor juicio crítico de mis humildes composiciones." See Solita Salinas de Marichal, *El mundo poético de Rafael Alberti* (Madrid: Gredos, 1968), p. 112.

18. See Velloso, *Conversaciones con Rafael Alberti*, pp. 255–256.

19. *Auto de Navidad* (Madrid: Aguilar, 1971), pp. 78–79. Music, p. 145.

20. See *Romancero tradicional de las lenguas hispánicas*, X, eds. D. Catalán, et al. (Madrid: Gredos, 1978), p. 421.

21. In a letter to Robert Marrast. According to Marrast, "le titre de *La novia del marinero* laisse deviner une oeuvre plus traditionnelle, plus folklorique, que *Ardiente-y-fría.*" *Aspects du théâtre de Rafael Alberti* (Paris: Société d'Edition d'Enseignement Supérieur, 1967), p. 12.

22. According to Manuel Bayo (see below) a copy of the play has been found, but he gives no reference for it.

23. Marrast, *Aspects*, pp. 19–21.

24. *En España con Federico García Lorca*, pp. 46–47.

25. "La *Santa Casilda* de Rafael Alberti," *ABC* (January 27, 1931), p. 36. Cited in part by Marrast, *Aspects*, p. 21, and in part by Louise B. Popkin, *The Theatre of Rafael Alberti* (London: Tamesis, 1975), p. 38.

26. *Romancero hispánico*, II, p. 429.

27. From the Archives of Menéndez Pidal in Madrid.

28. See *Romancero tradicional*, X, pp. 113–115. In 1977, 14 additional versions of this ballad were collected during a field trip in León and Santander, and have been published in the *Archivo Internacional Electrónico del Romancero (AIER)*, II, eds. Suzanne Petersen, et al. (Madrid: Gredos, 1982), pp. 40–56.

29. This dramatized version of Lorca's poem was recalled from memory with telling intonation by Diego Catalán, who saw the representation at the Instituto Escuela as a child of five or six years of age.

30. *OC*, I, p. 301.

31. Eugenio de Olvarría y Huarte, "El Folk-lore de Madrid," *Biblioteca de las tradiciones populares*, II, ed. Antonio Machado y Álvarez (Sevilla: Alejandro Guichot, 1884), p. 49.

32. The text of this play, thought to be lost for many years, was recovered and sent by Alberti to Manuel Bayo, who published it with a short introduction: "Una obra escénica inédita de Rafael Alberti," *Revista de Occidente*, 128 (November, 1973), pp. 151–158. All the following quotes are from this source.

33. The play was also performed by the "Teatro Popular" of the Misiones Pedagógicas two days after the "sublevación" against the Republic, on July 20, 1936, in Madrid's Teatro Español. See Bayo, p. 151.

34. Ramón Menéndez Pidal, *Flor nueva de romances viejos*, 20th ed. (Madrid: Espasa-Calpe, 1965), p. 78. The complete version, pp. 78–80.

35. For a thorough study of this ballad's history, see Diego Catalán, "*El Enamorado y la Muerte*: De romance trovadoresco a romance novelesco," in *Por campos del Romancero* (Madrid: Gredos, 1970), pp. 13–55.

36. *Aspects*, p. 22.

37. *Por campos del Romancero*, p. 23.

38. The syntax of Menéndez Pidal's hemistich, however, would not be supported in oral tradition. See *Por campos*, pp. 53–54.

39. The text of the play has been published by Robert Marrast as a sequel to Alberti's Havana lecture. (See n. 3 in chapter 1.) Gonzalo Menéndez Pidal gave Marrast the only known copy of this work, which was typewritten, with notes in Alberti's handwriting. See *Aspects*, p. 25. All quotations in the text refer to Marrast's edition, hereafter cited as *PP*.

40. *La arboleda perdida*, p. 237.

41. As late as 1935, "Federico y Elizalde trabajaban asiduamente en el piano...sobre esta versión musicalizada." *Federico y su mundo*, p. 276.

42. According to a personal interview (July, 1982) with Jimena Menéndez Pidal, who directed the performances of the Instituto Escuela during these years.

43. *PP*, p. 65.

44. In a taped interview with Manuel Bayo, cited in González Martín, p. 184.

45. *TC*, pp. 143–144.

46. Rodríguez Marín, *Cantos populares españoles*, I, pp. 95–96.

47. Alonso de Ledesma, *Juegos de Noches Buenas a lo divino* (Barcelona: Sebastián Cormellas, 1605). *Romancero y cancionero sagrados*, ed. Justo de Sancha, in *Biblioteca de Autores Españoles*, 35 (Madrid: M. Rivadeneyra, 1872), p. 158, no. 394.

48. *Biblioteca de Autores Españoles*, 42, p. 333.

49. See Joaquín Díaz, *100 temas infantiles* (Valladolid: Centro Castellano de Estudios Folklóricos, 1981); text and music, pp. 149–152.

50. *PP*, pp. 80–81.

51. Interview cited in González Martín, p. 184.

52. See *Aspects*, pp. 13–19.

53. Sergio Hernández de Soto, "Juegos infantiles de Extremadura," in *Biblioteca de las tradiciones populares españolas*, III (Sevilla: Francisco Álvarez, 1884), ed. A. Machado y Álvarez, pp. 91–94 ("La viudita," "El conde de Cabra"). A very similar version is published by E. de Olvarría y Huarte, "El Folk-lore de Madrid" in vol. II of the same collection, previously cited, pp. 47–48. Only one of the *coplas* had appeared in Rodríguez Marín's *Cantos populares*, I (1882), p. 50, among the "Rimas infantiles": "Soy biudita, / lo manda la ley, / quiero casarme / y no hayo con quién. / Ni contigo, / ni contigo, / sino contigo / qu' eres mi bien."

54. Such presuppositions lead to seeing the work as no more than a "nonsense play" of "essentially non-dramatic character," and as "a series of loosely related episodes involving numerous characters." See Popkin, p. 40.

55. The game-song continues to live in the oral tradition with the same beginning, according to Joaquín Díaz, *100 temas infantiles*, pp. 153–154.

56. *PP*, pp. 83–84.

57. *PP*, p. 55.

58. This information supplied to Marrast by María Teresa León. See *Aspects*, p. 19.

59. The name, as in the case of the other characters, is suggested by popular tradition. For a number of children's games that begin with "Pipirigaña," see Hernández

de Soto's collection in *Biblioteca de tradiciones populares*, II, pp. 137–139; and Rodríguez Marín, *Cantos populares*, I, pp. 48–49.

60. *PP*, p. 41.

61. González Martín, p. 184. The *aleluyas* were the equivalent of comic strips and were enormously popular in the nineteenth century. Printed on thin cheap paper, dyed pink, green, or blue to disguise its poor quality, they consisted of rough comic prints, each captioned underneath by a *copla*. Margarita Ucelay has elucidated the function of the *aleluya* in her edition of Lorca's *Amor de Don Perlimplín con Belisa en su jardín* (Madrid: Cátedra, 1990), pp. 13–17.

62. At this point in the interview, Alberti recited the prologue. See González Martín, p. 185.

63. See the description of the *Romance de ciego* in chapter 4.

64. *PP*, pp. 41–43.

65. González Martín, p. 186.

66. *OC*, III, p. 404.

67. Antonio Gallego Morell, *García Lorca: Cartas, postales, poemas y dibujos* (Madrid: Editorial Moneda y Crédito, 1968), p. 53; ed. C. Maurer, *Epistolario*, I, pp. 81–82.

68. *Federico y su mundo*, p. 301; *OC*, III, p. 403.

69. Gallego Morell, p. 97; Maurer, *Epistolario*, II, p. 90.

70. Arturo de Hoyo's "cincuentenario" edition of the *OC* includes the 1930 and 1933 versions. Mario Hernández documents the four performances for these (in Madrid, December of 1930; again in Madrid in 1933; with the Lola Membrives company in Buenos Aires, in 1933; and with the Lola Membrives company in Madrid, 1935). See the introduction to his edition of *La zapatera prodigiosa* (Madrid: Alianza, 1982), pp. 9–44 and pp. 191–213.

71. I use the 1930 edition of the *OC*, II, p. 305. Hereafter cited as *ZP*.

72. *TC*, pp. 105–106. See also the equivalent "Prólogo hablado" to the *Retablillo de don Cristóbal*, *OC*, II, pp. 675–676.

73. *OC*, III, p. 404.

74. *ZP*, Act I, p. 309.

75. Quoted by Mario Hernández in his edition of *La zapatera*, p. 34. The *criada* Dolores Cebrián, remembers Lorca thus: "Cuando en la televisión oigo a uno que va por los pueblos preguntando a las gentes las cosas del lugar, me acuerdo del señorito Federico, que también le gustaba preguntar a mi Encarna y a mí por las cosas de mi tierra y de mis gentes." Daniel Devoto appreciates in *La zapatera* "la más extraordinaria colección de expresiones tradicionales jamás oídas en una obra literaria...." See "Las zapateras prodigiosas," in *Lecciones sobre Federico García Lorca*, ed. Andrés Soria Olmedo (Granada: Comisión Nacional del Cincuentenario, 1986) p. 73.

76. *OC*, III, p. 566.

77. In the collection of *Entremeses* by Miguel de Cervantes, ed. Eugenio Asensio (Madrid: Castalia, 1970), p. 62. Francisco García Lorca points out the connection between these two works in *Federico y su mundo*, pp. 309–310.

78. *OC*, III, p. 405.

79. *Entremeses*, p. 72.

80. *ZP*, p. 306.

81. *ZP*, p. 323.

82. *ZP*, p. 332.

83. *ZP*, pp. 334–335.

84. The Niño first warns La Zapatera about "las coplas que te han sacado," *ZP*, p. 340. The *copla* is a quatrain arrangement of the eight-syllable *romance* line.

85. *ZP*, p. 343. The music is that of the "Zorongo gitano," in Onís, pp. 137–139.

86. *ZP*, p. 343. "Estafermo" was also part of Dolores Cebrián's vocabulary, along with "garabato de candil," "chupaletrinas," "corremundos" and "judío colorado." See M. Hernández, *La zapatera prodigiosa*, p. 34.

87. *ZP*, Act II, p. 348.

88. *ZP*, Act II, pp. 352–353.

89. *ZP*, Act II, p. 351.

90. *ZP*, Act II, pp. 353–357.

91. *ZP*, p. 355.

92. *ZP*, pp. 324–325. Although not included on the recording Lorca made with La Argentinita, he performed this song, traditional not only in the province of Granada, at the

Residencia de Estudiantes and in the homes of friends on a great number of occasions. Moreno Villa, *Los autores como actores*, p. 65. Onís, p. 113.

93. *ZP*, pp. 359–360.

94. *OC*, III, p. 404.

95. November 30, 1933. Cited in *Federico y su mundo*, p. 302; *OC*, III, p. 403.

96. *OC*, III, p. 581. Mario Hernández reconstructs the entire performance, in reality a fusion of three different songs Lorca knew, including these verses:

> Si eres hija del sueño,
> paloma mía,
> a la hora del alba
> verte querría.
> Morena, dímelo,
> si eres casada o no;
> si eres casada, niña
> de mi corazón.
>
> Yo no quiero más premio
> ni más corona
> que ser dueña absoluta
> de tu persona.
>
> Corazón que no quiera
> sufrir dolores
> pase la vida entera
> libre de amores.
> Libre de amores,
> ay, vida mía,
> libre de amores.

See his edition of *La zapatera prodigiosa*, pp. 168–169 and pp. 174–175.

97. *OC*, III, p. 581. García Lorca's analogy for the process of oral transmission is both original and accurate: "Las canciones son como las personas. Viven, se perfeccionan y, algunas degeneran, se deshacen....", p. 580.

98. *OC*, III, pp. 576–577. Mario Hernández and Arturo de Hoyo correct earlier editions of the *OC* which originally gave *el siglo XVIII* as Larca's date for the origin of "Los pelegrinitos." In the case of the "Canción castellana," the sixteenth century is most likely accurate, since the song has the air of the "cancioneros antiguos." But the correction *siglo XVIII* to *siglo XVI* does not make sense in the case of "Los pelegrinitos," since the *romance* most probably originated in the nineteenth century. In the same interview, Lorca described plans for other "canciones escenificadas" to be staged in the near future; there is no record that these plans were carried out. "Pienso escenificar lo que se llama 'villancicos,' villancicos de Góngora, de Lope de Vega, de Tirso de Molina, muy breves y muy sabrosos, con un sentido profundo y una grata envoltura, que espero serán verdaderamente gustados por el público...."

99. Cited by Mario Hernández, ed., *La zapatera prodigiosa*, p. 42.

100. *Federico y su mundo*, pp. 302–303. Lola Membrives kept the original.

101. Carlos Morla Lynch, pp. 446–449, gives an account of the performance.

102. Laffranque, pp. 454–455.

103. The session included *Los dos habladores* and the *Retablillo de don Cristóbal*. Laffranque, p. 457 and p. 459.

104. Laffranque, pp. 456–459.

4

The Context of Popular Balladry and Song

Both Alberti and García Lorca drew upon a tradition of popular culture that has disappeared with the advance of the twentieth century. Though well known to Spaniards from a range of social classes at the beginning of the century, the popular poetry and stories once hawked through the streets and circulated on cheap paper are almost unknown to them as the century ends. Today one no longer sees the blind men and their *lazarillos*, or guides, who used to traverse the small towns and villages distributing *hojas volanderas* and *pliegos sueltos*, while proclaiming the subjects of their wares in a loud chant. It is almost impossible now to find one of the last of these blind vendors, or perhaps his helper, sequestered in a poor dwelling of some Castilian town, who formerly sang for a living in the public squares and marketplaces of the most remote villages. Nevertheless, the memory of the *ciego* is still present in many towns in Spain. Spaniards of the Generation of 1898, and even of the Generation of 1927, could still witness the sale of this kind of printed matter in the outlying districts of the larger cities. Certain writers of these generations dedicated a portion of their work to recording the *ciego* and his ·wares. Perhaps their interest was a sign of the imminent disappearance of a figure who had been familiar for centuries.

The Singer and Seller of Tales:
The *Romance de ciego*

Miguel de Unamuno and Pío Baroja have left us two interesting *costumbrista* descriptions of the *romance de ciego* which deserve to be quoted at length. In Unamuno's novel, *Paz en la guerra*, published in 1897, we read:

> Hacía una temporada que le había dado a Ignacio con ardor por comprar en la plaza del Mercado, al ciego que los vendía, aquellos pliegos de lectura, que sujetos con cañitas a unas cuerdas se ofrecían al curioso; pliegos sueltos de cordel. Era la afición de moda entre los chicos, que los compraban y se los trocaban.
>
> Aquellos pliegos encerraban la flor de la fantasía popular y de la historia; los había de historia sagrada, de cuentos orientales, de epopeyas medievales, del ciclo carolingio, de libros de caballerías, de las más celebradas ficciones de la literatura europea, de la crema de la leyenda patria, de hazañas de bandidos, y de la guerra civil de los Siete Años. Eran el sedimento poético de los siglos, que después de haber nutrido los cantos y relatos que han consolado de la vida a tantas generaciones, rodando de boca en oído y de oído en boca, contados al amor de la lumbre, viven, por ministerio de los ciegos callejeros, en la fantasía, siempre verde, del pueblo.
>
> Ignacio los leía soñoliento y sin entenderlos apenas. Los de verso cansábanle pronto y todos tenían para él muchas palabras inentendibles. Sus ojos, para dormirse, reposaban a las veces en alguno de los toscos grabados. Pocas de aquellas legendarias figuras se le pintaban con líneas fijas: a lo más la de Judith levantando por el cabello la cabeza de Holofernes; Sansón atado a los pies de Dalila; Simbad en la cueva del gigante, y Aladino explorando la caverna con su lámpara maravillosa; Carlomagno y sus doce pares "acuchillando turbantes, cotas y mallas de acero" en el campo en que corría la sangre como cuando está lloviendo; el gigantazo Fierabrás de Alejandría, "que era una torre de huesos", y que a nadie tuvo miedo, inclinando su cabezota en la pita bautismal; Oliveros de Castilla, vestido ya de negro, ya de blanco o rojo, con el brazo ensangrentado hasta el codo y mirando desde la plaza del torneo a la hija del rey de

Inglaterra; Artús de Algarbe peleando con el monstruo de brazos de lagarto, alas de murciélago y lengua de carbón; Pierres de Provenza huyendo con la hermosa Magalona a las grupas del caballo; Flores, el moro, llevando de la mano a la playa y mirando a Blancaflor, la cristiana, que mira al suelo; Geneveva de Bravante, semidesnuda y acurrucada en la cueva con su hijito, junto a la Cierva; el cadáver del Cid Ruy Díaz de Vivar, el Castellano, acuchillando al judío que osó tocarle la barba; José María deteniendo una diligencia en las fragosidades de Sierra Morena; las grullas llevando a Bertoldo por el aire y sobre todo esto, Cabrera, Cabrera a caballo con su flotante capa blanca.[1]

And Pío Baroja, in his article describing the "Carteles de feria y literatura de cordel":

En las aldeas y pueblos de España, desde hace muchísimo tiempo no hay barracas con figuras de cera. Este espectáculo era uno de los más sensacionales y folletinescos de la época. En algunas partes, se sustituían las barracas por unos carteles horriblemente pintados, en donde se representaban escenas de crímenes, inundaciones, rayos, pedriscos y otras calamidades públicas.

Generalmente, tales carteles estaban pintados por los dos lados; en uno de ellos se veían los personajes de un crimen, el asesino que mataba a una mujer o a sus propios hijos y volvía tranquilamente a su casa, y luego se le veía preso en la cárcel, y al último aparecía sentado en el banquillo fatal, donde le habían dado garrote. En el otro lado se trataba de un fenómeno cósmico o atmosférico, de un eclipse o de una aurora boreal con los colores del arco iris.

El más característico que recuerdo de estos carteles es uno que vi en Sigüenza, hace treinta y tantos años.

A un lado se representaba el crimen de Don Benito, en varias escenas, con el trágico fin en el patíbulo de los dos criminales importantes: García de Paredes, hijo de una familia noble de Extremadura, y el amigo y compinche suyo, tipo shakesperiano, llamado Castejón. Entre los dos mataron a una pobre costurera, Inés María, y a su madre.

El hombre que comentaba el cartel recitaba con voz lastimera un romance, del que no recuerdo más que estos dos versos puestos en boca del asesino y dirigidos a la víctima:

Entrégate, Inés María, que tu madre ya murió.

Los romances explicativos de asesinatos que recitaban los hombres que llevaban carteles no eran casi nunca antiguos, porque los horrores lejanos interesaban poco al público. Eran, en general, de hechos recientes.

Yo he oído romances sobre ese crimen de Don Benito, sobre el del Huerto del Francés, Rosaura la de Trujillo, Cintabelde, Higinia Balaguer, protagonista del suceso de la calle de Fuencarral, que fué famosísimo en España, y de otros, como el del exprés de Andalucía.

Además, en esos cartelones se comentaban asuntos políticos de actualidad. Uno de ellos estaba dedicado a la sublevación del general Villacampa, y se contaba cómo la hija de éste se presentaba en casa de Sagasta, jefe del Gobierno por entonces, vestida de negro, a pedir el indulto de su padre, y el viejo político lloraba enternecido.

También había un cartelón del submarino Peral, con las conquistas que íbamos a hacer los españoles cuando este submarino anduviera por el fondo de los mares y encontrara en él restos de naufragio, como el de los galeones de Vigo....

De tales relaciones, la que recuerdo más completa es la aparición de la Fiera Corrupia.

Varias veces estuve escuchando las narraciones horripilantes y a veces cínicas de dicha fiera fantástica.

La Corrupia tenía forma de dragón rojo, con siete cabezas, siete cuernos y unos candeleros con velas en cada cabeza. Era evidentemente la bestia del Apocalipsis, más o menos camuflada, que venía a la plaza pública a presentar sus respetos a la gente....

Esta Fiera Corrupia, otras veces Correpia, descendiente espúrea de la Bestia del Apocalipsis, tenía diversos avatares. Perdía, sin duda, en otros carteles y romances el carácter de su origen bíblico....

El monstruo evolucionó con el tiempo, y en otros romances se le llamó Crupecia o Curpecia: "Horrorosos estragos ocasionados por la Fiera Curpencia, que apareció en Melilla, en el río de la Plata."

No sabemos qué río será éste, o si el autor del letrero confundió
Melilla con Buenos Aires.

A juzgar por el grabado que encabezaba el romance, la Fiera
Curpecia era un monstruo femenino, con cuatro cuernos, alas de
murciélago, dos patas y dos garras suplementarias a cada lado. Su
voracidad era terrible. El hombre del cartel que vendía los romances,
hombre, sin duda, de gran cultura histórica, aseguraba que la fiera
comía más que el animal llamado Heliogábalo.[2]

Typically the *ciego* narrated or chanted his text (accompanying himself on
a guitar, if he owned one) in front of a gathering in the marketplace or public
square, while his *lazarillo* pointed to scenes from the *romance*, depicted visually
like a cartoon on a big poster board attached to a pole. This was the *cartelón del
ciego*.[3] Doubtlessly the graphic illustration of the ballad's characters and events,
in combination with the oral performance of the *ciego*, contributed to the sale of
the printed *pliegos* of the texts themselves.

The "pliegos de lectura, que sujetos con cañitas a unas cuerdas" and sold by
the *ciegos*, could be found until the 1930's, together with the "Historia de Bertoldo,
Bertoldino y Cacaseno" and a popular edition of the *Quijote*, in many rural
homes.[4] Many *pliegos* have since been lost through use or negligence; others
were burned by Franco's troops when they took Republican territory.[5] Today the
pliegos de cordel are bibliographic rarities treasured and traded by an urban elite.

The sale of the *cupón*, or lottery ticket, as a means of living, today reserved
only for blind men, has taken the place of the old "privilegio" of selling the
literature of "caña y cordel," once the exclusive right of the *ciegos*.[6] The blind
singers of ballads inherited a long guild association tradition which dates back to
the Middle Ages.[7] At least since that period, sightless men had supplemented
their migratory begging with various occupations for which the ear, the memory,
and the voice were essential. The blind *rezador*, for whom the Arcipreste de Hita
says he composed *cantares*,[8] continued, in the following centuries, to invite
requests for prayers from the devout and charitable members of his audience. And
we cannot forget the *ciego* in *Lazarillo de Tormes*, who "en su oficio era un

águila," and who knew more than a hundred prayers, which he would sing in "un
tono bajo, reposado y muy sonable."[9]

During the mid-sixteenth century, the *ciego* makes an appearance in various
works of the *teatro menor*, soliciting alms in exchange for singing psalms and
prayers from his extensive repertory, which he announces:

> Ayuda, fieles hermanos,
> al ciego lleno de males:
> los salmos penitenciales
> si mandáis rezar, cristianos,
> Dios os guarde pies y manos,
> vuestra vista conservada;
> la oracion de la enparedada
> y los versos gregorianos,
> las Angustias, la Pasión,
> las almas del Purgatorio,
> la oración de San Gregorio,
> la santa Resurrección....[10]

In Juan de Timoneda's *Entremés de un ciego y un moço y un pobre, muy gracioso*,
we find a similar petition:

> Mandad, señores, rezar,
> la muy bendita oración
> de la sancta encarnación
> del que nos vino a saluar,
> otra oración singular....[11]

However, by the beginning of the seventeenth century, according to Lope de Vega,
the *ciego*'s merchandise is already written. In *La octava maravilla*, Act I, we learn
of these "papeles impresos":

> Don Juan.   ¿Qué es eso,
>   Motril? ¿Es papel?

Motril.	Y impreso.
Don Juan.	Muestra.
Motril.	Si no le trujera.
Don Juan.	¿Qué es esto?
Motril.	Historia trovada.
Don Juan.	¿Versos son?

Motril.
            ¡Y qué tan buenos!,
de un hombre que cuando menos
dicen que parió en Granada.

Don Juan.   ¿Hombre parir? ¿Quién lo afirma?

Motril.   *Los ciegos que ven*, señor.

Don Juan.   ¡Que se sufre tanto error!
mas con esto se confirma
la barbaridad de España.

Motril.   ¿Está de molde y te burlas?

Don Juan.   Cómo esas cosas de burlas
sufre el molde y acompaña.
      Luego dicen que reniega
un cristiano y que el demonio
le aparece en testimonio
de que a sus vicios se entrega.
      Luego es martir, y aparece
en su tierra a un licenciado,
y el vulgo necio, atezado
lo celebra y encarece....[12]

In Lope's *Servir a señor discreto*, written sometime between 1610–1618, the *coplas de ciego* are equivalent to other forms of merchandise:

Girón.
> ¿Quién compra la obra nueva,
> recién impresa y famosa,
> della verso y della prosa?
> ¿Quién la compra? ¿quién la lleva?

. . . .

Doña Leonor.
> ¡Coplas! pensé que traía
> puntas de Flandes y Holandas.

Girón.
> Ni se de puntas ni bandas,
> porque yo trato en poesía.

Doña Leonor.
> ¿Véndese ya?

Girón.
> Por nosotros.

. . . .

Doña Leonor.
> ¿De qué trata ese papel?

Girón.
> Cinco elogios milagrosos
> de capitanes famosos
> vienen escritos en él.

. . . .

Doña Leonor.
¡Buena, para ser de ciego![13]

And in his *Santiago el Verde* (1615), the market reality of the *ciego*'s enterprise is clearly evident:

Rodrigo.   Dad por mi vida, maestro.
Esa historia para coplas
a un ciego que la pregone
y a un neçio que la componga.

García.   Ya, señor, la escribe un nezio
y otro çiego la pregona.

Rodrigo.   No se como se consiente
que mil inbentadas cosas
por ynorantes se bendan
por los çiegos que las toman.
Allí se cuentan milagros,
martirios, muertes, desonrras,
que no han passado en el mundo,
y al fin se vende y se compra.[14]

Although Lope and other Siglo do Oro poets and dramatists complain (as would writers during the Enlightenment) that "el molde" was suffering from the frightful "historias trobadas" sold by the blind men, the fact is that many poets came forward to write for them. As Cervantes observed in *La gitanilla*, there were poets "para ciegos, que les fingen milagros y van a la parte de la ganancia."[15]

Between the *ciego rezador* and the blind seller of the *pliegos de cordel* there exists a certain continuity; however, the differences between their functions outweigh the similarities.[16] From the end of the sixteenth century on, the *ciego* is but a link in the chain of production and distribution of this material, destined for consumption by the poor. The blind singer becomes dependent on the most revolutionary cultural process of the century—the industrialization and mercantilization of the word through the medium of the printing press. The *pliego suelto* is the result of the discovery, by both printers and booksellers, that the real business of the press lay not in the reproduction of great codices (as Guttenberg believed) for a select minority of international readers (for example, the Bible in Latin), but in the diffusion of an endless number of cheap texts within national linguistic boundaries. The blind sellers of *pliegos sueltos* constitute the last step in the effort to expand the borders of this widening market, since they were meant to sell the printed word even to people who did not read.

In his *Ensayo sobre literatura de cordel*, Julio Caro Baroja recognizes that "la literatura de cordel decimonónica y primisecular es un resultado final. Es el final de una larga selección de elementos que pasan de la prensa ilustrada a la prensa humilde."[17] He sums up this process with an important distinction:

> ...que la Literatura de cordel es una Literatura más bien *popularizada* que de origen estrictamente *popular*, o si se quiere, folklórico. Su transmisor principal, el ciego, puede ser poeta a veces. Otras no es más que *actor* mínimo y vendedor de obra ajena. A fines del siglo XIX comerciaba con textos de origen medieval y renacentista, con restos del teatro clásico, con obras de ciegos de los siglos XVII y XVIII, con composiciones de autores, más o menos conocidos, de mediados del siglo XIX y con obras suyas o de algún compañero de profesión de infortunio.[18]

From the end of the sixteenth to the beginning of the twentieth centuries, the *romance de ciego* and the narrations sung in *coplas* comprise one of the most popular genres of *subliteratura, infraliteratura* or *paraliteratura* (as it has been variously called),[19] produced and marketed in urban centers for mass consumption. As with other consumer items, the manufacture of this literature tries to take into account the tastes of the consumer (actual or supposed). But to an even greater degree it tries to impose a "culture," not the culture inherited or created by the users of these items, but one from outside their sociocultural sector. The idea is to impress the potential buyer with elements that are different, strange, and extraordinary, as much in the content as in the form of expression.

Thus nothing could be further from the truth than affirmations such as:

> El ciego llevaba en su cargamento...cuanto fuera del gusto de su
> público. Siempre y cuando fuera expresado en lenguaje sencillo y
> directo, de manera elementalísima.... La literatura de cordel...acoge
> temas y tópicos de la literatura culta expresados de manera directa.
> Sin ser poesía tradicional, conserva ciertas características de aquélla,
> interesa por su función de transmisor de corrientes literarias e
> ideológicas. El público decide el contenido y la forma....[20]

Although "el vulgo necio" was the target for the consumption of the *literatura de cordel*, the consumer had little to do with the development or elaboration of this genre, whether in the late nineteenth or late sixteenth centuries. Moreover, given the vigilance of the Counter Reformation, which zealously expurgated the contents of any literature destined for the *pueblo*, it is clear that the literature intended specifically for "el vulgo" would be subjected to rigorous scrutiny and censorship at all times. In terms of ideology, the *pliego de cordel* could not fail to be a vehicle for the interests of the censors.[21] Genuinely oral literature is quite another matter; the possibilities for the centers of officialdom to intervene in its "voice" are limited.

If the ideological content of the printed *pliego de cordel* reproduces the dominant value system, the same holds true for its form of expression. The language used in the tales, *romances*, and *coplas de ciego* is based on the language that emerged at the end of the sixteenth century and that we usually identify with the Baroque *comedia*. The difference between the two is one of quality and not kind: the language of the *literatura de cordel* is *vulgar*, not because it adapts itself to the poetic or linguistic tendencies of the *pueblo*, but because its creators are less talented than the writers who meet with success in the theater and novel. The passing of centuries affects only the stylistics of the genre: the language of the *romances* and *coplas* of the last half of the sixteenth century is, of course, less "Baroque" than the language of the early seventeenth century. But studies of the *literatura de cordel* show that, even in the eighteenth and nineteenth century, there is no break with the linguistic and poetic heritage of the previous century. Rather, sales continue through new editions of materials originating in the late sixteenth and seventeenth centuries.

The *romances* and other materials carried by the *ciegos* were consumed by generations upon generations of *campesinos* and residents of the larger *pueblos* in much the same way they consume radio and television programs today. As a part of this process, certain individuals in these communities memorized a large number of *romance de ciego* texts. Often illiterate, these individuals were capable of retaining an enormous quantity of verses in their memories, usually having heard or read them (or having heard them read) only a few times. Even today *recitadores* with exceptional memories can be found in the *pueblos* of the provinces. In some cases they have learned the texts from other *recitadores*; in others they manage to hear the *romances*, or buy them, from the *ciegos* during the 1930's. In either case, these long narratives constitute a genre distinct from the *Romancero* of oral tradition. Although they are repeated orally, and although they are stored in the memories of men and women of the *pueblo* (preferably men), they are not *poesía popular*, but rather *poesía popularizada*.

The mere repetition of these texts does not alter what Menéndez Pidal called the "plebeyo" literary style of their language—the vocabulary, syntax, and method of narration, as well as certain rhetorical figures and a moralizing tendency, are very far from the language, style, and ideology which distinguish the poetic materials *re*created through the oral tradition. The distinctive features of the *literatura de cordel* are borrowed from the culture of the urban bourgeoisie, however much its authors may have intended their products for popular consumption. In contrast to the poetry of oral tradition, the poetry of the *pliegos* is not subject to *re*creation as it passes from memory to memory. The only changes it undergoes are deformations due to problems in comprehension and/or to lapses of memory. Those who know and transmit this poetry do not make it their own through the creative process of variation. The following fragments of *romances de cordel*, which have been collected orally, provide a good illustration. For example, "Rosaura la de Trujillo," one of the ballads Pío Baroja mentioned:

Sobre una alfombra de flores   cercada de hermosas plantas,
en donde las avecillas   tienden sus pintadas alas
y con música bella   al rey del cielo dan gracias,
en acá este prado meno,   en este mar de abondancia,
en este pecho que cubre   dos mil afligidas causas
como la que contaré,   si el alto cielo me ampara,
y porque sepáis su nombre   será preciso nombrarla.
En la gran Sierra Morena   de tantos delitos capa
fuérame a cazar un día,   cansado de andar a caza.
Arrimado a un duro tronco   escurriendo en cosas varias,
sintí una voz tenebrosa   que sonaba en las montañas
. . . .
y Rosaura en un convento   en ejemplar vida pasa.[22]

The same attempt at a "writerly" style can be observed in "Dionisia Pérez Losada":

De la celestial Princesa   que es de gloria coronada,
del Pilar divina aurora   pide mi pluma la gracia
para hacer notario el caso   con toda su circunstancia,
servir de ejemplo y enmienda   a los de conciencia mala;
que en Zaragoza la ilustre,   que ya está bien elogiada,
por imagen tan divina   que fue del cielo bajada,
vivía Dionisio Pérez   con Catalina en Losada.
El cielo les dio una hija   del corazón prenda amada,
la criaron con cariño   y a la virtud inclinada
. . . .
seamos todos devotos   con el corazón y el alma.[23]

Not all the *romances de cordel* are directed to a strictly individual moral message. "La fiera Cuprecia," which fascinated Pío Baroja, is put to the service of a much wider religious didacticism:

Una historia más antigua   ni en Africa ni en Grecia,
se ha visto fiera tan mala   como la fiera Cuprecia.
Este monstruo sanguinario   se vio por primera vez
por una joven de España   valiente y noble mujer.

En Melilla se encontraba   lavando muy descuidada
cuando se halló de improviso   por la Cuprecia atacada.
Su padre y un hermanito   se hallaban cortando leña,
(y) a los cuales destrozó   (y) aquella maldita fiera.
Su hermano quiso escapar   pero la fiera enseguida
también se apoderó de él,   destrozándole enseguida.
La joven quiso escapar   a dar parte decidida;
y al pueblo pudo llegar   angustiada y afligida.
(Y) a casa del señor juez,   aquella joven hermosa,
(y) al punto parte le dio   de aquella fiera horrorosa.
El señor juez le pregunta   por las señas de la fiera
y ella, con dulces palabras,   le dice de esta manera:
—Tiene boca de león,   los cuernos de toro bravo,
pelo como una mujer   y las alas de pescado,
las uñas como puñales,   las orejas de carnero,
y en el rabo una cruceta   que causa terror y miedo.
Yo descuidada me hallaba   cuando la fiera salió
del río dando bramidos,   y a mi padre destrozó.
Mi hermano quiso escapar   pero la fiera enseguida
también se apoderó de él   destrozándole enseguida.
Entonces el señor juez   ordena con ley severa
que salgan cincuenta moros   por ver si matan la fiera.
. . . .
—Señorita, no se atreva;   mire que la va a matar.
—Callad, moros del demonio,   no gritar con tanto alarde,
que sois más grandes que Judas,   asquerosos y cobardes.
—Caramba con la blanquita,   dicen todos ofendidos,
que aunque somos de color   también somos bien nacidos.—
Pero la joven, entonces,   sin atender a palabras,
y toda la morería   l'iba siguiendo detrás.
Detrás de un árbol se pone   la española decedida
y hace un certero disparo   cayendo la fiera herida.
Luego coge su machete,   con arrogante valor,
y le corta la cabeza   (y) a aquel animal feroz.
¡Viva la gente española,   gritaba la morería,
que jamás se ha visto en ella   bajeza ni cobardía![24]

The *romances* and kindred narrations faithfully memorized from the *pliego de cordel* are notable for their wordiness, (the above ballad is twice as long as quoted), elaborate vocabulary, extended syntax, lack of variation, and generally monotonous style. But not every text proceeding from a *pliego* is frozen forever in this stultifying structure.

The *Romance vulgar*: Steps toward Traditionalization

In contrast to the texts just seen, we find some *romances* in the modern oral tradition which, though based on the old narrations from the blind singer, are undergoing a process of adaptation to the language of popular traditional poetry. What signals this process is the presence of the most distinctive feature of any traditionalized material: the "openness," or *apertura*, of its text.

Although the transmission and divulgation of ballads through the press and through the oral tradition are usually two separate and independent processes, occasionally there are points of contact and crosses between the two. All of the literary modes have left some trace on the repertory of the modern oral tradition. There are traditional *romances* based on troubadoresque texts from the beginning of the sixteenth century (and let us not forget the contributions of Gil Vicente and Juan del Encina to the modern oral tradition),[25] as well as ballads based on the *romancero nuevo* of the late sixteenth and early seventeenth centuries (including some of Lope's inventions),[26] and *romances* which have descended from texts "arranged" by anthologists in different periods. Today, we also find traditionalized *romances* which have their origins in the printed matter circulated by the *ciegos* from the sixteenth through the eighteenth centuries.

These ballads of late origin, which begin to live in the oral tradition, make up what is called the *Romancero vulgar*. They conserve some of the stylistic features and original language of the *Romancero de ciego*, but they begin to show variation at the level of the ballad's discourse—condensing the syntax, picking up traditional formulaic expression—and even show new imagination and/or invention in terms of the content or the plot of the narration.   An example of the traditionalization of a ballad is provided by these two versions of "El capitán burlado":

Doña Antonia de la Rosa,   de la hacienda monedada,
va montada en su alcarroza,   cuatro caballos la halan,
cuatro caballos mermejos,   que el alto cielo arrodeaban.
Han entrado por la iglesia,   hizo reverencia hallada,
cogiendo el agua bendita   por mano de una criada.
Y el general de Opinión,   que dentro la iglesia estaba,
viéndole esas acciones   se enamoró de la dama.
. . . .
. . . .   Le preguntó a la criada:
—¿Dónde es aquella hermosura   y aquella linda e sagrada?
—Pues, hija de un tal don Pedro,   que en la ciudad tiene fama.
—Pues, pronto quiero yo a don Pedro,   pronto escribirle una carta,
que a la hora de comer   voy a comer a su casa.—
La niña dijo que sí   aunque no es de buena gana.
Aún no es la mesa pronta,   ya el general está en casa.
Tratón de poner la mesa,   el mantel de fina grana,
en cada punta un pañuelo,   también un cuchillo en véina.
En medio de comer,   el general preguntaba:
—¿Dónde está la dueña Antonia,   que a esta mesa no se hallaba?
—La dueña Antonia es muy chica,   a esta mesa no alcanzaba.
—Pero, por el alto cielo   . . . .—
De allí se salió don Pedro,   lleno de color y rabia,
allá dentro del aposento   a donde su hija estaba:
—¡Oh, Antonia de mi vida,   lindo espejo de mi cara!,
el general de Opinión   y el mercader que está en casa
jura por el alto cielo   y por la cruz de su espada,
que has de ir en su retaguardia,   si la muerte no la ataja.
—No tenga pena, mi padre,   de eso no se le dé nada;
váyase usted a la cocina   y tráigame una criada,
la más bien hecha de cuerpo   y la más bonita de cara;
yo le pongo de mis ropas   y le pongo de mis galas,
le pongo mantos de seda   que a doblón costó la vara;
yo me pongo toca sucia   y camisa remendada

y zapatos de dos suelas   como mozo de soldada,
me pongo a fregar mi loza   y también a barrer mi casa,
también a servir a la mesa   como una humilde criada.—
Caminan siete leguas,   no se dijeron palabra,
al cabo las siete leguas   el general preguntaba:
—¿Qué lleva, la doña Antonia,   que del color va mudada?
—No soy la doña Antonia,   doña Antonia llaman mi ama,
yo vengo a servir a usted   como una humilde criada.
—¡Vuelva atrás, la soldadesca,   vuelva atrás, la retraguarda,
que el que mantiene a la hija,   que mantenga a la criada!
Dígale usted a doña Antonia   que se vaya enhoramala,
que se vaya a roer huesos   y cáscaras de granada,
que la que quiere ser buena   no le falta modo y maña.[27]

The pace of the narration accelerates in spite of the increase in repetition, as we see in this version:

En esta çuidad vivía   un caballero de fama,
y a él lo llaman don Pedro   y a su mujer doña Juana
y una hija que tenía   doña Antonia se llamaba.
Yéndose un día pa misa   con una de sus criadas,
el general preguntó   y el general preguntaba:
—¿Quién es esa niña linda?   ¿quién es esa niña dama?
—Esta es hija de don Pedro,   que en la ciudad tiene fama.—
Y él como sabía hacerlo   y al pronto escribe una carta:
que si quería que fuera   un día a comer a su casa.
Tratan de poner la mesa   y en una sala adornada,
la mesa era de bronce   y el mantel de fina grana,
una botella con vino   y una garrafa con agua.
El general preguntó   y el general preguntaba:
—¿Dónde está la doña Antonia,   que a esta mesa no llegaba?
—Doña Antonia es tan pequeña   que a esta mesa no alcanzaba.
—Pues nada más que por eso   la tengo 'e llevar pa España.—
Se levanta de la mesa,   lleno de cólera y rabia
y se va paso entre paso,   donde doña Antonia estaba.
—¿Qué trae, mi padre querido,   qué trae, mi padre del alma?

—Lo que traigo es, mi hija,   que te quieren llevar pa España.
—Cállese, padre querido,   de eso no se le dé nada,
que la que quiere ser buena   no le falta modo y maña.
Váyase usted a la cocina,   coja una de las criadas,
póngale mi ropa de oro   pa que reluciendo vaya,
yo me pondré ropas sucias   y camisa remendada
y le serviré a la mesa   como una de las criadas.—
Ya la niña está compuesta,   ya el general caminaba;
miró el general pa tras   la vido muy agoniada:
—¿Lo qué trae, la doña Antonia,   que viene tan agoniada?
—Yo no soy la doña Antonia,   doña Antonia llaman mi ama.
—Pues si usted no es doña Antonia,   yo de usted no quiero nada,
que el que mantiene a la hija,   que mantenga a la criada.—
Se montó en un pino verde   por ver si la divisaba
y lo que vido fue el polvo   del carro que la llevaba.[28]

The following is an illustration of what happens when printed *romances* "de
sucesos" or "de crímenes" undergo fusion in the oral tradition. In this case, we see
the transformation of two separate texts, published in 1663, into one modern oral
version, "La Rueda de la fortuna y los Presagios del labrador":

La rueda de la fortuna   y de la fortuna rueda,
a vuelta y media que distes   me trajistes a esta tierra.
No me pesa haber venido   ni tampoco estar en ella,
que he visto la mejor dama   que había en toda esta tierra.
La he visto cogiendo rosas   en una linda pradera
y yo como tunantillo   le pedí la mejor dellas.
—Mira, mira, el picarillo,   cómo pide el sin vergüenza.
—No se asuste Vd. señora,   que es costumbre de mi tierra,
los chavales como yo   pedimos a las doncellas,
y ellas nos dan para guantes,   nosotros zapato y medias,
y ellas nos dan para ligas   de vuelta y media la pierna.
—Si quieres conversación   ven a mi casa por ella;
mi marido no está en casa   que se marchó pa' la feria.
Y a eso de la medianoche   llegó el marido a la puerta
y ya la encontraba cerrada,   la que siempre estaba abierta.

Con la punta de su espada   hizo un agujero en la puerta.
—Por aquí cabe mi brazo,   por aquí cabe mi pierna,
po'aquí cabe mi caballo,   llevándolo yo de la rienda.
Iba paso contra paso   y al subir las escaleras
en el medio de la sala   había una luz
que parecía un difunto   cuando le alumbran con cera.
Iba paso tras de paso   al cuarto de la morena
y la encontraba dormida   y al mancebito con ella.
—¡Qué falta tienes, mujer,   de andar en estas quimeras?
Tú, si te hace falta pan   lo tienes en la panera
y si te hace falta vino   lo tienes en la bodega
y si te hago falta yo   haberme puesto dos letras.
En estas mismas razones   lo quería ayudar ella.
La pegó tres puñaladas   y la dejó muerta en tierra.
Allí la dejó cadaver   y al mancebito con ella,
y una niña que tenía   la lleva a casa 'e su suegra.
—Tenga, suegra, esta niña,   esta niña cuide de ella.
Si sale como su madre   más vale que se muriera.
—¿Qué tienes contra mi hija   que tanto mal dices de ella?
Cuando veniste a buscarla   no tenías esa idea.
—En mi casa quedó muerta   y el mancebito con ella.
El que quiere carne fresca   vaya a mi casa por ella;
a ochavo vendo la libra   y a maravedí la media.[29]

Originally, the ballad of the adulteress was a typical *romance de ciego* of the seventeenth century, replete with devils and daggers and the blind man's conventional *exordium*: "Tomad exenplo casadas / en oyendo esta tragedia."[30] In time, the laborious introduction was forgotten, and the ballad joined with "La Rueda de la fortuna." It is possible that the two texts were published together in a single *pliego* at some point, and thus may have entered the oral tradition in a hybrid state. In any event, once circulating orally, the verbal padding disappears. The new version shows not only economy of style and imagination in solving the problem of how to enter a locked house without being detected, it takes on as well the traditional poetic recourses to formulae, incremental repetition, and direct dialogue.

The *Romance noticiero* of the
Nineteenth and Twentieth Centuries

The nineteenth-century *ciegos* also carried the chronicle of newsworthy events (or "sucesos") through the villages, towns, and outlying districts of cities, narrating not only crimes (either new or renovated) and other deplorable matters, but also taking part in the ideological disputes of the day. According to Julio Caro Baroja, "Después de 1823, es decir, a partir de la reacción absolutista fernandina hay en casi todas las regiones de España dos sectores populares: uno absolutista, chapado a la antigua y otro revolucionario, liberal o no."[31] Caro Baroja sums up the literary activities of the *ciego* at mid-century as originally described by Antonio Ferrer del Río and Juan Pérez Calvo in *Los españoles pintados por sí mismos* (Madrid: 1851, pp. 374–378):

> Fue también el ciego decimonónico cantor, según las tornas, del absolutismo o de la libertad. Llevaba unas veces sobre el sombrero la cinta blanca y un ostentoso letrero que decía "Viva el Rey y la Religión". Pero tras defender el trono y el altar y cantar la "Muerte de Elio" y el "julepe", se colocaba la cinta morada con una gran divisa de "Constitución o muerte", cantando el "Trágala" o el "Himno de Riego". Moderados, progresistas, conservadores o "ayacuchos", los ciegos servían de correveidiles y aun de espías. En torno a la Imprenta Real o Nacional de Madrid se agrupaban para coger al vuelo las noticias que a veces alteraban o falsificaban. Pudieron ser verdaderas las victorias de Prim, anunciados por ellos...pero tres veces hicieron morir a Zumalacárregui, una vez hicieron fusilar a Cabrera por los suyos y aun otra anunciaron que don Carlos el pretendiente había sido envenenado por un fraile.[32]

For the most part, this combative poetry has vanished without a trace, but the impact of ideological subject matter was greater than Caro Baroja thought when he wrote, (with characteristic aloofness regarding popular ideology), "A la gente popular parece que le interesaba más el testamento de don Juan de Austria que lo que en el Norte hacían Zumalacárregui o Espartero. Con respecto a épocas posteriores se puede decir lo mismo."[33] Certain ballads relating to the Carlist wars persist in the oral tradition, such as this one, in orthodox *romance* meter, describing the misconduct of political factions from a liberal perspective:

Atención pido, señores,   para poder explicar
la vida de los carlistas   es muy digna de contar.
Cuando van por los pueblos   no cesan de preguntar:
—¿Dónde está el señor alcalde,   dónde está ese liberal?
Que se presente al momento,   que tiene que racionar:
quinientos hombres venimos,   quinientas libras de pan
y otras tantas de carnero,   si no hay vaca que matar;
cebada pa los caballos   también nos tiene que dar,
cigarros y cajetillas   y papel para fumar.
Ahora nos vamos a Estella,   aquel cuartel general,
donde están las buenas chicas   que las queremos chingar.
. . . .[34]

Other topics were sung in more unusual meters. One that has enjoyed a wide diffusion in the oral tradition is *La muerte de Prim*. Due to its nimble seven-syllable line, it is much more lively than most *coplas noticieras*.

Al salir de Palacio
le dijeron a Prim,
vaya usted con cuidado
que le quieren herir.

Si me quieren herir
o me quieren matar,
entregaré la espada
al otro general.

Como hombre valiente
a la calle salió.

> Le pegan cuatro tiros
> a boca de cañón.
> . . . .[35]

The account of Prim's death has been elaborated with many details and variants. For example:

> En la calle del Turco
> a las diez de la noche,
> a Juan Prim lo mataron
> metidito en su coche.
>
> El coche era de plata
> donde iba metido.
> Al romper los cristales
> le pegan cuatro tiros.
>
> Cuatro tiros le pegan,
> cuatro balas le sacan
> y al tiempo de morir,
> lo llevan a su casa.
> . . . .[36]

A version collected by Tomás Navarro Tomás begins:

> En la calle del Turco
> han matado a Prim
> sentadito en su coche
> con la guardia civil.
> . . . .[37]

Another invents a different cause of death:

> En la calle del Turco
> malhirieron a Prim,

> por un dedo en su mano
> causa fue de morir.
> . . . .[38]

Variants also proliferate in the account of the reaction of Prim's wife and children, clearly indicating the song's acquisition of traditional poetics. Only a few versions retain the memory of the political machinations:

> Aunque soy chiquitito
> y no tengo edad
> la muerte de mi padre
> juro la he de vengar.
>
> . . . .
>
> Al hijo de Serrano
> propio desafió
> con padrinos al campo
> pero al fin le mató.
>
> Serrano ha jurado
> que había ' vengar la aición
> contra el hijo de Prim
> n'el Café de la Unión.
>
> Libertad pide el hijo,
> pide el hijo de Prim,
> que ha de vengar la muerte
> o prefiere morir.
>
> Libertad pide el pueblo,
> libertad, libertad.
> La muerte de su padre
> jurada tiene ya,
> la muerte de su padre
> ella se vengará.[39]

Other versions take on purely folkloric traits, and, instead of relegating all the words and reactions to the "eldest son," divide them into three, according to the laws of traditional structure.[40]

Al subir la escalera
dijo el hijo mayor:
La muerte de mi padre
tengo que vengar yo.

Al subir la escalera
dijo el hijo de enmedio:
La muerte de mi padre
tengo que vengar yo.

Al subir la escalera
dijo el hijo menor:
La muerte de mi padre
tengo que vengar yo.

Aunque soy chiquitito
y no tengo edad
La muerte de mi padre
tengo yo que vengar.[41]

The *noticierismo* of the theme outlasted the Restoration.

An account of the Anarchists' frustrated attempt to assassinate Alfonso XII in 1878 is told from the point of view of the would-be assassin, whose execution gives rise to a cry for freedom:

Bajó del coche   con gran valor.
Subió al tablero   sin detención.
El señor cura: —Piense usté en Dios.—
La centinela   se desmayó.
Antes de morir, Antonio   estas palabras habló:
—Pobrecitos madrileños,   bien os acordaréis de mí.

Si yo no he sido,   otro será,
que al rey Alfonso   le han de matar.
Si yo no he sido,   otro será,
porque es muy grande   la Sociedad.

Yet not all political accounts have their origins in revolutionary propaganda. The "Sublevación de Asturias de 1934," also sung by the *ciegos*, appears to side with the government, as shown by these verses recited by a woman who remembers the arrival of the *ciego* in her *pueblo*, selling and singing:

En Cataluña y Asturias
se prepara un movimiento,
que fracasó por completo
ya desde el primer intento.
Contaban con muchas armas
y bastantes municiones,
se lanzaron a la calle
sin mirar contemplaciones.[42]

On the other hand, "La heroína de Oviedo" is clearly revolutionary, as we see in this version collected by Jon Juaristi:

Si algún día vas a Asturias
descúbrete, compañero,
por la muerte que han tenido
esos valientes mineros.

Esos valientes mineros
de la provincia de Oviedo
han demostrado a toda España
que no han conocido el miedo.

De Madrid salió la historia
de Agustina de Aragón.

Una mujer asturiana
la superó con valor.

Una mujer heroína
que luchaba contra el tercio
con una ametralladora,
en una calle de Oviedo.
. . . .[43]

The *ciegos* also purveyed *coplas* concerning "El escándalo Lerroux," providing a list of the names of its protagonists, and including an *estribillo* that parodies "La Cucaracha":

El estraperlo, el estraperlo,
ya no puede funcionar,
porque no tiene, porque le falta
ayuda de Salazar.

Estando Strauss en Holanda
Lerroux en San Rafael,
se le planteó el negocio
de don Ricardo Sampere.

Quiere lavarse las manos
el señor José María,
pero don Aurelio dice
que es también de la pandilla.
. . . .[44]

The *romance de suceso* and the *romance noticiero* remained vigorous in the tradition throughout the nineteenth century and well into the twentieth, as long as the *ciego* and his *lazarillo* carried and sang them through the towns and countryside. Within this branch of the tradition, two ballads inspired García Lorca and Alberti: "Mariana Pineda" (referring to a "suceso" of 1831), and "El fusilamiento de García y Galán" (referring to a "suceso" of 1930).

Notes

1. Included by Antonio Rodríguez Moñino, "Textos sobre literatura de cordel (Siglos XVI–XX)," in his *Diccionario bibliográfico de pliegos sueltos poéticos (Siglo XVI)* (Madrid: Castalia, 1970), pp. 115–116.

2. Published in *Revista de Información Médico Terapeútica*, Año XXII (1947), nos. 21–22, pp. 1024–1027.

3. See the illustration to Pío Baroja's article, p. 1025.

4. According to the testimony of field notes made by ballad collectors during the first two decades of this century (materials stored in the Archives of Menéndez Pidal).

5. In the late seventies and early eighties field researchers heard accounts of the book burnings during the Civil War. I am greatly indebted to Diego Catalán for much of this and the following discussion.

6. According to Julio Caro Baroja, *Ensayo sobre la literatura de cordel* (Madrid: Revista de Occidente, 1969), p. 59: "En 1787 hubo discusión respecto a si los ciegos debían disponer del caudal de invenciones literarias y musicales de esta clase, como la había pedido *El Correo de los Ciegos*, defendiendo los 'autores' Martínez y Ribera en un memorial los derechos de estos." Caro Baroja cites another case illustrating this "privilegio" on p. 69, n. 71: "Por el año de 1790, en una esquina de la calle Nueva, de Málaga, tenía un puesto donde vendía libros, romances y estampas un buen hombre que se llamaba Juan de Balenzuela, el cual era ya de sesenta y cuatro años de edad. Este 'pregonaba' la mercancía que tenía en venta según su calidad. Mas he aquí que un ciego, llamado Mateo Mata, hizo un llamamiento al Cabildo para que le aplicara una real provisión, dada por la Chancillería de Granada a 25 de agosto de 1789, en que solo quedaban autorizadas las personas privadas de la vista a vender públicamente 'romances, almanaques, calendarios, diarios, tablas de jubileos y otros papeles sueltos, ni que los impresores y libreros los entregasen para su venta a otros que no fuesen ciegos'. El Cabildo, considerando el caso, vino a hacer una excepción con Balenzuela, aunque en teoría diera la razón al ciego Mata...."

7. Caro Baroja, *Ensayo*, pp. 41–70, and Rodríguez Moñino, pp. 85–126, have brought together an impressive array of literary citations and testimonials concerning the *ciegos* and their efforts to earn their living through their voices, in the streets and squares of both cities and towns from the Middle Ages to the early twentieth century.

8. "Cantares fiz' algunos, de los que disen los çiegos." Juan Ruiz, Arcipreste de Hita, *El Libro de buen amor*, II, ed. Julio Cejador y Frauca (Madrid: Clásicos Castellanos, 1913), st. 1514, p. 228. Two examples of these prayers are in lines 1710–1728, pp. 287–293.

9. In the "Tratado primero," *Lazarillo de Tormes*, ed. Angel González Palencia (Zaragoza: Clásicos Ebro, 1953), p. 30.

10. *Farsa del molinero*, in Diego Sánchez de Badajoz, *Recopilación en metro* (Sevilla: 1554), fol. 109r; ed. facsim. of the Real Academia Española (Madrid: 1929). Cited by Rodríguez Moñino, pp. 85–86; Caro Baroja, *Ensayo*, p. 49.

11. Included in his *Turiana* (Valencia: 1563), fol. 3; ed. facsim. of the Real Academia Española (Madrid: 1936). Cited by Rodríguez Moñino, pp. 86–87; Caro Baroja, p. 48. Another example can be found in Timoneda's *Un passo de dos ciegos y un moço muy gracioso para la noche de navidad*, also included in the same edition of his *Turiana*.

12. Cited by Rodríguez Moñino, pp. 87–88, from the Nueva edición de la Real Academia Española, VIII, p. 255. Morley and Bruerton give 1609 as the date for the play, *Cronología*, p. 62 and p. 88.

13. Act I, scene 9, in *Biblioteca de Autores Españoles*, 52 (Madrid: M. Rivadeneyra), p. 72. Cited by Rodríguez Moñino, pp. 88–90. The date, from Morley and Bruerton, p. 66 and p. 268.

14. Act III. Cited by Rodríguez Moñino, p. 91, from *Teatro antiguo español*, IX (Madrid: 1948), p. 109.

15. Caro Baroja, *Ensayo*, p. 54.

16. As noted above, by the time of the Arcipreste de Hita's writing, there were already "autores" who wrote for the *ciegos*, or *ciegos* who sang literature composed specifically for distribution through them. The Arcipreste, however, rejects the marketing of this kind of literature. See sts. 1629–1630 of *El Libro de buen amor*.

17. *Ensayo*, p. 439.

18. *Ensayo*, p. 433.

19. See María Cruz García de Enterría's discussion in *Sociedad y poesía de cordel en el Barroco* (Madrid: Taurus, 1973), pp. 41–44.

20. Iris Zavala, *El texto en la historia* (Madrid: Nuestra Cultura, 1981), p. 167.

21. Again, contrary to Iris Zavala's statement, p. 156: "Es vocero de las ideologías de esa masa informe y anónima que crea la historia."

22. Version from La Cruz Santa (Tenerife), recited by "Señá" María Lorenzo Pérez, 70 years old, in 1952–53. Published in *La Flor de la Marañuela*, II, ed. Diego Catalán, et al. (Madrid: Seminario Menéndez Pidal and Gredos), no. 652, p. 240.

23. Version de Lanzarote, n.p., in *La Flor de la Marañuela*, II, no. 672, p. 247.

24. Version from Lomeña-Basieda (Santander), sung by Juliana Díez, 67 years, in July, 1977. Published in *Voces nuevas del Romancero castellano-leonés*, in vol. II of *AIER*, no. 146, pp. 308–309.

25. In chapters 2 and 3, respectively.

26. See, for example, "Mira, Zaide, que te aviso," *Catálogo General del Romancero*, 2, no. 58, pp. 305–307.

27. Version from Icod el Alto (Tenerife), recited by Mercedes Suárez López, 82 years old, in 1953. *La Flor de la Marañuela*, I, no. 205, pp. 211–212.

28. Version from Las Mercedes (Tenerife), recited by "seña" Victoria in 1954. *La Flor de la Marañuela*, I, no. 204, p. 210. The song "Anda jaleo," or "El contrabandista," included on Lorca's and La Argentinita's recording, begins: "Yo me subí a un pino verde / por ver si la divisaba, // y sólo divisé el polvo / del coche que la llevaba...."

29. Unpublished version in the Archives of Menéndez Pidal, from Vierdes (León), recited by Jacinta Redondo, collected by Diego Catalán and Alvaro Galmés in August, 1946. Another fragmented version can be found in *AIER*, II, no. 81, p. 149.

30. See *Las Fuentes del Romancero General*, II, ed. Antonio Rodríguez Moñino (Madrid: Real Academia Española, 1957), pp. 92–95.

31. *Ensayo*, p. 292.

32. *Ensayo*, p. 60.

33. *Ensayo*, p. 295.

34. Version from Sejas de Aliste (Zamora), recited by a young woman about 20 years old, collected by Diego Catalán and Alvaro Galmés in the summer of 1948. Unpublished. In the Archives of Menéndez Pidal there are five other older and more complete versions.

35. In other versions, "Si me quieren herir / que me dejen hablar." This unpublished version is from Coin (Málaga), prior to 1920.

36. Unpublished version from Mochinejo (Málaga), prior to 1920.

37. Collected in 1910 in Fermoselle (Zamora). Unpublished.

38. Unpublished; from Teverga (Oviedo).

39. Teverga (Oviedo).

40. See the "Law of Three," in Axel Olrik's "Epic Laws of Folk Narrative," *The Study of Folklore*, ed. Alan Dundes (Englewood Cliffs, NJ: Prentice-Hall, 1965), pp. 129–141.

41. Unpublished, n.p.

42. Both texts appear in Diego Catalán, "El Romancero de tradición oral en el último cuarto del siglo XX," *El Romancero hoy: Nuevas fronteras* (Madrid: Gredos, 1979), p. 255.

43. This and the following are unpublished versions from Las Arenas (Bilbao), sung by María Teresa Linacero, 58 years old, on August 23, 1982.

44. According to the informant, "estas coplas las cantaban los ciegos, por Bilbao, y circulaban impresas."

5

The Stage Model of the "Cartelón de ciego"

The large and varied field of *poesía popularizada*, though undervalued and usually ignored, forms a pervasive backdrop to the literary experiments that Alberti and García Lorca set out to stage during a period of increasing political awareness. Both poets took the *ciego* and his *cartelón* as a model for the stage and, in both instances, picked subjects for their plays that were politically sensitive, or, in Alberti's case, incendiary.

Mariana Pineda: The Ballad of Tradition and Lorca's Stage Portrait

Following his experiments with the *teatro de guiñol*, Lorca began work on *Mariana Pineda* in 1923. In a letter to Antonio Gallego Burín, he wrote "Tengo el proyecto de hacer un gran romance teatral y ya lo tengo resuelto."[1] The date here is important, as it invalidates the theory that the play was written in reaction to Primo de Rivera's *pronunciamiento* on September 17, 1923. However, the ensuing repressive political climate and heavy censorship did contribute to the delay in the play's opening. Originally scheduled for late 1924 or early 1925, the play's première did not take place until June, 1927, in the Teatro Goya in Barcelona. Margarita Xirgu played the leading role, and the set and costume designs were carried out in collaboration with Salvador Dalí.[2] *Mariana Pineda* marks Lorca's first attempt at writing serious tragedy, and more importantly for my purpose, it is the first evidence of his attraction to oral narrative poetry as a vehicle of theatrical communication.

Mariana Pineda (b. 1804) was publicly executed in Granada during the wave of reaction that followed Fernando VII's return to the throne. In the process of dismantling the Constitution of 1812, Fernando persecuted Liberal leaders ruthlessly. When the makings of a Liberal flag were found in the home of the young widow and mother, she was charged with conspiracy against the State, found guilty, and garroted on May 26, 1831.[3] In García Lorca's play, we see her private dilemma: either to inform authorities of the names of liberal conspirators, or to face death and the abandonment of her children.

> Todos los héroes del siglo XIX español que tienen estatua han tenido
> también su dramaturgo. La única que no lo tenía era Mariana
> Pineda, quizá porque está necesitaba su poeta.[4]

There can be no doubt that Lorca's play is inspired directly by a ballad of oral tradition on the noble sacrifice of Granada's heroine. In a letter to Melchor Fernández Almagro, he wrote:

> Desde niño estoy oyendo esa estrofa tan evocadora de
>
> > *Marianita salió de paseo*
> > *y a su encuentro salió un militar...*
>
> Yo quiero hacer un drama procesional.... Una especie de cartelón de
> ciego *estilizado*. Un crimen, en suma, donde el rojo de la sangre se
> confunda con el rojo de las cortinas. Mariana, según el romance y
> según la poquísima historia que la rodea, es una mujer pasional hasta
> sus propios polos, una *posesa*, un caso de amor magnífico de
> andaluza en ambiente extremadamente *político...* Ella se entrega al
> amor por el amor, mientras los demás están obsesionados por la
> Libertad.[5]

The author also declares his sources when he subtitles the work, "Romance popular en tres estampas." Years later, during a repeat performance of the play in 1933, he offered the following testimony of his childhood encounter with the ballad in the *pueblo* of Fuentevaqueros, and later in the streets of Granada.

> *Mariana Pineda* fue una de las más grandes emociones de mi infancia. Los niños de mi edad, y yo mismo, tomados de la mano en corros que se abrían y cerraban rítmicamente, cantábamos con un tono melancólico, que a mí se me figuraba trágico:
>
> > ¡Oh!, qué día tan triste en Granada,
> > que a las piedras hacía llorar
> > al ver que Marianita se muere
> > en cadalso por no declarar.
>
> > Marianita, sentada en su cuarto,
> > no paraba de considerar:
> > "Si Pedrosa me viera bordando
> > la bandera de la libertad."
>
> .... Un día llegué, de la mano de mi madre, a Granada: volvió a levantarse ante mí el romance popular, cantado también por niños que tenían las voces más graves y solemnes, más dramáticas aún que aquellas que llenaron las calles de mi pequeño pueblo....[6]

At the turn of the century the ballad of "Marianita Pineda" was widely known in the province of Granada. Don Manuel Gómez Moreno, the archaeologist and art historian (born in Granada in 1870), provided Menéndez Pidal with a copy of the song as he remembered it, sung repeatedly by the children in Granada around 1900:

> Marianita encerrada en su cuarto
> no paraba de considerar
> si Pedrosa la viera bordando
> la bandera de la libertad.

. . . .

Que me quiten mis hijos delante
que me quiten que no los vea yo,
que me quiten cien veces la vida,
¡qué dolor, qué dolor, qué dolor![7]

Throughout the 1920's the ballad continued to be very popular in the "corros de niñas" of Granada and Málaga, as several versions sent to Menéndez Pidal testify. In this version from Granada, sung by a sixteen-year-old girl, we find the same ballad *exordium* that Lorca remembered:

Una tarde muy triste en Granada
que a las piedras hacía llorar
de ver que a Marianita la llevan
a la horca por no declarar.
. . . .
—Si declaro moriremos muchos
y así sola muero yo no más.
Una tarde salió de paseo
al encuentro salió un militar:
—¿Dónde va usted, Marianita, sola?
Hay delito, vuélvase usté atrás.
Marianita se metió a su cuarto
la bandera se puso a bordar;
la han pillado con ella en la mano
y a la horca la llevaban ya

. . . .

Another version from Málaga, sung by Victoria García Zumaquero at the age of fourteen, is especially interesting, as it makes manifest the connection between the ballad of "Marianita Pineda" and the "Himno de Riego," which the liberal tradition would succeed in imposing as the national "anthem" of the Second Republic.

Marianita encerrada en su cuarto
no paraba de considerar
si Pedrosa la viera bordando
la bandera de la libertad.

Constitución o muerte
será nuestra divisa:
si algún traidor avisa
la muerte sufrirá.

Marianita al palacio la llevan;
una escolta la va acompañando
y sus hijos la siguen gritando:
—Vente a casa, querida mamá.

Que me quiten mis hijos delante,
que me quiten que no los vea yo,
que me quiten cien veces la vida,
¡Qué dolor, qué dolor, qué dolor!

—Mariana, tu crimen es grande,
si declaras tú no morirás.—
Y responde la joven graciosa:
—Muero, muero, por no declarar.

. . . .

These circle game versions from Andalucía have reduced the story to only a few of the many strophes it originally contained. Although the oral tradition alone does not permit us to "restore" the ballad as Lorca knew it, the comparison of various versions I have seen with Lorca's play does allow us some idea of the historical details it included.[8]

Lorca obviously knew much of the history of Mariana, which provided him with important details concerning the liberal conspiracy—the figure of Pedrosa ("alcalde del crimen de la chancellería de Granada"); the escape of Álvarez de

Sotomayor from jail, first disguised (with Mariana's help) as a friar, and later as a "contrabandista"; the discovery of the flag in the Albaicín district; Mariana's imprisonment in the convent of Santa María Egipciaca—all of which are recounted in the first historical biography of Mariana Pineda, published five years after her execution.[9] But in Lorca's rendition of the story, Mariana's rejection of Pedrosa's sexual advances near the end of the second act proves to be the pivotal point of the play. When Pedrosa declares "Nadie sabrá lo que ha pasado. Yo te quiero mía, ¿lo estás oyendo? Mía o muerta,"[10] her refusal of him is equivalent to choosing death. Lorca has cast the omnipresent political loyalty of the ballad into terms of sexual fidelity and individual honor. For his portrayal of Pedrosa's vehement and vengeful persecution of Mariana, Lorca obviously takes his cues from the *romance*. History attributes Pedrosa's relentless action to political reasons alone.

Six versions of the ballad, which offer notable variations, ascribe responsibility for informing authorities of Mariana's complicity (and the subsequent search of her house) to Pedrosa. For example:

> Ay, Pedrosa, cómo me has perdido,
> No me has sido constante y leal:
> el registro que en mi casa ha habido
> nuevas pruebas de soplo me da.[11]

This verse casts a new aspect on the story, which various independent versions develop in more detail. The Sephardic version from Tetuán stops short of attributing other than political reasons to Pedrosa's actions, and comes to a close with

> Oh, Pedrosa, qué cruel has sido,
> que la vida por fin la quitó
> a la pobre de la Marianita
> que en el mundo tres hijos dejó.

However, other versions are not satisfied that a purely political motivation can justify Pedrosa's cruelty. A version from Cartagena (Murcia), and another from Infantes (Ciudad Real), provide the following explanation:

> Marianita era de Granada,
> su belleza debió de inspirar
> a Pedrosa, coronel infame,
> su lujuria insolente y audaz.

The pompous vocabulary and elaborate syntax of these lines betrays the "vulgar" literary origins of the *romance noticiero*. Added to this strophe in the Cartagena version is another of the same pattern:

> No pudiendo vencer sus virtudes
> por los medios y orden natural,
> la denuncia, persigue y apresa
> por vengarse, cayendo en el mal.

The version from Infantes, in turn, gives an account of the fear and distrust aroused in Mariana by Pedrosa's close surveillance.

> Si el traidor de Pedrosa me ronda
> mis ventanas, puertas y balcón.

Thanks to a version from El Hoyo (Ciudad Real), we learn just how Pedrosa discovers that Mariana is making the flag:

> Marianita mandó a su criada
> por un cuarto de seda en color.
> Se ha encontrado a Pedrosa en la calle,
> Marianita, ¡Jesús, qué dolor!

The version from El Bohoyo (Ávila) explains the treacherous Pedrosa's previous intentions, and justifies Mariana's fear and suspicion:

> Si tuviera una llave ganzúa
> y tu cuarto pudiera escalar
> para entrar en tu cuarto a deshora
> y en tu lecho poder descansar.

And the already quoted version from Cartagena tells of Pedrosa's proposal to Mariana, once he has her in his power:

> —Los rebeldes— responde Pedrosa
> no merecen nuestra caridad;
> pero acaso podré perdonarla
> si lo dicho quiere declarar.
>
> —No es posible, la muerte mil veces;
> yo no quiero mi honra manchar,
> que me pesa sin honra la vida
> y no es vida la infamia aceptar.

But it is above all in the version from Infantes, collected by Diego Catalán and Alvaro Galmés in 1947, and sung, as they note, "en colaboración: viejas, mujeres y chicas y niñas," in which the aspect of sexual war between Pedrosa and Mariana is most clearly developed:

> Yo no muero porque yo soy libre
> ni tampoco que soy liberal;
> sólo muero porque no has podido
> de mi cuerpo tu gusto lograr.

Here the political context of her death has disappeared, and the situation is expressed as an individual conflict of sexual interest.

An additional personal situation can be found in García Lorca's play: the love relationship between Mariana and Pedro de Sotomayor. As Guillermo Díaz Plaja observed in 1927, in the play, "la figura señera de Mariana tiene a un lado el amor malo de Pedrosa, y al otro—como para equilibrar el trance—el amor vehemente y magnífico de Pedro de Sotomayor, el galán apuesto y liberal...."[12]

For this dramatic "balance," Lorca does not take recourse to the ballad of tradition. Although the history of Mariana Pineda relates how she helped her cousin, Álvarez de Sotomayor, to flee from prison,[13] there is no mention of anything other than a mutual political interest. The assumption of the romance between Mariana and Sotomayor is Lorca's interpretation of her role in the liberal captain's escape. Lorca's interest in the figure of Mariana does not stem from her ideological position.[14] For this reason he gives her these words during the final scenes of the play:

> Yo bordé la bandera por él. Yo he conspirado
> para vivir y amar su pensamiento propio.
> Más que a mis propios hijos y a mí misma le quise.
> ¿Amas la Libertad más que a tu Marianita?
> ¡Pues yo seré la misma Libertad que tú adoras!
>
> . . . .
>
> ¡Yo soy la Libertad porque el amor lo quiso![15]

But this "amor" does not exist in the ballad. Instead there is a repeated insistence that Mariana's adherence to the liberal movement overrides all other ballad situations presented. Mariana sacrifices her own children

> A sus hijos la ponen delante
> por ver si algo pueden conseguir.
> Y responde, muy firme y constante:
> No declaro, prefiero morir.[16]

rather than sacrifice allegiance to her fellow "libres":

> A la grita que las gentes daban
> Marianita de esta suerte habló:

> Es en vano lo que ustedes piden
> que a mis libres no descubro yo.[17]

Several versions of the ballad also bring into focus the pathos of the children's imminent abandonment.

> Huerfanitos sin padre ni madre,
> hijos míos de mi corazón,
> hoy fallece la que tanto tiempo
> con sus pechos os alimentó.[18]

Versions which include the children's tearful entreaty to their mother are even more pathetic:

> Al cadalso va la Marianita
> y sus hijos la lloran detrás:
> Madre nuestra, declara y no mueras,
> ¡qué solitos nos vas a dejar![19]

Many others extend the anguish to those present at the execution:

> Marianita al cadalso la suben
> y decían todos a una voz:
> Marianita, mira por tus hijos,
> ¡Marianita, declara, por Dios![20]

These and other versions provide the evidence to explain the ballad's survival in the oral tradition. Pedrosa's intervention, though rarely forgotten, tends to lose its importance during the course of the ballad's life. Yet the loss of this historical detail in the process of the ballad's traditionalization does not suppose a loss of political meaning. Clearly the success of "Marianita Pineda" depended always on its message of liberty. The emphasis on Mariana's steadfast commitment to liberty over life assured the ballad's continued existence during times of political repression, including the Franco years.

Another reason for the endurance of this ballad's theme is the pathos inherent in the situation of the young widow and mother with small children, highly exploited in the oral tradition, as we have seen. This is the aspect of the ballad that García Lorca takes for his play, not the Mariana described in the official nineteenth-century poetry written in her honor: "Envuelta en altisonantes endecasílabos, acrósticos y octavas reales, surgía constantemente Mariana Pineda cubierta de férrea armadura...."[21] An example of what Lorca refers to here is the following sonnet entitled, "A la inmortal heroína de Granada," composed by Pío Pita y Pizarro:

> Del alma libertad el fuego enciende
> El pecho de Mariana generosa
> Y del patriota vuela presurosa
> Al socorro, y de muerte le defiende.
>
> El sagrado pendón alzar pretende
> De la Patria, en la lucha peligrosa:
> Prepárele su mano valerosa
> Y del combate la señal atiende.
>
> Cuando un traidor perjuro fementido
> La tregua inerme el enemigo fiero
> Que al punto a horrible muerte la condena.
>
> Sube al negro cadalso con erguido
> Noble rostro, asombrando al mundo entero
> Y deja de su gloria a España llena.[22]

García Lorca wanted to free Mariana from all the ponderous patriotic trappings of her official image. Thus for the conception of his play, he turns to the song of his childhood:

> Inicié mi labor con el romance popular que cantaban en las calles las
> voces puras y graves de los niños, y terminaba musitándose tras de

las celosías y de las rejas en un tono de oración que me arrancaba
lágrimas:

> ¡Oh!, qué día tan triste en Granada
> que a las piedras hacía llorar.[23]

Thus the play opens with the ballad lifted directly from oral tradition as Lorca
remembered it, sung by a chorus of girls' voices offstage. And, at the end of this
"prólogo," the invisible chorus repeats the ballad's first two lines,

> ¡Oh, qué día tan triste en Granada
> que a las piedras hacía llorar![24]

which reproduces their two possible positions in the versions of the ballad we have
seen—as *exordium*, or as closure. Obviously Lorca was struck by the strange
mixture of poetry and violence found in these verses from the Cartagena version,
for between the *exordium* and the *remate* a little girl appears onstage and sings
them alone:

> Como lirio cortaron el lirio,
> como rosa cortaron la flor,
> como lirio cortaron el lirio,
> más hermosa su alma quedó.[25]

A variant from Palazuelo verges on the surrealistic:

> Como lirio cortaron tres rosas,
> como lirio cortaron el sol,
> como el lirio cortaron tres rosas,
> más hermoso su cuerpo quedó.

The ballad is also responsible for introducing one of the play's primary
metaphors. For example, the poetic reverberations of "¡Oh!, qué día tan triste en
Granada, que a las piedras hacía llorar," suggest the rain that is a pervasive

backdrop throughout the last half of the second act. The rain accompanies the revelation of Mariana's complicity in the liberal cause, and reinforces the tragic notion of her assured death. Lorca has deliberately planted the metaphor as a form of tragic prophecy during the first act with "Lloverá, aunque Dios no quiera,"[26] and he draws out the association between rain and tears at the end of the second act, with Mariana's anguished "Mírame y llora. ¡Ahora empiezo a morir!"[27] Within this context we are meant to understand the reference in the third act to "una niña llorando."[28] By the final curtain, when the ballad is repeated, the image of rain as tears has of course been strengthened.

Another of the recurring metaphors of the play is unknown to the ballad in the versions I have seen. Throughout the dialogue Lorca scatters numerous references to Mariana's white and fragile neck. Since the ballad has informed the audience from the start that she is to die on the gallows, these allusions seem almost mechanically placed. In the first act, Mariana's friend Amparo kisses her on the neck and exclaims:

> Porque este cuello, ¡oh, qué cuello!,
> no se hizo para la pena.[29]

The gesture and accompanying lines have a contrived and artificial effect. Lorca makes a reference to the content of the story but not in terms of the ballad's vocabulary. In a similar melodramatic fashion, he portrays the treacherous Pedrosa, as going for the throat, not only of Mariana's beloved Pedro—"Pero Pedrosa ya buscará su garganta"[30]—but of Mariana's own throat as well:

> Me mira la garganta, que es hermosa
> y toda mi piel se estira.[31]

In the second act, the association between the cut flowers of the ballad and Mariana's neck is made clear, if not obvious, in Pedrosa's threat to Mariana:

> Me has despreciado siempre; pero ahora
> puedo apretar tu cuello con mis manos,
> este cuello de nardo transparente...[32]

Other references carefully extend the association. Yet throughout the play we find that this imagery is always referential and associative; the language of the ballad is never directly interwoven with the text. By the third act, Lorca has imbedded enough prior references to justify these lines, spoken by Mariana when she still clings to the idea of her salvation:

> Tengo el cuello muy corto para ser
> ajusticiada. Ya ve. No podrían.
> Además, es hermoso y blanco; nadie
> querrá tocarlo.[33]

"Tengo el cuello muy corto para ser ajusticiada" belongs, in fact, neither to Lorca nor to the ballad, but to history. This was, according to Mariana Pineda's first biographer, her incredulous response on hearing of the petition for her death sentence.[34]

Obviously history provides most of the plot for the play. But the ballad contributes some important details of its own. The characterization of Pedrosa and his coercive sexual interest is drawn directly from the ballad. Even more important, the ballad represents the figure of Mariana as a human, pathetic "Marianita," who was closer to García Lorca's essential interest. In addition to these characterizations, Lorca lifts the ballad's narrative structure and fleshes it out with his own poetic language. He adds his visual composition of costumes, staging, and sets, and thus actualizes the ballad onstage. Finally, he invents the love affair between Mariana and Sotomayor as part of his attempt to humanize the heroine of monuments and commemorative plaques. In view of this relationship, he consequently deemphasizes Mariana's role as mother, a role the modern Romancero, with its characteristic interest in family relationships, most naturally stresses. In the play, the children are seen in a closer relationship to Clavela than to Mariana.

Other passages based on popular tradition can be found in the play, though these are unrelated to the ballad of "Marianita Pineda." In the first act, for instance, Amparo regales Mariana with a separate ballad account of her stay in Ronda, which begins:

> En la corrida más grande
> que se vió en Ronda la vieja.
> Cinco toros de azabeche
> con divisa verde y negra...[35]

During the second act, one of the liberal conspirators relates the capture and death of General Torrijos.

> Torrijos, el general
> noble, de la frente limpia,
> donde se estaban mirando
> las gentes de Andalucía,
> caballero entre los duques,
> corazón de plata fina,
> ha sido muerto en las playas
> de Málaga la bravía.
>
> . . . .
> Muy de noche lo mataron
> con toda su compañía...[36]

Both of these ballads are Lorca's invention, narrative and elegiac in the style of the Siglo de Oro *comedia*.[37] But the idea for them is not: Lorca had heard traditional ballads on the same or similar themes, which he described as "la poesía recia y varonil que acompaña a aquellos caballeros románticos del amor y la libertad en el siglo XIX, la que recoge la muerte bellísima de Torrijos, contraste de aquella otra que pinta una corrida de toros en Ronda la Vieja...."[38] Act II opens with the "Romance del bordado," recited together by Clavela and Mariana's children as a bedtime story. Lorca clearly intends the *romance* to be a "play within the play," in lyrical miniature. We see how the apostrophic introduction imitates the "oraciones de ciego," but thereafter the ballad takes on the traditional lyric style:

Bendita sea por siempre
la Santísima Trinidad,
y guarde al hombre en la sierra
y al marinero en el mar.
A la verde, verde orilla
del olvarito está
una niña bordando.
¡Madre! ¿Qué bordará?
Las agujas de plata,
bastidor de cristal,
bordaba una bandera,
cantar que te cantar.
Por el olivo, olivo,
¡madre, quién lo dirá!,
venía un andaluz
bien plantado y galán.
—Niña, la bordadora,
mi vida, ¡no bordar!,
que el duque de Lucena
duerme y dormirá.
—No dices la verdad:
el duque de Lucena
me ha mandado bordar
esta roja bandera
porque a la guerra va.
—Por las calles de Córdoba
lo llevan a enterrar
muy vestido de fraile
en caja de coral.
La albahaca y los claveles
sobre la caja van,
y un verderol antiguo,

> cantando el pío pa.
> —¡Ay, duque de Lucena,
> ya no te veré más!
> La bandera que bordo
> de nada servirá.
> En el olivarito
> me quedaré a mirar
> cómo el aire menea
> las hojas al pasar.
> —Adiós, niña bonita,
> espigada y juncal,
> me voy para Sevilla,
> donde soy capitán.—
> Y a la verde, verde orilla
> del olivarito está
> una niña morena,
> llorar que te llorar.[39]

In this case Lorca borrows lines from traditional song and weaves them into his own tiny dramatic creation. Very likely he had this song in mind:

> A Atocha va una niña—*¡carabí!*,
> hija de un capitán—*carabí, hurí, hurá,*
> *Elisa, Elisa de Mambrú.*
> ¡Qué hermoso pelo lleva!
> ¿Quién se lo peinará?
> Se lo peina su tía
> con mucha suavidad,
> con peinecito de oro
> y horquillas de cristal.
> Elisa ya se ha muerto,
> la llevan a enterrar.
> La caja era de oro,
> la tapa de cristal.
> Encima de la tumba
> un pajarito va,

cantando el pío, pío,
cantando el pío, pa.[40]

All three of Lorca's ballad inventions constitute independent lyric interludes, acting as rests during the unfolding of the dramatic developments. They do not impel the plot forward and, except for the moment of poetic foreshadowing we find in the "Romance del bordado," they do not contribute dramatically to the play's structure. These passages can and do stand alone and, as such, are evidence of Lorca's gift for fusing his own language with the language of oral poetry.

The question is not only what Lorca uses from the ballad, but how he decides to use it. The most immediately apparent decision he makes is to place the children's song at the beginning and close of the play, *re*creating the ballad's *exordium* and *remate* structure at the stage level. It is a careful construction, conscious and deliberate, and not particularly subtle. The ballad distinctly marks the perimeters of the play, but fails to function as a vehicle for its forward motion.

In choosing to use the ballad as a frame, Lorca reveals an essentially static conception of his play. That he was aiming primarily for an exterior, visual realization of Granada's heroine is revealed in his stage directions. He meant *Mariana Pineda* to be a portrait. Instead of "acts," he uses the pictorial term, "estampas." He then specifies that the opening scene is to "encuadrado en un margen amarillento, como una vieja estampa."[41] Likewise, the second act is to be "en grises, blancos y marfiles, como una antigua litografía."[42] Not only the sets, but the onstage action itself is conceived with an eye to its purely visual effect. Lorca repeatedly poses the characters, enclosing them within an elaborately framed visual space:

MARIANA se sienta en una silla, de perfil al público, y FERNANDO junto a ella, un poco de frente, componiendo una clásica estampa de la época.[43]

And again:

> Unos se sientan y otros quedan de pie, componiendo una bella estampa.[44]

This division into "prints"—the general emphasis on visual composition with the particular signification of "portrait"—serves to slow the dramatic pulse and arrest our imaginative participation in it. Though the ballad as an opening is provocative, sets the tone and provides the theme for the play, Lorca does not integrate it into the dramatic development. He merely presents the ballad, without additions or alterations. Throughout the play's interior he alludes to the romance, but never once incorporates it directly. Instead the ballad remains an external referent for the events and dialogue taking place onstage. The structural principle inherent in Lorca's direct and unaltered appropriation of traditional song reflects a static conception of the play as a whole.

Although Lorca knew the ballad of "Marianita Pineda" as a turn-of-the-century "canción de corro," the ballad's *noticiero* character and its close relationship to the *romance de ciego* did not escape him. The ballad's meter is not that of the *romance de pliego de cordel* but rather that of the political "news" ballad, which, during the nineteenth century, had incorporated other metric systems. The metric pattern of "Mariana Pineda" coincides with that of the "Himno de Riego." However, the original language of the ballad, as well as its ambience of pathos, point to its "vulgar" literary origin.

Thus Lorca had good reason to conceive his play in terms of the *romance de ciego* model and to attempt to reproduce the visually emphatic *cartelón de ciego* onstage. Given his poetic sensibilities in 1923, he eschews the loud, garish, declamatory aspects of the *ciego* model (which fascinated Valle Inclán) in favor of a more refined, exquisite version.

> Yo veía dos maneras para realizar mi intento: una, tratando el tema con truculencias y manchones de cartel callejero (pero esto lo hace insuperablemente don Ramón), y otra, la que he seguido, que responde a una visión nocturna, lunar e infantil.[45]

At this point in his development as a dramatist of "lo popular," he respects the autonomy of the oral text, and simply attaches it to his play in the form of a children's song. We see that other versions of the ballad from the oral tradition provide additional material at great length, but Lorca artfully selects its most lyric moment as the introduction to his drama. Much in the style of the *romances viejos* compiled for the *Cancioneros* of the early sixteenth century, he truncates the ballad but otherwise does not alter it. Hence the mysterious power of the opening scene—which serves his intentions perfectly.

This early attempt at exploiting a popular ballad for staged representation suffers from a conflict between method and goal. The *romance de ciego* format works against Lorca's poetic ends. The ballad of "Marianita Pineda" suggests metaphors for the play, but these extended associations prove weaker than the language of the ballad itself. The lyrical opening and closure remain on the level of external adornment, a static frame. Other poetic passages of popular inspiration occur only at intervals in the play, but they are isolated instances serving as contrasts to the dramatic action. The audience recognition and response that is evoked by this traditional poetry tends to be cut off by a shift in tone, theme, or imagery. There is no one central impulse to regulate the play, but rather a series of scenes in succession. Our response has no way to grow with the action on the stage.

Lorca himself recognizes the shortcomings of *Mariana Pineda* in 1929, when the play was presented for the first time in Granada: "Mi drama es obra débil de principiante, y aun teniendo rasgos de mi temperamento poético, no responde ya en absoluto a mi criterio sobre el teatro."[46] Yet the work has the indisputable value of attempting a kind of theater unknown to urban Spanish audiences at that time.[47] It risks keeping alive a collective historical inheritance, both in its form and its content.

We see here the beginning of one very important aspect of Lorca's dramatic art, an art which seeks out a way to its audience, though as yet Lorca has not discovered the audience he is looking for. Popular traditional poetry is the vehicle of this intended communication; later, in his work with "La Barraca," he will come to identify his audience as the people who not only recognize it, but produce it and use it, and to whom it rightfully belongs.

The Ballad of *García y Galán*
and Alberti's Dramatization

At the time Lorca was completing revisions of *Mariana Pineda*, the *dictadura* of Primo de Rivera was only in its initial stages. As years went by, the increasing unrest with his "provisional" directorate, sparked by organized and violent student demonstrations (starting in 1927), brought about the resignation of Primo de Rivera in January, 1930. Alfonso XIII, in a final attempt to prop up the tottering monarchy, replaced him with General Berenguer, whose more moderate rule was nicknamed the *dictablanda*. By the time Alberti began work on his play *Fermín Galán* in the spring of 1931, the perspectives for change had risen sharply throughout the country.[48]

The premature military uprising in Jaca against the government of Berenguer on December 12, 1930, resulted in the quick execution of its leaders, Captains Fermín Galán and García Fernández, by a firing squad two days later.[49] The unexpected harshness of the reprisal (Primo did not execute his opponents) provoked widespread public indignation, and shortly thereafter the popular tradition transformed García and Galán into ballad heroes, sacrified in the cause for freedom, just as it had done with Mariana Pineda a century before.

The ballad of "El fusilamiento de García y Galán" is a *noticiero* account of the death of these two soldiers, described in *coplas*, and still sung today in many different regions of Spain. I use several versions of this ballad collected between 1977 and 1982 during field trips organized by the Seminario Menéndez Pidal.[50] The ballad begins with an allusion to Franco (Ramón) and Rada, two officer pilots who attempted an uprising at the Cuatrovientos air force base on the day following the execution:

> A las dos de la mañana
> en Madrid se presentó
> Franco con su aeroplano
> y Rada con su avión.[51]

Immediately, however, the narration centers on the death sentence of García and
Galán:

> Mandaron un telegrama
> a García y a Galán
> que a las dos de la mañana
> los iban a fusilar.[52]

Curiously enough, the ballad supposes that the two condemned men are able to
return home and take leave of their loved ones in person:

> García vuelve a su casa
> y le dice a su mujer:
> —Traeme ese traje de gala
> que me lo voy a poner.
>
> . . . .
>
> La verdad no te lo digo
> pero te voy a abrazar;
> trae la niña que me bese
> que me van a fusilar.[53]
>
> Galán fue en ca' su novia
> y un abrazo le pidió:
> —Dame un abrazo, Emilia,
> dámelo de corazón
> que afusilan al tu amante
> por defender la nación.[54]

The narration ends with the appearance of García's daughter on the scene,
proclaiming the revolution:

> García tenía una hija
> que apenas sabía hablar;

> va gritando por las calles
> ¡Que viva la libertad!
> Que viva la libertad
> y muera el fascio traidor
> que a mi padre lo mataron
> por defender la nación.[55]

We have seen the pathetic emphasis of the *romancero vulgar* before, in the ballad of Mariana Pineda. The only verses of "García y Galán" which manage to override this dominant tone of pathos are the ones alluding to the execution:

> Ya se sienten los disparos
> desde los montes de Jaca.
> Matan los republicanos,
> los más valientes de España.
>
> . . . .
>
> Las guitarras guardan luto,
> cuerdas no quieren tocar,
> porque dicen que mataron
> a García y a Galán.[56]

Possibly one or more versions of this ballad were what Alberti heard in the months following the rebellion:

> Ese grito, que zigzagueaba, callado y sigiloso, iba a agolparse, apretado de valor y heroísmo, en la garganta de los Pirineos, estallando al fin un amanecer entre las nieves de Jaca. ¡Viva la República! Es Fermín Galán quien lo ha gritado. Fermín Galán, a quien el fervor popular, naciente, va a incorporar al cancionero de la calle.[57]

However, as we shall see, he clearly did not base his play *Fermín Galán* on any of the versions he may have heard. On the other hand, the following verses seem to have made an impression on him:

> ¿Quiénes son esas señoras
> que tan enlutadas van?
> Es la madre de García
> y la suegra de Galán.
>
> . . . .
>
> La virgen del Pilar dice
> que no quiere monarquía,
> quiere ser republicana
> como Galán y García.[58]

Shortly after the execution of García and Galán, while traveling in Cádiz, Alberti began work on a set of his own *romances* in response to the tragedy. "Llevaba en mi bolsillo unos romances sobre la vida de Fermín Galán, nacido por aquellas tierras del Sur, en la isla de San Fernando."[59]

Alberti's idea for a *romancero* on the events at Jaca was doubtlessly stimulated both by the "cancionero de la calle" and by the enormous success of García Lorca's *Romancero gitano*. The similarity of the ballads of the *Romancero de Fermín Galán* and the *Romancero gitano* with the ballads of tradition derives primarily from the use of the traditional eight-syllable line. In all other respects, these are *romances cultos*, products of the imagist poetic sensibilities of the Generation of 1927. For example, in the following verse, Alberti reflects nothing in common with the *romance* of oral tradition, yet he echoes Lorca perfectly:

> Noche negra, siete años
> de noche negra sin luna.
> Primo de Rivera duerme
> su sueño de verde uva.[60]

Prompted also by the considerable success and controversy of his modern version of an *auto sacramental, El hombre deshabitado*, in February, 1931,[61] Alberti conceived the idea of a play depicting the life of the military hero and the events of the aborted *pronunciamiento*. The model he chose for this play is the *romance de ciego*, as he tells us explicitly: "Me puse a trabajar de firme. Mis propósitos eran conseguir un romance de ciego, un gran chafarrinón de colores subidos como los que en las ferias pueblerinas explicaban el crimen del día."[62]

Fermín Galán signals the point at which Alberti's literary consciousness and political conscience become manifestly one. His judgment in choosing the form of the narrative *romance vulgar* to convey an openly political position marks a critical moment of transition between his art for the sake of art, and his art as an integral part of his ideology.

> Recién llegado a Madrid, corrí, lleno de cívico entusiasmo a proponerle a Margarita [Xirgu] el convertir aquellos romances míos sobre el héroe de Jaca en una obra de teatro, obra sencilla, popular, en la que me atendría, más que a la verdad histórica, a la que deformada por la gente ya empezaba a correr con visos de leyenda.... Lleno de ingenuidad, y casi sin saberlo, intentaba mi primera obra política.[63]

Margarita Xirgu, whom Alberti described as "la actriz republicana, la verdadera amiga de los poetas y escritores,"[64] accepted the role of Fermín Galán's mother (a role suggested by the ballad), and the play opened in Madrid's Teatro Español on June 1, 1931. Alberti's own *romances*, printed on thin paper of various colors in the form of *aleluyas*, were sold to the spectators at the theater's entrance.[65]

Alberti's structural use of the *romance de ciego* is external and literal. The seated audience faces a curtain painted to resemble the frontispiece of a *pliego de cordel*, with the title of the work at the top, and the price below, underneath a large bordered illustration, or *estampa*, of two soldiers facing a firing squad.

> En primer término del escenario, telón pintado: con colores populares, de aleluya callejera, el fusilamiento de Fermín Galán y

> García Hernández, sobre un fondo de alegoría republicana. Arriba,
> en la parte alta del telón, un gran letrero que dice: "ROMANCE DE
> FERMÍN GALÁN Y LOS SUBLEVADOS DE JACA." Abajo, en
> uno de los lados, este otro más pequeño: "Precio: 5 cénts."[66]

The conventions of the street ballad are further replicated by placing a blind man
and a boy in front of the curtain, facing the audience:

> En el centro de la escena, rígido, con su guitarra, *El Ciego*, y *El
> Niño*, distraído, llevando en una mano un pliego de romances en
> papeles de colores, y en otra, una escudilla de metal.[67]

In the same manner as the "Lector" in *El Enamorado y la Muerte* and the
"Pipirigallo" in *La pájara pinta*, El Ciego and El Niño pronounce the exterior level
of the narration, which mediates between the audience and the action of the play's
interior. In this case, they announce the "suceso" currently for sale:

> ¡Compren, si quieren llorar!
> ¡Oigan, si quieren llorar!
> ¡Romance de Fermín Galán y
> los sublevados de Jaca! ¡A
> cinco céntimos![68]

El Ciego's subsequent exhortation to the child recalls the typical pathos of the
romance vulgar, and at the same time reflects the traditional poetic recourse to the
description of nature as sympathetically responsive to human events:

> Más pena, niño, más pena
> en ese pregón, más pena.
> Haz que se paren los pájaros,
> que los cielos se detengan,
> que lloren las nubes agua
> y lloren sangre las piedras.[69]

Similarly, we saw how the "día triste" in *Mariana Pineda* "a las piedras hacía llorar."

The time of the dramatic action at this opening point is soon after the execution of García and Galán. The characters Alberti has appear on stage in response to the "pregón" are representative of the *pueblo* as he then envisions it: students, workers, and an old woman, who shout, "¡Abajo Berenguer! ¡Muera el Rey!" El Niño recites:

> Republicana es la luna,
> republicano es el sol,
> republicano es el aire,
> republicano soy yo.[70]

Still at the exterior level, El Ciego begins to narrate the life of Fermín Galán with a lexicon and imagery which clearly do not belong either to the ballad of the *pliego* or to the oral tradition, but which apparently fit the poetics of Alberti's generation:

> Vió la luz Fermín Galán,
> su luz primera, en la Isla.
> Cádiz, tacita de plata,
> le regaló su bahía.[71]

However, the epithet for Cádiz, "tacita de plata," has been collected from the oral tradition of popular lyrics. For example:

> En la bahía de Cádiz
> ha entrado una fragata
> con un letrero que dice:
> "Cádiz, tacita de plata."[72]

The blind man's narrative in front of the curtain is a preview of the scene that is to follow. Nothing is left to the audience's perception. He describes the pensive melancholy of the young Galán, and even the scenery:

Ved ya cómo se le acerca,
cómo le pregunta, tímida,
—dime, Fermín, di, ¿qué tienes?—
cómo luego lo acaricia
y cómo Fermín le habla
frente al mar de la bahía.
De azul, oyéndolo todo,
Cádiz está de rodillas.
¡Miradlos![73]

The possibility of unimpeded dramatic development is cut short by anticipating the substance of the scene before it takes place. The scene then amplifies the narration into three dimensions.

When the curtain (or first page of the *pliego*) is lifted, the audience views more deeply into the play. The scene before them is the dock of the Isla—the time leaps backwards to Galán's boyhood. From this movement in and back, Alberti will bring the action progressively forward in periodic historical episodes drawn from history and legend (scenes of Galán's military service in North Africa, his imprisonment in Montjuich, his post in Jaca, and his role in the developments in the conspiracy for the Republic).[74] Interspersed with these are truly comic sketches of his own imagination, satirizing army officers in Melilla and the guests at a cocktail party in the palace of aristocrats. Some of these episodes contain high moments of poetic persuasion, while others exhibit characteristic Albertian exuberance, spilling over into broad farce. In each case, the episode is prefigured by El Ciego's exterior narration at the front of the stage. The effect, decidedly antidramatic, duplicates the static rhetorical passages of the *romance de ciego*.

Two episodes in particular failed egregiously with the public and the press, although for different reasons. The seventh episode in the second act takes place in the sanctuary at Cillas, where Republican soldiers sought refuge after their rout by Berenguer's forces. In terms of the play, the tragedy rightfully should stem from this moment. But the possibility of pathos is crushed when Alberti has the statue of the Virgin come alive and step off the altar in response to the soldiers' prayers for mercy:

> Hijos, yo velaré por vosotros. Lavaré vuestras heridas
> con lagrímas de mis ojos. Haré de mis tocas vendas y agua
> dulce de mis lloros. Republicana es la Virgen y acude en
> vuestro socorro.
>
> (Baja del altar, quitándose la toca y desgarrándola en tiras.)[75]

Possibly Alberti could have saved the scene from the public's indignation at this point had the Virgen performed a conventional miraculous healing of the wounded Republican soldiers, but he extends his revolutionary feelings too far for the sensibilities of his audience when he transforms the Virgen into a brave "guerrillera":

> Yo defiendo a la República
> y a los revolucionarios.
> ¡Abajo la Monarquía!
> Salid conmigo a los campos.
> ¡Dadme un fusil o un revólver,
> una espada o un caballo!
> Quiero ser la Coronela
> de todos los sublevados.[76]

By the end of the second act, the "Santuario" (the "vieja iglesia") has become a "hospital de sangre," and the Virgin's cloak has become a flag wrapped around a bayonet.

Although the exaggerated visual and rhetorical melodrama of this and other scenes is entirely in keeping with the stylistics of the *romance de ciego* genre, Alberti later recognized the limitations of transposing it from its street context (where the play's overtly political platform would be appropriate) to the interior of urban, commercial theater.

> El primer acto pasó bien, pero cuando en el segundo apareció el
> cuadro en el que tuve la peregrina idea de sacar a la Virgen con fusil
> y bayoneta calada, acudiendo en socorro de los maltrechos

sublevados y pidiendo a gritos la cabeza del rey y del general
Berenguer, el teatro entero protestó violentamente: los republicanos
ateos porque nada querían con la Virgen, y los monárquicos por
parecerles espantosos tan criminales sentimientos en aquella Madre
de Dios que yo me había inventado.[77]

Once the political lines have been drawn so firmly, the remainder of the play
serves only to underscore them.   After the tenth and final episode, surely
representative of Alberti's verbal agility at its best, the antagonized audience rushed
the stage in an uproar.   One scene in this episode was based on an actual event that
must have occurred only days before the play's opening: "La duquesa de la
Victoria, en pleno 'cock-tail' patriótico, pega una blanca bofeteada a una señorita,
hija de marqueses, que algo mareada se atrevió a clavar en su cabeza una
minúscula bandera tricolor."[78]   Alberti gives the anonymous young lady the
name "Señorita Guirigay," and has her wear the flag, which the duchess then takes
from her and rips to shreds.   In the midst of the ensuing blows, the Señorita cries:

> ¡Abajo los monárquicos!
> El azul que hay en mis venas,
> yo lo prefiero encarnado.
> ¡Mueran los duques, los condes![79]

The audience, of course, knew exactly which members of Madrid's aristocratic
social set were being satirized.[80]

Alberti rounds out the final episode with perhaps his wittiest attack.   He
presents a Cardinal (whom the audience immediately recognized as Cardenal
Segura, archbishop of Toledo and arch enemy of the Republic) in a drunken stupor,
offering a toast in a funny, fractured Latin:

> Nos, repudiam anarquistas,
> repudiam sindicalistas,
> despreciavit comunistas,
> et amavit catequistas.[81]

At this point the metal fire curtain had to be lowered to keep the audience off the stage.

Theater critics unanimously denounced the play. Díez-Canedo, perhaps the strongest supporter of the new generation's experiments in the theater, found nothing wrong with Alberti's choice of the ballad format, but rather with the indiscriminate jumble of tragic and satiric scenes. Alberti's decision to portray a militant Virgin, he wrote, "acaba de asestar un golpe decisivo al interés dramático."[82] Jorge de la Cueva attempted to compare Alberti's play with the new Soviet theater. "Hay en el teatro ruso un propósito de arte, un dinamismo escénico, una fuerza, un poder representativo y sintético que falta por completo en la obra del señor Alberti."[83] Another reviewer could only fume: "...está fuera de la literatura, del arte, del teatro y de la poesía. No cabe crítica serena ante aquel cúmulo de despropósitos."[84] But the closest statement of the problem came from Melchor Fernández Almagro:

> Puesto que se trata de una obra...en relaciones directas con la plaza
> pública, ¿es lógico que se la emplace en un teatro de tradicionales
> exigencias literarias y ante un público que no es, ni tiene por qué ser,
> el inocente y sencillo de las encrucijadas de las plazas?....
> Imaginemos que estábamos, efectivamente, en un aldeón castellano
> escuchando la cantata de un ciego.... Pues bien: la obra, en general,
> no es conmovedora tampoco: no se trata de un fruto sano y popular,
> sino de un producto plebeyo.[85]

Fernández Almagro correctly observes that the context of the commercial theater imposes a referent entirely different from that of street theater or the performance of a *romance de cartelón*, but he mistakenly assumes that his own aesthetic criteria would be shared by a villager. Had Alberti's real audience been the *pueblo* he depicted in *Fermín Galán*—the old women, the students and workers—the play's reception might well have been different. Alberti's own critique reveals the core of the problem:

Mi mayor equivocación consistió sin duda en haber sometido un romance de ciego, cuyo verdadero escenario hubiera sido el de cualquier plaza pueblerina, a un público burgués y aristocrático, de uñas todavía sectario en cierto modo y latentes en él, aunque no lo supiera, todos los gérmenes que en el curso de muy pocos años se desarrollarían hasta cuajar en aquel sangriente estallido que terminó con el derrumbe de la nueva República.[86]

Fermín Galán was Alberti's last attempt to write for commercial theater until several years after the "sangriente estallido." And never again was he to confront that particular audience in Madrid.

Notes

1. See Maurer, *Epistolario*, I, pp. 89–90. The confusion in dates (Laffranque, p. 420; Gallego Morell, p. 123) is resolved by a letter written to Melchor Fernández Almagro before September 11, 1923. See n. 5 below. According to Francisco García Lorca: "Fechada el 8 de enero de 1925, *Mariana Pineda* había sido ya leído en su integridad a un grupo de amigos en 1924." *Federico y su mundo*, p. 285.

2. Laffranque, "Bases," p. 424. Gibson's biography, vol. I, includes a photo (no. 51, ff. p. 480) of Dalí's set, courtesy of Antonina Rodrigo. In October of the same year, Xirgu's company opened the play in Madrid. *Mariana Pineda* was first published in *La Farsa*, II, no. 52 (September 1, 1928).

3. Partial documentation of the trial proceedings can be found in Antonina Rodrigo, *Mariana de Pineda* (Madrid: Alfaguarra), 1965.

4. *OC*, III, p. 577.

5. September, 1923. Gallego Morell, pp. 55–56. Maurer, *Epistolario*, I, pp. 84–85.

6. *OC*, III, pp. 586–587.

7. These and the following texts from the Archives of Ramón Menéndez Pidal. Ballad collecting in Granada was no doubt stimulated by Menéndez Pidal's visit there in

September, 1920. García Lorca organized an excursión to the "barrios gitanos" and helped Menéndez Pidal with the task of collecting. "En las cuevas del Sacro Monte hallé otro filón," notes Menéndez Pidal. "'La Santa,' anciana de 60 años, me dio un regular repertorio." *Romancero tradicional*, V (1971), pp. 62–63. A full description of this ballad collecting session is given in the note on pp. 67–68. In part, "La falta de tiempo fue salvada por la oferta de recogerlos que nos hizo el joven Federico García Lorca, quien se mostró muy animado y amable en preparnos esta excursión, que le revelaba un escondido aspecto de Granada desconocido de los granadinos."

8. The 22 versions that I have seen, some extensive and others very fragmentary, originate in very diverse regions of the Peninsula: 5 from Andalucía, 1 from Cartagena, 6 from Castilla la Nueva, 1 from Segovia, 1 from Soria, 1 from León, 1 from Ávila, 1 from Orense, and 3 from Vizcaya. Others come from Latin America (1 version from Puerto Rico, c. 1927) and from the Spanish-speaking Jewish communities of Morocco (from Tetuán, prior to 1905–1906).

9. José de la Peña y Aguayo, *Doña Mariana Pineda. Narración de su vida, de la causa criminal en la que fue condenada al último suplicio y descripción de su ajusticiamiento* (Madrid: 1836; subsequent printings: Albacete, 1842; Granada, 1870). Cited in Rodrigo, *Mariana de Pineda*, p. 338. This work may have been suggested to Lorca by Antonio Gallego Burín, who was a student of Granada history. In a letter to Gallego Burín, Lorca asked for

> una biografía de ella y algunos datos sobre la conspiración. Como tú comprenderás, el interés de mi drama está en el carácter que yo quiero construir y en la anécdota, que no tiene que ver nada con lo histórico, porque yo me lo he inventado yo. Yo quiero que tú me guíes en lo referente a Pedrosa, y que me digas dónde puedo enterarme del estado de Granada en aquella época.

See Mauer, *Epistolario*, I, pp. 89–90.

10. I use the edition of *Mariana Pineda* in *OC*, II (hereafter cited as *MP*), p. 239.

11. With minor variations, in versions from Cartagena (Murcia), Palazuelo (León), Riaza (Segovia), Infantes (Ciudad Real), Alameda (Ciudad Real), and Tetuán.

12. In an interview published in *La Gaceta Literaria*, cited by Rodrigo, *Mariana de Pineda*, p. 235.

13. "Relato de la fuga de don Fernando Álvarez de Sotomayor," in the historical biography by Peña y Aguayo already cited; reproduced in Rodrigo, *Mariana de Pineda*, pp. 277–290.

14. Lorca is explicit on this point: "Yo he cumplido mi deber de poeta oponiendo una Mariana viva, cristiana y resplandeciente de heroísmo frente a la fría, vestida de forastera y librepensadora del pedestal." *Federico y su mundo*, p. 289.

15. *MP*, p. 266 and p. 272.

16. With minor variations, in versions from Riaza, Palazuelo, Cartagena, Infantes, Tetuán and Puerto Rico.

17. Version from Infantes.

18. In versions from El Hoyo (Ciudad Real), Palazuelo, and Cartagena.

19. In versions from Riaza, El Hoyo, and Tetuán.

20. Version from Munera (Albacete), recited by Juan José Márquez, 47 years of age, and collected by D. Catalán. Variants of this strophe can be found in versions from Cartagena and Infantes.

21. *OC*, III, p. 587.

22. See Rodrigo, *Mariana de Pineda*, p. 228.

23. *OC*, III, p. 588. Lorca may have also heard the extraordinary image, "hace llorar a las piedras," in the form of a *frase popular*. It appears as such in the late nineteenth-century collection of Olvarría y Huarte, *Biblioteca de las tradiciones populares*, II, p. 24, accompanied by this note from the folklorist Adolfo Coelho: "Alguem podería ser tentado de vêr n'essa locuçâo nâo um simples facto de lingagem, mas um echo mythico; por exemplo, na morte de Balder choram todas as cousas creadas, homens, animaes, plantas e pedras. *Edda de Snorr*, 68."

24. *MP*, p. 166. Lorca took charge of directing this chorus himself. Antonina Rodrigo, *García Lorca en Cataluña* (Barcelona: Planeta, 1975), p. 100.

25. *MP*, p. 166.

26. *MP*, p. 178.

27. *MP*, p. 242.

28. *MP*, p. 250.

29. *MP*, p. 178.

30. *MP*, p. 183.

31. *MP*, pp. 193–194.

32. *MP*, p. 239.

33. *MP*, p. 256.

34. Peña y Aguayo, p. 107. Cited in Rodrigo, *Mariana de Pineda*, p. 146. See also *Federico y su mundo*, p. 289.

35. *MP*, pp. 176–177.

36. *MP*, pp. 225–226. A published version of the "El Fusilamiento de Torrijos," beginning "El general Torrijos / cuando recibe el pliego / le dice al mensajero / si hay alguna traición...," can be seen in *AIER*, II, p. 132.

37. Indeed, the last two verses cited recall the *estribillo* of Lope's *El caballero de Olmedo*.

38. *OC*, III, p. 588. The *romances* in *Mariana Pineda* correspond to the same cycle of Lorca's poetic production as the *Romancero gitano*, published in 1928 but composed during 1924–1927. Thus they logically are included by Mario Hernández in his edition of Lorca's *Romancero gitano*, vol. I of *Obras de Federico García Lorca*, pp. 107–112.

39. *MP*, pp. 205–207.

40. The underscored refrain is repeated at the end of every line throughout the song. Olvarría y Huarte, "El folk-lore de Madrid," *Biblioteca de las tradiciones populares*, II, p. 71. Variants of the song, known in the Canary Islands as "Mambrú se fue a la guerra" and also "Carabí," can be seen in *La Flor de la Marañuela*, I, pp. 355–356; II, pp. 167–168. Versions from the peninsula are found in *AIER*, II, pp. 218–221. The name "Mambrú" is the Spanish adaptation for the French pronunciation of the Duke of Marlborough.

41. *MP*, p. 165.

42. *MP*, p. 202.

43. *MP*, p. 191.

44. *MP*, p. 219.

45. *Federico y su mundo*, p. 290.

46. *OC*, III, p. 414.

47. Consider Torrente Ballester's description of the audience's reaction to *Mariana Pineda* in Oviedo:

> Dos filas de butacas y alguna gente arriba: ¿Quién fue Mariana Pineda y quién es García Lorca? Una niña vestida de blanco, con pollera corta, canta un romance en un escenario cuyas decoraciones, al mismo tiempo que llaman la atención, previenen al espectador de la naturaleza inusual del espectáculo.... Al cuarto verso, los escasos espectadores arrugan la frente y se miran.... A mi lado, cuchichea un señor: "Debe de ser una cosa escrita por uno de esos poetas de ahora." Unos minutos después, Carmen Carbonell, que era entonces una mocita preciosa, recitó el romance de la fiesta de toros en Ronda, y cuando llegó a aquello de "parecía que la tarde—se ponía más morena," el estupor cuajó como un cristal de hielo, y, acto seguido, los espectadores se desentendieron de la obra. Al terminar había uno que aplaudía en el patio de butacas y otro, no sé quien, en las alturas.

Quoted by Antonina Rodrigo, "Mariana de Pineda, Federico García Lorca: Relación personaje-autor," in *Hommage/Homenaje a García Lorca* (Toulouse: Université de Toulouse-Le Mirail), pp. 50–51.

48. Herr, pp. 140–155.

49. For a personal testimony of the failure of the Republican committee's plans to coordinate the "sublevación," see José Rico Godoy, "No pudimos convencer a Galán," in a special issue commemorating the fiftieth anniversary of the Second Republic, *Historia 16*, 6, no. 60 (April, 1981), p. 85.

50. I have participated in two of these field trips—one in the summer of 1980, in the west of Asturias and northeastern León, the second to the east of Orense and southeastern Galicia, in the summer of 1982. The objectives and methods of the Seminario's field work are described by Flor Salazar and Ana Valenciano, "Arte nuevo de recolección de romances tradicionales," in *AIER*, 1, pp. lxi–lxxxii. For published versions of the ballad, see Diego Catalán, "El romancero oral en el último cuarto del siglo XX," *El Romancero hoy: Nuevas fronteras*, p. 254, and *AIER*, II, pp. 145–146.

51. Version sung by Aurora Linacero, 56 years of age, and collected by Jon Juaristi in Las Arenas (Bilbao) on August 23, 1982.

52. Version from Guímara (León), sung by Agustín Martínez, 68 years old; collected by J. Antonio Cid on September 22, 1979.

53. Version from Chano (León), sung by Ramero Martínez (56 years old), and "un corro de hombres, en la taberna." Collected by J. Antonio Cid on September 22, 1979.

54. Version from Friera (Orense), recited by Ceferina Granja, 75 years old, and collected by Koldo Biguri, et al., on July 18, 1982. The recitation was followed by her personal commentary: "Y esto vino ahora…todo esto, de García y Galán…. Lo pedían, lo pedían los obreros. ¡La democracia!"

55. Version from Guímara.

56. Version from Guímara.

57. Rafael Alberti, *El poeta en la España de 1931, seguido del Romancero de Fermín Galán y los sublevados de Jaca* (Buenos Aires: Editorial Araújo, 1942), p. 22.

58. Version from Guímara. The last quatrain robs and recasts the old *coplas* referring to the siege of Zaragoza during the War for Independence: "La virgen del Pilar dice / que no quiere ser francesa, / que quiere ser capitana / de la tropa aragonesa." Partially cited by Pierre Vilar, *Historia de España*, trans. M. Tuñón de Lara (Paris: Librairie Espagnole, 1963), p. 75.

59. *El poeta en la España de 1931*, p. 26.

60. *El poeta…seguido del Romancero de Fermín Galán*, p. 52. Alberti read this poem in its increasingly satirical entirety to the Ateneo in Cádiz in March. Before the reading began, a student stood up and demanded that the poet Pemán leave the hall. The following day, Alberti was stopped in the street during a student demonstration and asked to repeat the verses. See pp. 28–29. Also *La arboleda perdida*, pp. 289–290.

61. For a judicious yet favorable review of Alberti's first full-length play, see Enrique Díez-Canedo, *Artículos de crítica teatral. El teatro español de 1914–1936*, IV (Mexico: Joaquín Mortiz, 1968), pp. 113–117. The review originally appeared in *El Sol*, April 27, 1931. Alberti provoked a scandal when, after the final curtain call, he appeared on stage shouting "¡Viva el exterminio! ¡Muera la podredumbre de la actual escena española!" The resulting riot forced Benavente and the Quintero brothers to leave the theater before the arrival of the police. See *La arboleda perdida*, pp. 283–285.

62. *La arboleda perdida*, p. 292.

63. *La arboleda perdida*, p. 292.

64. *La arboleda perdida*, p. 292.

65. According to Alberti in an interview with Manuel Bayo, in González Martín, pp. 103 and 193.

66. Rafael Alberti, *Fermín Galán. Romance de ciego, en tres actos, diez episodios y un epílogo* (Madrid: Chulilla y Angel, 1931), p. 11. Hereafter cited as *FG*.

67. *FG*, p. 11. A photograph of the *ciego* and the boy standing in front of the painted curtain, which first appeared in *Ahora* on June 2, 1931, has been reproduced in Víctor Fuentes, *La marcha al pueblo en las letras españolas, 1917–1936* (Madrid: Ediciones de la Torre, 1980), p. 136. What strikes the eye is the rigidity, both in the posture of the *ciego*, and in the rectangular frame of the *estampa*.

68. *FG*, p. 13.

69. *FG*, p. 14. The sympathetic response can be found in "El Conde Niño," or in these verses from "El Infante Arnaldos": "Marinero que la guía / diciendo viene un cantar, // que la mar ponía en calma, / los vientos hace amainar; // los peces que andan al hondo / arriba los hace andar // las aves que van volando / al mástil vienen posar." *Flor nueva*, p. 247.

70. *FG*, p. 14. Alberti first heard these verses in Cádiz where he had gone to give a reading at the Ateneo in March, 1931. "El folklore de la primera República, resucitado, se atrevía, en rincones de cante jondo y tabernas ocultas, a agitar sus guitarras. Allí aprendí esta copla." *La arboleda perdida*, p. 289.

71. *FG*, p. 15.

72. Mercedes Díaz Roig, *El Romancero y la lírica popular moderna* (México: El Colegio de México, 1976), p. 187. Additional information in the bibliography, p. 278: "*Colección Díaz*: colección manuscrita de canciones y coplas recogidas entre los españoles residentes en México y otras sacadas de discos y libros, México, 1969–1974."

73. *FG* p. 18.

74. Alberti has not revealed the sources for this biographical information.

75. *FG*, pp. 133–134.

76. *FG*, pp. 134–135.

77. *La arboleda perdida*, p. 293.

78. *El poeta en la España de 1931*, p. 26.

79. *FG*, p. 197.

80. According to Alberti, the scene was repeated in Madrid's Retiro a few days after the play's opening, when "una dama muy estirada" stepped down from her horse-driven carriage and slapped Margarita Xirgu in the face, "¡Tome! Por lo de *Fermín Galán!" La arboleda perdida*, p. 294.

81. *FG*, p. 193 and p. 199. The hostility Cardinal Segura had for the Republic is documented in Víctor Manuel Arbeloa, "Iglesia y República: Diálogo imposible," in the special issue of *Historia 16* already cited, pp. 70–77.

82. Díez-Canedo, p. 118. In the same review, which appeared in Madrid's *El Sol* on June 2, 1931: "Y es, efectivamente, un romance, dicho por un cantor popular, el hilo que engarza los diez episodios de esta historia, que intentan ser, en su corporeidad escénica, voluntariamente exagerados sus rasgos patéticos y sus efectos satíricos, lo que las ingenuas pinturas de un cartelón, lo que las chillonas estampas de un pliego de aleluyas, realizadas con fuertes colorines."

83. In *El Debate*, June 2, 1931, cited in Marrast's *Aspects*, p. 60. A year later, Alberti would travel to Germany and the Soviet Union with a grant from the "Junta para Ampliación de los Estudios" to study new European theater, including Brecht.

84. Luis Araújo Costa, *La Epoca*, June 2, 1931. Reprinted in its entirety in *Aspects*, p. 69.

85. *La Voz*, June 2, 1931; in *Aspects*, pp. 59–60.

86. *La arboleda perdida*, p. 294.

6

The Integration of Theatrical Experience:
The "Teatro para llegar a todos"

The flowering of artistic ideas and activities in the late 1920's comes to fruition in the period 1932–1935. *Fermín Galán* in 1931 represents the last theatrical work of the early stage of Alberti's political awakening. In the years that follow, his first political revelations develop into deep political commitment. After trips to Berlin and Moscow, Alberti turned his attention mainly to *poesía comprometida* and to the journal *Octubre*, which he and María Teresa León founded in 1933 as an outlet for the Asociación de Escritores y Artistas Revolucionarias.[1] For Lorca these years mark his arrival as a dramatist fully conscious of his resources, and as a director increasingly aware of his goals: to renovate and revitalize the theater that belongs to the authentically Spanish tradition. Also in these years Lorca was to reach his widest public, both throughout Spain and in Latin America.

Lorca and La Barraca: The Discovery
of the "Pueblo" as "Público"

In 1931 plans were made for two traveling theater groups to be organized and financed by the government of the Second Republic as part of a far-reaching educational reform. The Patronato de Misiones Pedagógicas, headed by Manuel B. Cossío, embodied many of the old *Institucionista* ideals. Its stated goals were to "difundir la cultura general, la moderna orientación docente y la educación ciudadana en aldeas, villas y lugares, con especial atención a los intereses espirituales de la población rural."[2] In addition to mobile libraries and a museum of paintings copied from the Prado, the Misiones Pedagógicas took movies, records, choral groups (under the direction of Eduardo Martínez Torner), and a theater (under the direction of Alejandro Casona) to some of the most remote and forgotten villages in Spain.[3] Another itinerant theater, La Barraca, was created with a subsidy from the Ministerio de Instrucción Pública, headed at that time by Fernando do los Ríos, and was placed under the direction of Federico García Lorca and Eduardo Ugarte in March of 1932.[4]

La Barraca proved to be the perfect laboratory for Lorca's developing ideas about theater and the relation of author to audience. At first he conceived it as an extension of his *teatro de guiñol* and as still another outlet for the performance of *canciones populares*,[5] but as the project took shape, La Barraca became a vehicle for the open-air presentation of seventeenth-century *comedias* and *entremeses* within the twentieth-century context of developing socialism. When asked how La Barraca was organized, Lorca stressed its nature as a collective:

> Aquí no hay ni primeras ni segundas figuras; no se admiten los divos. Formamos una especie de falansterio en que todos somos iguales y cada cual arrima el hombro según sus aptitudes. Si uno hace de protagonista, otro se encarga de distribuir los bastidores, otro se convierte en un organizador de los efectos luminosos, y el que parece que no sirve para nada está, sin embargo, haciendo a maravilla el oficio de conductor de camiones. Una democrática y cordial camaradería nos gobierna y alienta a todos.[6]

He also described how invitation performances would be held on the first night for the wealthiest members of a town; on subsequent nights, little or nothing would be charged so that the working people could attend.[7] But it was not just the internal organization of La Barraca that reflected socialist ideas. The external relation of author and audience led García Lorca to a crucially important discovery:

> Hay un solo público que hemos podido comprobar que no nos es adicto: el intermedio, la burguesía, frívola y materializada. Nuestro público, los verdaderos captadores del arte teatral, están en los dos extremos: las clases cultas, universitarias o de formación intelectual o artística espontánea, y el pueblo, el pueblo más pobre y más rudo, incontaminado, virgen, terreno fértil a todos los estremecimientos del dolor y a todos los giros de la gracia.[8]

Lorca's idea was to take theater out of its exclusively urban domain, where it was stratified by commercial interests and bourgeois values, and return it to its traditional roots. In order to travel the roads between cities and rural communities, La Barraca, in the manner of the early caravan theater in Lope de Rueda's time, dispensed with elaborate sets and depended primarily on a platform and a simple black curtain for staging most of the works. In the larger towns plays were sometimes staged indoors. Whatever decorated backdrops were used had to be "montables" and "desmontables" and easily loaded onto the back of a truck.

The plays performed by La Barraca were almost all works of the sixteenth and seventeenth centuries. As director, Lorca respected the language of the originals, but cut the scenes of purely local and historical reference which would be pointless to a twentieth-century audience.[9] Otherwise, he made no concessions to the public's understanding of the work. Rather, he paid close attention to the audience's reception of the undiluted *comedia* language.

The fresh reactions of the rural audience, in particular, provided Lorca with new insights into the special relation between author and audience.

> Y es curioso el íntimo placer, la atención recogida de los aldeanos, que le pegarían al que hiciera el menor ruido que les hiciera perder una palabra, con que en los pueblos aparentemente más atrasados de España se escuchan nuestras representaciones, que son el verdadero trasunto, la más fiel y revivida versión de nuestro teatro clásico.[10]

The reactions and interpretations of the *campesinos* signalled a direction for the dramatist to follow in his pursuit of a dialogue mediated by the play. For Lorca the process entailed a clearer understanding of his intended audience. Describing the work of La Barraca for an interview in 1934, he said:

> Claro que le gusta al público. Al público que también me gusta a mí: obreros, gente sencilla de los pueblos, hasta los más chicos, y estudiantes y gentes que trabajan y estudian. A los señoritos y a los elegantes, sin nada dentro, a esos no les gusta mucho, ni nos importa a nosotros. Van a vernos y salen luego comentando: "Pues no trabajan mal." Ni se enteran. Ni saben lo que es el gran teatro español. Y luego se dicen católicos y monárquicos y se quedan tan tranquilos. Donde más me gusta trabajar es en los pueblos. De pronto ver un aldeano que se queda admirado ante un romance de Lope, y no puede contenerse y exclama: "¡Qué bien se expresa!"[11]

That is, the public García Lorca addresses himself to is the one most receptive to the resonances of ageless popular and traditional material. The anonymous songs and ballads Lope so deftly incorporated into his plays, and that provoked such a spontaneous reaction in the twentieth-century "aldeano," are the materials that Lorca himself knew and loved so well.

According to Luis Sáenz de la Calzada, one of the university students who comprised the theater troupe (and whose memories provide the most detailed description available of La Barraca's activities between 1932 and 1936),[12] Lorca had an active hand in every aspect of the theatrical productions. As director and choreographer he selected and reworked the plays for production, added musical interventions, and freely interpolated songs and dances whenever suggested by the text. As choreographer he sometimes consulted and collaborated with La Argentinita and her sister, Pilar, who taught *sevillanas* and other dances to the student members of the troupe.[13] As actor he played the role of the black-veiled Sombra in La Barraca's first production, the *auto sacramental* version of Calderon's *La vida es sueño*.[14] Dámaso Alonso was present at one of the first performances of the *Auto*, in the town of Almazán, and recorded the audience's reaction:

> A todo atiende Federico, al tono de voz, a la posición en escena, al efecto de conjunto…. En la plaza de un pueblo, a poco de comenzar la representación a cielo abierto, se pone a llover implacablemente, bien cernido y menudo. Los actores se calan sobre las tablas, las mujeres del pueblo se echan las sayas por la cabeza, los hombres se encogen y hacen compactos: el agua resbala, la representación sigue: nadie se ha movido.[15]

Various pieces of *teatro menor* were staged by García Lorca with La Barraca, including Lope de Rueda's *La Tierra de Jauja* and *La Egloga de Plácida y Victoriano* of Juan del Encina.[16] To all of these Lorca added music and song, "cancioncillas antiguas que Federico con un acierto insuperable, sabía colocar en el momento justo."[17] Some of the *entremeses* were by now more than familiar to him (such as Cervantes' *Los dos habladores* and the *Retablo de las Maravillas*), having first produced them a decade earlier in Granada with Manuel de Falla. To these he added others by Cervantes, *La cueva de Salamanca* and *La guarda cuidadosa*. On certain occasions three *entremeses* were presented together as a group to fill one drama session; at other times they were represented individually in conjunction with a larger work in the classic *comedia* manner. Lorca's innovations and irrepressible spirit in staging the *entremeses* were not always understood or appreciated. "A María de Maeztu no le gustó la representación; comentó que no se podía tratar tan irrespetuosamente a D. Miguel de Cervantes; que bailar los Entremeses constituía poco menos que un delito."[18]

Lorca also selected the full length *comedias* performed by La Barraca: *El burlador de Sevilla* by Tirso de Molina;[19] and two by Lope, *Fuenteovejuna* and *El caballero de Olmedo*. What seems to have interested him above all in the first two were the weddings. García Lorca equalled Lope in his stage mastery of these celebrations: "no he visto a nadie disfrutar como a él montando una boda en un escenario."[20] Weddings offered the maximum opportunity to meld song with dance, music with text, and to orchestrate the whole into one harmonious *espectáculo*.

Ahora bien, una boda en escena no era cosa que Federico dejara irse
así como así, sino que aprovechaba para sacar de ella lo más hondo,
lo más popular...que una boda rural puede tener en sus entrañas....
La celebración de la boda, ese "despierte la novia, despierte la
novia", era una verdadera fiesta para Federico

¡ea, tañed y cantad
pues que para en uno son![21]

In fact, the *bodas* were complete theatrical events, entire unto themselves, and
could be represented separately from the *comedia* with equal success:

La cosa salía bien; no hubo lugar donde la boda de *Fuenteovejuna* no
se aplaudiera a rabiar.... "Federico: especialista en bodas", le
dijimos, sobre todo cuando, de manera totalmente diferente, montó
la de Aminta y Patricio en *El burlador de Sevilla*. No, no se puede
explicar por qué movía a los personajes como lo hacía, de dónde
sacaba sus canciones que eran, en todo caso, las adecuadas, y cómo
imprimía a la escena una movilidad perfecta que hacía, insisto, que
el público prorrumpiese siempre, y en todo caso, en incontenibles
aplausos.[22]

Lorca's adaptation of Lope's *Fuenteovejuna* was done with both an eye and
ear to the prevailing democratic spirit of the early years of the Republic. All
references to the Catholic Kings, including the final scene of pardon and
conciliation, were cut. The student actors were dressed in the same traditional
campesino clothing worn by members of the audience, with the exception of the
character of the Comendador, who wore a dark sports jacket bearing the emblem
of the Order of Calatrava on the left breast pocket.[23] However, Lorca did not
alter a word of Lope's language. The audience was visibly startled by Laurencia's
famous tirade that she delivers to rouse the men of the town to action:

¡Vive Dios, que he de trazar
que sólo mujeres cobren

> la honra, de estos tiranos,
> la sangre, de estos traidores!
> ¡Y que os han de tirar piedras,
> hilanderas, maricones,
> amujerados, cobardes!

Women of the *pueblo* in the early 1930's did not say "maricón," nor did they instigate collective rebellion against the established authority. That a dramatist said that they did so in centuries past was a surprising revelation, and brought forth spontaneous, show-stopping applause.[24]

García Lorca's intervention in Lope's *El caballero de Olmedo* was minimal. For the prophetic song, "Que de noche le mataron / al caballero," he used the music composed by Cabezón. In terms of the play's structure, he eliminated the final scene, in which the Rey Juan II orders the execution of the assassins, and ended the play at its highest moment of pathos, when Tello, who carries the dying Don Alonso, protests:

> ¿Qué dirá aquel noble viejo?
> ¿Qué hará tu madre y
> tu patria? ¡Venganza, piadosos cielos![25]

The tragedy is thus undiluted by the conventions of the *comedia*, which required the return to an established order.

For the commemoration of the three hundred years of Lope de Vega's death, La Barraca presented *El caballero de Olmedo* at the Universidad Internacional in Santander and in the surrounding towns, in August, 1935. As part of the performance "cuadernillos," printed in different bright colors, were distributed to members of the audience. These *Cantares de Lope de Vega*, as they were titled,[26] contained the texts of old traditional songs, arranged by Lorca. One of these was the "Trébole de la casada," including the verses: "Trébole, ay Jesús cómo huele / Trébole, ay Jesús qué olor." Another was:

No corráis, vientecillos,
con tanta prisa
porque al son de las aguas
duerme mi niña.
No corráis, vientecillos.[27]

Fuenteovejuna was also performed for the tricentenary, as well as an "escenificación" of Lope's version of the ballad, "Las almenas de Toro." The *romance*'s narrative sequences were recited offstage by García Lorca, while the actors, dressed in the emblematic "mono" of La Barraca, carried out the actions and recited the dialogue parts in front of a black curtain. The different roles were signified only by a helmet, or paper cut-outs attached to the uniform with ribbons.[28]

Apart from the special performances of Lope's works for the "Tricentenario," "Las almenas de Toro" was included in a separate function devoted to the Romancero. The *Fiesta del Romance*, as Lorca named it, was comprised of three *romances escenificados*. In addition to "Las almenas de Toro," Lorca staged the *romances* of "Conde Alarcos" and Antonio Machado's "La Tierra de Alvar González," thus bridging in one session a large spectrum of characteristic types in the *romancero* tradition. We have seen that "Las almenas de Toro" was already considered a *romance viejo tradicional* in Lope's time, and that it is still found in the oral tradition today. The *glosa* Lope invented for it represents a major activity of the *poeta culto* during scores of decades. The ballad of "El Conde Alarcos" presents a different example. Widely diffused in the modern oral tradition, it derives from an old troubadouresque text which was itself very well known in 1454.[29] And of course Antonio Machado's "La Tierra de Alvar González," cited by Alberti as another example of the "embestida" of *poesía popular* on the *poeta culto*, closely echoes the *romance de suceso* distributed by the *ciegos* in the *pliegos de cordel*. Not that Lorca's intent in staging these *romances* was didactic; rather, the *Fiesta del Romance* represents a synthesis of his understanding and appreciation of this genre in its many ramifications.

For the staging of the *Romance del Conde Alarcos*, Lorca divided the narrative segments (which were both recited and sung) between two lines of a chorus, dressed in white, standing to either side of a bare stage. The action took place in the center, illuminated by a series of changing colored lights which served to accent the developments of the text. For *La Tierra de Alvar González*, Lorca stood to one side of the platform and read the narrative sequences himself. In this case, his idea was to suggest a *romance de cartelón.* "Federico pensaba representarla tal vez como la canción del ciego que, con grandes cartelones, da información gráfica de lo que va cantando o contando."[30] Here, too, the text of the poem was printed and distributed to the audience after the performance, much in the manner of the *pliego de cordel.* Both "escenificaciones" were abundantly illustrated with music, which Lorca "había sacado de nuestro romancero musical."[31] Lorca's varied experience with the actual staging of *romances* provided him with a new understanding of their innate dramatic potential. In 1934 he exclaimed, "Este año hemos incorporado a nuestro programa una fiesta más. ¡Es tan vivo y tan dramático nuestro romancero!"[32]

La Barraca provided the testing ground for García Lorca's mature theatrical work. "Esta labor mía en La Barraca es una gran enseñanza," he stated in an interview with Juan Chabás. "Yo he aprendido mucho. Ahora me siento verdadero director."[33] In another interview he added, "Y además, a la vuelta de ensayos y experiencias siento que me voy formando como director de escena, formación difícil y lenta. Estoy animado a aprovechar esa experiencia para hacer muchas cosas."[34] By 1934 La Barraca had become central to his experience as a director and as a dramatist. "La Barraca para mí es toda mi obra, la obra que me interesa...."[35] In 1935, after three years of hard work in every possible aspect of theatrical production with La Barraca, Lorca was able to state with assurance: "Mi amor a los demás, mi profundo cariño y compenetración con el pueblo...me ha llevado a escribir teatro para llegar a todos y confundirme con todos."[36]

Bodas de sangre: The "Poema en Movimiento"

García Lorca's definition of and relationship to his audience underwent a profound change during the decade between *Mariana Pineda* and *Bodas de sangre.* The way in which Lorca implements traditional popular song in 1923 and in 1933 demonstrates an evolution not only in his understanding of the literature of the *pueblo*, but a new awareness of the social dimensions of theatrical art:

> Un pueblo que no fomenta su teatro, si no está muerto, está moribundo; como el teatro que no recoge el latido social, el latido histórico, el drama de sus gentes y el color genuino de su paisaje y de su espíritu, con risa o con lágrimas, no tiene derecho a llamarse teatro, sino sala de juego o sitio para hacer esa horrible cosa que se llama "matar el tiempo".[37]

Although Lorca added that "No me refiero a nadie ni quiero herir a nadie," it is clear that he was referring to the kind of theater perhaps best illustrated by Benavente, whose plays dominated the theaters of Spanish cities during the 1920's and early 1930's. This Europeanized type of theater generally depicted the customs and preoccupations of the upper- and middle-class drawing room. And it was probably Benavente's audience that Lorca had in mind when he said:

> En cuanto los de arriba bajen al patio de butacas, todo estará resuelto. Lo de la decadencia del teatro a mí me parece una estupidez. Los de arriba son los que no han visto *Otelo* ni *Hamlet*, ni nada, los pobres. Hay millones de hombres que no han visto teatro.[38]

He deplored the distortions imposed on urban theater by a market reality which regulated what was offered to the public.

> Escribir para el piso principal es lo más triste del mundo. El público que va a ver las cosas queda defraudado. Y el público virgen, el público ingenuo, que es el pueblo, no comprende cómo se le habla de problemas despreciados por él en los patios de la vecindad.[39]

Amusing and lightly satiric, the drawing-room comedy lacked the kind of authentic drama and deeply-rooted passion that Lorca wanted to portray.

> Hay que volver a la tragedia. Nos obliga a ello la tradición de
> nuestro teatro dramático. Tiempo habrá de hacer comedias, farsas.
> Mientras tanto, yo quiero dar al teatro tragedias.... Es nuestra hora.
> Hay que ser jóvenes y vencer.[40]

Bodas de sangre is the first of Lorca's mature tragedies, and, as such, represents the culmination of a decade's experience and activities in a wide range of theater—from the puppet stage, to the open-air "farándula," to the Coliseum in Madrid. Many of the structural problems in the utilization of traditional popular song that Lorca encountered in *Mariana Pineda* are resolved effortlessly in *Bodas de sangre*. In *Mariana Pineda*, Lorca worked generally as Guillén de Castro did in *Las mocedades del Cid*. We saw how, unlike Lope, Castro tacked on or simply inserted ballads at an appropriate moment in the plot. The language of the ballads in Castro's work is not woven with the dialogue of the play, so that the transition from his own language to that of popular traditional poetry has a slightly jarring effect. The *romances* in *Las mocedades* dilute the action of the play, creating obstacles to its ongoing movement. But in *Bodas de sangre* Lorca attains what Lope had achieved in *El caballero de Olmedo*: the seamless integration of song with text, in an unimpeded dramatic development—what Alberti called a poem "en movimiento."

Let us go back for a moment to the changes Alberti made in his presentation of the poets of 1927. They testify to Lorca's growth as a dramatist of Lope's order. In Berlin Alberti had introduced Lorca with these words:

> El granadino Federico García Lorca, músico, folklorista, que ha
> acompañado al piano y transcrito las canciones que ha oído, es el que
> más ha minado su obra del espiritu popular y el que, a su vez, le ha
> entregado más, a cambio. Su *Romancero gitano* es conocidísimo.[41]

In Havana in 1935, Alberti amended his original presentation in order to introduce a mature Lorca, experienced with both the methods and materials of popular tradition in the formation of a uniquely Spanish theater:

Federico no está ausente del mundo que le rodea. Su teatro, todo él
popular de intención, aunque no de expresión, está aireado de música
y versillos, vareado de garbo lopesco. No busca sus temas en lo
abstracto. *Yerma* y *Bodas de sangre* son sus *Romances gitanos* en
movimiento.[42]

Contrary to the lengthy gestation and many revisions of his first tragedy, Lorca
wrote *Bodas de sangre* inside of a week, with what must have been a spontaneous
productivity akin to Lope's.[43]   Furthermore, in contrast to the lukewarm
reception of *Mariana Pineda* (made even more problematic by the political
situation in 1927), *Bodas de sangre* was received with open praise and
enthusiasm.[44]   The play's first performance, in Madrid's Teatro Beatriz on
March 8, 1933, received this review:

Bodas de sangre obtuvo éxito extraordinario. Federico García Lorca
salió a escena, entre grandes ovaciones, al final de cada acto y en
otros momentos de la tragedia.... En *Bodas de sangre* nos
encontramos frente a frente con la tragedia popular, sin rodeos ni
artificios cortesanos de ninguna clase. Vive en ella juego de pasiones
elementales, rudas, animadas por ese poematismo alegórico que tanto
cultivaron nuestros autores del Siglo de Oro.... Ni que decir tiene
que en *Bodas de sangre* no suenan jamás esos tópicos, esas frases
hechas con que fastidian nuestros oídos los diálogos artificiosos de
teatro habitual.[45]

In *Bodas de sangre* the participation of traditional poetic elements is
absolutely essential to the dramatic action. Here we find the presence of traditional
song not at the level of adornment or even interludes, but at the very core of the
play.

Mucho se ha hablado de la participación de elementos populares en
la poesía y el teatro de García Lorca. Nunca el poeta, sin embargo,
había desarrollado tanto un elemento lírico de raíz tradicional—ni, a
mi juicio, con tanto acierto—hasta hacerlo crecer a proporciones

dramáticas.... Caracterizaríamos, pues, a *Bodas de sangre* como la
primera realización, en proporciones mayores, de una utilización de
elementos poéticos: la máxima, en este sentido, en su género....
Porque, como hemos dicho, no se trata de la simple incorporación de
elementos poéticos, sino de su dramatización.[46]

Francisco García Lorca's judgment is best illustrated by the well-known wedding
scene, in which all the differing facets of Lorca's theatrical art coalesce. The entire
scene is orchestrated around the deceptively simple song:

> Despierte la novia
> la mañana de la boda.

The repetition of these verses, in solo voice and in chorus, as a fragment and as
part of a larger lyrical pattern, provides a structure for the entire scene. Spoken
prose segments alternate with dance and song, while preparations for the wedding
take over the stage. Names of fruits and flowers mingle with the references to the
lace, silver, and shiny leather of festive dress:

> Que despierte
> con el ramo verde
> del amor florido.
> ¡Que despierte
> por el tronco y la rama
> de los laureles!
>
> Que despierte
> con el pelo largo,
> camisa de nieve,
> botas de charol y plata
> y jazmines en la frente.

. . . .

Despierte la novia,
que por los campos viene
rondando la boda,
con bandejas de dalias
y panes de gloria.

. . . .

Baja, morena,
arrastrando tu cola de seda.

Baja, morenita,
que llueve rocío la mañana fría.

Despertad, señora, despertad,
porque viene el aire lloviendo azahar.

. . . .

¡Ay mi niña dichosa!

Que despierte la novia.

¡Ay mi galana!

La boda está llamando
por las ventanas.

Que salga la novia.

¡Que salga, que salga!

¡Que toquen y repiquen
las campanas!

¡Que viene aquí! ¡Que sale ya!

> ¡Como un toro, la boda
> levantándose está![47]

The wedding scene brought the audience to its feet: "la sala entera estalla en una delirante ovación que obliga al autor a salir a escena.... Restablecido el silencio, y calmado el vendaval de entusiasmo, la representación sigue su curso."[48] The moment was Lorca's triumph.

This was "espectáculo" equal to Lope's in its integration of the plastic with the verbal and musical elements of theatrical art. However, the wedding was not the only model García Lorca learned from Lope. Another can be found in the form of a traditional song Lorca incorporates into the play, the *nana* sung by the Mujer and the Suegra in Act I.

That Lorca had long been interested in Spain's traditional lullabies is evident in his lecture/demonstration of "Las nanas infantiles," or "Canciones de cuna españolas," given at the Residencia de Estudiantes in Madrid, at Vassar College in New York, and again in Havana. In gathering these songs together, he tells us, "me puse a buscar los elementos vivos, perdurables, donde no se hiela el minuto, que viven un tembloroso presente."[49] It is precisely this quality that he captures and projects onstage with the "Nana del caballo" in *Bodas de sangre*.

It has often been pointed out that there exists a parallelism between one of the *nanas* Lorca used to illustrate his lecture (and which, according to Lorca, is "la más popular del reino de Granada"),

> A la nana, nana, nana
> a la nanita de aquel
> que llevó el caballo al agua
> y lo dejó sin beber.[50]

and the lullaby of his tragedy:

> Nana, niño, nana
> del caballo grande
> que no quiso el agua.[51]

What is essential to see is the extent to which Lorca utilizes the traditional *nana* to generate the rest of his play. Not only does he alter the first stanza, as shown, he elaborates it into a *glosa* which becomes a miniature poetic drama entire in itself:

SUEGRA.
> Nana, niño, nana
> del caballo grande
> que no quiso el agua.
> El agua era negra
> dentro de las ramas.
> Cuando llega al puente
> se detiene y canta.
> ¿Quién dirá, mi niño,
> lo que tiene el agua
> con su larga cola
> por su verde sala?

MUJER. (Bajo.)
> Duérmete, clavel,
> que el caballo no quiere beber.

SUEGRA.
> Duérmete, rosal,
> que el caballo se pone a llorar.
> Las patas heridas,
> las crines heladas,
> dentro de los ojos
> un puñal de plata.
> Bajaban al río.
> ¡Ay, cómo bajaban!
> La sangre corría
> más fuerte que el agua.

MUJER.

> Duérmete, clavel,
> que el caballo no quiere beber.

SUEGRA.

> Duérmete, rosal,
> que el caballo se pone a llorar.

MUJER.

> No quiso tocar
> la orilla mojada,
> su belfo caliente
> con moscas de plata.
> A los montes duros
> solo relinchaba
> con el río muerto
> sobre la garganta.
> ¡Ay caballo grande
> que no quiso el agua!
> ¡Ay dolor de nieve,
> caballo del alba!

SUEGRA.

> ¡No vengas! Detente,
> cierra la ventana
> con rama de sueños
> y sueño de ramas.

MUJER.

> Mi niño se duerme.

SUEGRA.

> Mi niño se calla.

MUJER.

> Caballo, mi niño
> tiene una almohada.

SUEGRA.
>Su cuna de acero.

MUJER.
>Su colcha de holanda.

SUEGRA.
>Nana, niño, nana.

MUJER.
>¡Ay caballo grande
>que no quiso el agua!

SUEGRA.
>¡No vengas, no entres!
>Vete a la montaña.
>Por los valles grises
>donde está la jaca.

MUJER. (Mirando.)
>Mi niño se duerme.

SUEGRA.
>Mi niño descansa.

MUJER. (Bajito.)
>Duérmete, clavel,
>que el caballo no quiere beber.

SUEGRA. (Levantándose, y muy bajito.)
>Duérmete, rosal,
>que el caballo se pone a llorar.[52]

For this microcosm of the "play within the play," a sign for the tiny world of his first toy theater, Lorca again takes recourse to traditional popular forms of expression. The song of the "verderol antiguo, cantando el pío pa" in *Mariana*

Pineda, and the shoemaker's *romance de ciego* in *La zapatera prodigiosa*, are earlier examples of this recourse. In *Bodas de sangre*, however, the *actants* visualized in the *nana* begin immediately thereafter to move in the three dimensions of the stage space.

Lorca's transformation of the traditional cradle song in *Bodas* was suggested by the inherent dramaticity of the song itself. This he tells us in his lecture, when he describes the lullaby of Andalucía as "la canción de cuna más racional, si no fuera por las melodías. Pero las melodías son dramáticas, siempre de un dramatismo incomprensible para el oficio que ejercen."[53] He then explains that this "dramatismo" is also due to "el hecho insólito de no darle agua," which creates "una rara angustia misteriosa."[54] It is this atmosphere of anguish that Lorca transports to the stage.

In his *re*creation of the *nana*, Lorca makes an important change in the figure of the horse. In the traditional lullaby, the horse is passive and entirely innocent. He is led to the water and then abandoned; thus he is the unknowing victim of the mysterious movements of the nameless "aquel." In Lorca's version, no "aquel" appears—rather, "el caballo grande" is a knowing animal, who refuses to drink from some secret and terrible knowledge. Thus the passive and innocent horse is transformed into an active agent of independent will. To describe "el caballo de la canción" as "puro e inocente" is to miss the central point of Lorca's transformation.[55] And this transformation proves to be the driving force of the tragedy.

In his lecture, Lorca describes his own imaginative reaction to the *nana*:

> Ese *aquel* y su caballo se alejan por el camino de ramas oscuras hacia el río, para volver a marcharse por donde empieza el canto una vez y otra vez... Siempre imaginará [el niño] el traje oscuro de *aquel* y la grupa brillante del caballo. Ningún personaje de estas canciones da la cara. Es preciso que se alejen y abran un camino hacia sitios donde el agua es más profunda....[56]

The song's capacity for visualization takes immediate shape in his mind. "El río," the "ramas oscuras," and "el agua más profunda" are all Lorca's invention, yet they retain their immediacy when they reappear in his poetic gloss.

In fact, Lorca's intent is to reproduce the imaginative effects of the original *nana* in his tragedy. The ambiguity of the faceless "aquel" is reintroduced as the anonymous "they" of "bajaban." The ambiguity is deliberate because it opens up the text to imaginative participation. In doing so, Lorca conserves one of the distinctive features of oral texts, its "openness." According to Lorca, the child is provoked to enter the arena of the song, to picture for himself, "y, según su experiencia visual, que es siempre más de lo que suponemos, perfila su figura. Está obligado a ser un espectador y un creador al mismo tiempo." The idea that the child directly participated in the *nana* was a reality to Lorca: "se obliga al niño a ser actor único de su propia nana."[57] These features are what prompted Lorca to incorporate the lullaby into *Bodas de sangre*. Based on his previous experiences with traditional popular song, it presented him with the perfect instrument to draw the spectator into the play, and to add another, qualitatively different dimension to the events visibly taking place onstage. Like the *cantar* in Lope's *El caballero de Olmedo*, the *nana* provokes the imagination at the same time that it presents the central imagery woven throughout the rest of the play. And, like Lope's *cantar*, the *nana* announces the tragic prophecy of death.

Many parallels exist between *El caballero de Olmedo* and *Bodas de sangre*. In both the culmination of the tragedy takes place at night. The night atmosphere, intensified through contrasting references to flowers and nature, becomes dominant and permeates the entire text. Both Lope and Lorca construct the conflict in terms of an overriding passion which acts like the pole of a magnet and draws the protagonist to his destruction. Finally, in both plays the protagonist is a horseman: in *El caballero de Olmedo*, Don Alonso's position is at the top of a disappearing medieval social order; in *Bodas*, the "caballo" makes Leonardo a "caballero" within the relatively narrow hierarchy of the rural *pueblo*.[58]

It is interesting that Lorca was impelled to associate the lullaby with death. In his lecture he describes the capacity of the *nana* to do violence to the child's imagination. "La canción de cuna europea no tiene más objeto que dormir al niño, sin que quiera, como la española, herir al mismo tiempo su sensibilidad."[59]   By "herir" he suggests that poetic sensibility is kinesthetically experienced as physical sensation. This idea is developed further in the association he makes between the *nana* and the razor's cutting edge:

> La tristeza de la canción de cuna rusa puede soportarla el niño...pero en España, no. España es el país de los perfiles.... Un muerto es más muerto en España que en cualquiera otra parte del mundo. Y el que quiere saltar al sueño se hiere los pies con el filo de una navaja barbera.[60]

Furthermore, he sees the *nana*'s potential for tragedy: "Se trata de una abstracción poética, y, por eso, el miedo que produce es un miedo cósmico."[61]   The traditional song provides Lorca a way to attempt the transcendence of tragedy.[62]

Fernando Lázaro Carreter correctly asserts that "el poeta granadino aprendió de Lope de Vega el uso estratégico de la canción popular."[63]   But more than this and worth emphasizing is that both Lope and García Lorca learned dramatic strategies from the traditional songs and ballads themselves. In both *El caballero de Olmedo* and *Bodas de sangre*, a song lifted from the oral tradition provides the generative core of the play. Whereas Lope buried the song at the climax of the dramatic action and wrote the rest of the play towards it, García Lorca sets the *nana* first and explodes the rest of the play out of the song.

In *Bodas de sangre* the song, introduced early (Act I, scene 2), provides the basic material out of which the tragedy is constructed. The figure of the horse introduced at the song's end is immediately identified with Leonardo, its rider. "Llevo más de dos meses poniendo herraduras nuevas al caballo...."[64]   The physical impossibility of placing a horse onstage allows the poetic possibility of imaginatively reconstructing its sign into a plurality of associations, above all power and elemental, unreasoning passion. At the level of poetic signification, the "caballo" becomes the actual vehicle of the tragedy.

The transgression of established codes begins when Leonardo's wife questions his movements: "Ayer me dijeron las vecinas que te habían visto al límite de los llanos," and adds, to his denial, "Pero el caballo estaba reventando de sudor."[65] The connection between the trespass of territorial limits and physical limits is strengthened when La Suegra enters, exclaiming: "Pero, ¿quién da esas carreras al caballo? Está abajo, tendido, con los ojos desorbitados, como si llegara del fin del mundo."[66] Thus, in a very brief sequence, the identification of Leonardo with the "el caballo" of the song, and the excess with regard to territorial and physical restrictions, have been mentioned by those who would conserve the natural boundaries of things, the two mothers. The stage is set for the information that La Novia, who exists outside these boundaries in both scenes, is soon to be married, and the revelation that she is Leonardo's former lover. The parameters of the tragic conflict are now set. The scene ends with the emphatic repetition of the *nana*, which introduces one small but important change. The horse "que no quiere beber" has now trespassed that prohibition:

> Duérmete, clavel,
> que el caballo se pone a beber.[67]

The forbidden thirst will be satisfied, the tragic prophecy will be fulfilled, and the vehicle for its fulfillment will be "el caballo grande."

This hidden "personaje" who "nunca da la cara" is present, at the level of the imagination, from the moment it is introduced in the *nana* until the ritualized hunt and death scene at the end. References to the imagery of the *nana* provide a trajectory for the free and unimpeded development of the conflict. The knife, which figures in the opening conversation between La Madre and El Novio, and which appears in the lullaby as "dentro de los ojos, un puñal de plata," becomes, in the final scene of Act III:

> Con un cuchillo,
> con un cuchillito
> que apenas cabe en la mano,
> pero que penetra fino
> por las carnes asombradas
> y que se para en el sitio

> donde tiembla enmarañada
> la oscura raíz del grito.[68]

The knife is the instrument by which two men kill each other, but the tragedy of *Bodas de sangre* is not the death of Leonardo and El Novio. Our sense of tragedy comes with the knowledge that man is a victim of original, unreasoning forces in the world. Once the prophecy has been announced in the *nana*, the play's development rests on the attempt to resist what gradually appears to be its inevitable realization.

By the end of Act I, the forecasted tragedy has been set into motion. Leonardo has appeared in the vicinity of La Novia. When La Criada asks her, "¿Sentiste anoche un caballo?" and when La Novia replies, "Sería un caballo suelto de la manada," the implication is that a horse loose from the herd would be merely a chance deviation from the norm. But La Criada knows it was more than chance, that it was a deviation of intent. "No. Llevaba jinete."[69]

The "caballo" introduced in the *nana* brings freedom of movement to Leonardo, which posits as well freedom from social restrictions. He is the first to arrive at La Novia's house on the day of the wedding, for he could bypass the other guests, "Los pasé con el caballo." He can leave the main road to which his wife and others are restricted. "Yo vine a caballo. Ella se acerca por el camino." Yet this freedom encloses danger, as La Criada is quick to point out: "Vas a matar al animal con tanta carrera." Her warning is given the force of prophetic inevitability with Leonardo's reply, "¡Cuando se muera, muerto está!"[70]

Through association with the "el caballo grande," Lorca defines the character of Leonardo as independent of and superior to the existing order. This becomes apparent when the party is preparing to leave for the church, and Leonardo declares to his wife, "Yo no soy hombre para ir en carro."[71] The horse confers a measure of social position in that it is a measure of wealth, and thus signifies an undeniable status within the confines of a rural community. "Un hombre con su caballo," says La Novia in Act II, "sabe mucho y puede mucho para poder estrujar a una muchacha metida en un desierto."[72] Not Leonardo alone, but Leonardo "con su caballo" are the sources of unrestricted power.

The *nana* is also responsible for the contrast between Leonardo and El Novio. In comparison to the passion and vitality that "el caballo" lends to Leonardo, Lorca continually associates El Novio with dryness and hardness, with "las piedras." We see this in the gift of the "azahar" he makes to his bride in the second scene of Act II. "Es todo de cera. Dura siempre. Me hubiera gustado que llevaras en todo el vestido."[73] That the flowers are false and made of wax is an indication that El Novio has little or no understanding of what it means to be alive and temporal. El Novio's distance from animal and natural forces is underscored when he mentions his relatives who have come from the coast for the wedding.

> NOVIO.
>> Hubo primos míos que yo ya no conocía.
>
> MADRE.
>> Toda la gente de la costa.
>
> NOVIO. (Alegre.)
>> Se espantaban de los caballos.[74]

The fear of "los caballos" expressed in his next of kin sharpens the contrast between the two characters and deepens the conflict foretold in the lullaby.

At the moment when La Mujer discloses (at the end of Act II), "Es que no le encuentro y el caballo no está tampoco en el establo,"[75] we know that the horse has become the vehicle for the flight of Leonardo and La Novia. "¡Han huído! ¡Han huído! Ella y Leonardo. En el caballo. Van abrazados, como una exhalación."[76] The revelation provokes the final recognition of what has become a power of mythic proportions.

> ¿Quién tiene un caballo ahora mismo, quién tiene un caballo? Que
> le daré todo lo que tengo, mis ojos y hasta mi lengua...[77]

La Madre's startling and violent language—the sacrifice of her eyes and even of her tongue, her only defensive weapon against the knife that stains her past—

reveals the extent to which the horse of the lullaby has become the central symbol of the play.

In the final act, the original prophecy of the lullaby is recalled and fulfilled. The woodcutters evoke the words of the song ("La sangre corría / más fuerte que el agua") when, through an earthly philosophizing, they present the explanation and the justification of the tragedy:

> LENADOR 1.
> Se estaban engañando uno a otro y al fin la
> sangre pudo más.

> LENADOR 2.
> ¡La sangre!

> LENADOR 1.
> Hay que seguir el camino de la sangre.

> LENADOR 2.
> Pero la sangre que ve la luz se la bebe la tierra.

> LENADOR 1.
> ¿Y qué? Vale más ser muerto desangrado que
> vivo con ella podrida.[78]

Lorca makes of this "sangre" the enduring life-striving of the world. During the hunt for the fleeing lovers, the horse has become the agent of transcendent freedom:

> NOVIO.
> Yo sentí hace un momento el galope.

> MOZO 1.
> Sería otro caballo.

NOVIO. (Dramático.)
Oye. No hay más que un caballo en este mundo,
y es éste.[79]

Thus the question of a man's responsibility as the conscious "jinete" in controlling and supressing the energy and instincts of "el caballo" is proportionately insignificant in light of the titanic struggle for expression of a man's individual truth. In the end, the imposition of conventional social restraints are ultimately ineffective in keeping Leonardo from La Novia's door.

Pero montaba a caballo
y el caballo iba a tu puerta.
Con alfileres de plata
mi sangre se puso negra,
y el sueño me fue llenando
las carnes de mala hierba.
Que yo no tengo la culpa,
que la culpa es de la tierra
y de ese olor que te sale
de los pechos y las trenzas.[80]

The poetic opposition between "el agua," or the forces of "la sangre," and "el caballo" as first presented in the lullaby, is resolved in the final scene. Lorca has La Novia describe Leonardo as "un río oscuro, lleno de ramas," thus neatly stitching the *nana* into the final pattern of the tragedy.[81] And, as predicted in the lullaby ("dolor de nieve"), Leonardo meets an icy death. "Era hermoso jinete / y ahora montón de nieve."[82]

The lyrical fragments of the lullaby have been fused with their concrete dramatic counterparts, and now the integrated concepts rise to a level of transcendence in the final act. The enormous difficulty of writing tragedy in the modern world—to describe the original, unreasoning forces in a world where man has to such a great extent subordinated the elements within and around him—is successfully solved in *Bodas de sangre*. Through the elaboration of the traditional *nana*, Lorca fuses the modern and tragic visions—man both dictates and falls victim to his own fate.

Notes

1. Fuentes, p. 57. In *Octubre* Alberti published two brief theatrical sketches, the *Dos farsas revolucionarias*, in 1934. Entitled *Bazar de la Providencia* and *Farsa de los Reyes Magos*, both are open satires of high church officials. See Popkin, pp. 73–84.

2. From the *Memorias del Patronato de Misiones Pedagógicas*, cited by Tuñón de Lara, *Medio siglo*, p. 398.

3. A history of the activities of the Misiones, including photographs which were stored in the Archives of the Junta para Ampliación de Estudios, can be seen in Eleanor Krane Paucker's "Cinco años de misiones," *Revista de Occidente*, Extraordinario I, nos. 7–8 (November, 1981), pp. 233–268. The photos document the reactions of the rural audiences to the first theater most of them had ever seen. Also of interest is the photo documentation Víctor Fuentes includes in his study.

4. Laffranque, p. 433. Gibson, II, pp. 159–164, provides details.

5. Lorca's ideas greatly influenced the final outcome of the project. See *Federico y su mundo*, p. 439; Morla Lynch, pp. 127–128.

6. *OC*, III, p. 511.

7. In an interview with Mildred Adams, *OC*, III, pp. 506–508.

8. *OC*, III, pp. 595–596.

9. "No he refundido, sino que he cortado, lo que es muy distinto. Las obras maestras no pueden refundirse." *OC*, III, p. 591.

10. *OC*, III, p. 595.

11. *OC*, III, p. 608.

12. *"La Barraca": Teatro Universitario* (Madrid: Biblioteca de la Revista de Occidente), 1976.

13. "La música, generalmente, la buscaba Federico....en cuanto a los bailes que bailaban los actores, tanto en *Fuenteovejuna* como en *El Burlador*, para mí tengo que habían surgido de la mente coreográfica de Federico; únicamente el poeta recurrió a Encarnación y a Pilar López, para las sevillanas de *El Retablo de las Maravillas*." Sáenz de la Calzada, p. 230.

14. Sáenz de la Calzada, pp. 50–58, includes photographs of Lorca in costume. Gibson's study also shows Lorca acting the part of La Sombra, II, plate 16.

15. Cited in Jorge Guillén's prologue, *OC*, I, p. xvi. Sáenz de la Calzada recalls the same performance, and adds, p. 58: "Algunos quisieron abrir los paraguas que, en previsión de la lluvia que se anunciaba, habían llevado a la plaza, pero no se lo permitieron los demás espectadores: ello no indica sino que, a pesar de lo conceptuoso del mecanismo poético de Calderón, a la gente sencilla, sin letras, le gustaba el teatro, y le gustaba aunque se hallara marginado de su ámbito de información, de su mundo perceptible."

16. Dámaso Alonso also attended this performance. According to García Lorca, "Pues Dámaso Alonso también se quedó prendado viendo una égloga de Juan del Encina. Quiere fundar un teatro como el de La Barraca en la Universidad de Barcelona." *OC*, III, p. 608.

17. Sáenz de la Calzada, p. 62. See also p. 61, p. 85, and pp. 95–96.

18. Sáenz de la Calzada, p. 61.

19. Lorca notes, "Unamuno vió *El burlador de Sevilla,* y tanto le gustó que, encontrándonos luego en Zamora, quiso oír y ver de nuevo la obra de Tirso." *OC*, III, p. 607.

20. Sáenz de la Calzada, p. 80.

21. Sáenz de la Calzada, pp. 70–71. These traditional verses from *Fuenteovejuna* also appear in the *folía* of *Peribáñez* and in other *comedias*. Correas includes them in his *Vocabulario de refranes*.

22. Sáenz de la Calzada, p. 71. Lope's weddings were also staged separately from his plays in the early 1930's by the Instituto Escuela, according to Jimena Menéndez Pidal, in a personal interview (July, 1982). Antonio Sánchez Romeralo recalls having participated in the performance of Lope's *bodas* while a student at the Instituto; in a personal interview (April, 1983).

23. Suzanne Byrd, "The Twentieth Century *Fuente Ovejuna* of Federico García Lorca," *García Lorca Review*, 5, no. 1 (Spring, 1977), p. 34.

24. "Recuerdo que cuando pronunciaba, a voz en cuello, los siguientes versos [cited in text] desde el público llegaba nítido al escenario un ¡Uuuuhhh!.... Cuando acababa su recitado la gente aplaudiá a rabiar, teniéndose siempre que interrumpir la escena." Sáenz de la Calzada, p. 67.

25. Sáenz de la Calzada, p. 101; Blecua, p. 111.

26. According to Mario Hernández, in his edition of Lorca's *Canciones, 1921–1924*, in *Obras de Federico García Lorca*, vol. 6 (1982), p. 23, "Montesinos, esta vez en colaboración con García Lorca, antologiza en un leve folleto, *Cantares de Lope de Vega*, impreso en 1935 para repartir durante las actuaciones de La Barraca."

27. Sáenz de la Calzada, p. 155. The "cuadernillos" were adorned by an illustration of "una campesina cerniendo trigo" done by the artist Alberto.

28. Sáenz de la Calzada, pp. 92–95.

29. For the old tradition of this ballad, see *Romancero hispánico*, I, pp. 356–361. Modern versions have been found in León, Asturias, Extremadura, Portugal, Galicia, Cataluña, Morocco, Salónica, Chile, and Brazil. In 1919 Jacinto Grau wrote a tragedy, *El Conde Alarcos*, based on a *romance de ciego* version of the ballad dating from the eighteenth century. A review written for *El Debate* on November 10, 1919, criticized Grau for not having based his play on the "romance anónimo del pueblo." From the Archives of Menéndez Pidal.

30. Sáenz de la Calzada, p. 89.

31. Sáenz de la Calzada, p. 88. The author specifies only that "gran parte de ella correspondía al romance de Delgadina" and that "La música es de un dramatismo verdaderamente sobrecogedor, que carga su incisivo acento en la acción...."

32. *OC*, III, p. 608.

33. *OC*, III, p. 608.

34. *OC*, III, p. 605.

35. *OC*, III, p. 594.

36. *OC*, III, p. 360.

37. *OC*, III, p. 459.

38. *OC*, III, p. 615.

39. *OC*, III, p. 673.

40. This interview was given shortly after Lorca finished work on *Bodas de sangre*. *OC*, III, pp. 605–606.

41. Berlin, p. 100.

42. Havana, pp. 31–32.

43. Francisco García Lorca, "Prologue," p. 20. See also *Federico y su mundo*, p. 334. Morla Lynch, p. 285.

44. The play's reception in the province was a little less enthusiastic. Andrew Anderson documents reviews of *Bodas de sangre* in Valencia, San Sebastián, and Zaragoza. See "Representaciones provinciales de dramas de García Lorca en vida del autor," *Segismundo*, nos. 41–42 (Madrid, 1985), pp. 269–281.

45. Antonio Espina in *Luz*, March 9, 1933, p. 13; reprinted in I.-M. Gil, *Federico García Lorca*, pp. 469–473. Carlos Morla Lynch writes, "El triunfo ha sido decisivo, contundente, terminante. No admite discusión," and gives a detailed description of the performance, pp. 329–335.

46. *Federico y su mundo*, pp. 340–341.

47. *Bodas de sangre*, Act II, *OC*, II, pp. 699–799. Hereafter cited as *BS*.

48. Morla Lynch, p. 332.

49. *OC*, III, p. 282.

50. Lorca collected six different versions of this song. *OC*, III, pp. 290–292.

51. *BS*, p. 713. I believe the first to point it out was Roberto G. Sánchez, *García Lorca: Estudio sobre su teatro* (Madrid: Ediciones Jara, 1950), pp. 129–130.

52. *BS*, pp. 713–716. Carlos Ramos-Gil also notes the similarity between the "nanas del caballo" and "las glosas de los clásicos," *Claves líricas de García Lorca* (Madrid: Aguilar, 1967), p. 146.

53. *OC*, III, p. 290.

54. *OC*, III, p. 291.

55. Sánchez, p. 130.

56. *OC*, III, p. 291.

57. *OC*, III, p. 291 and p. 293.

58. Other relationships between the two plays have been investigated by David K. Longhran, "Lorca, Lope and the Idea of a National Theater: *Bodas de sangre* and *El caballero de Olmedo*," *García Lorca Review*, 8, no. 2 (Fall, 1980), pp. 127–136.

59. *OC*, III, p. 284.

60. *OC*, III, p. 285.

61. *OC*, III, p. 289.

62. That Lorca's work transcends the category of a "rural Andalusian drama" and achieves the more universal statue of tragedy is the subject of two articles by Andrew A. Anderson, "De qué trata *Bodas de sangre?*," in *Hommage/Homenaje a Federico García Lorca* (Toulouse: Université de Toulouse-Le Mirail, 1982), pp. 53–64, and "García Lorca's *Bodas de sangre*: The Logic and Necessity of Act Three," *Hispanófila*, no. 90 (1987), pp. 21–37. Anderson argues against the most narrow Aristotelian reading of the play, however.

63. "Apuntes sobre el teatro de García Lorca," *Papeles de Son Armadans*, 28, no. 52 (July, 1960), p. 20. The author comments on the parallelism of the wedding scenes in *Fuenteovejuna* and *Bodas de sangre*.

64. *BS*, Act I, p. 716.

65. *BS*, p. 717.

66. *BS*, p. 718.

67. *BS*, p. 722.

68. *BS*, p. 798.

69. *BS*, p. 733.

70. *BS*, pp. 739–740.

71. *BS*, p. 752.

72. *BS*, p. 743.

73. *BS*, p. 759.

74. *BS*, p. 758.

75. *BS*, p. 766.

76. *BS*, p. 771.

77. *BS*, p. 771.

78. *BS*, p. 773.

79. *BS*, p. 779.

80. *BS*, pp. 784–785.

81. *BS*, p. 796.

82. *BS*, p. 797.

Epilogue
"La hora marcada"

The change in political circumstances and the rising divisive climate during the *bienio negro* of the Second Republic demanded changes in the attitudes of the artists of the Generation of 1927. By 1935 a different perspective appears in the work of the two poet dramatists considered in this study. Alberti's statements in Havana that year, after his second trip to Moscow, indicate that the end of the "virginidad del pueblo" is near:

> El canje de la poesía culta y la popular puede seguir produciéndose en España indudablemente por la virginidad de su pueblo. El lento proceso histórico hasta la formación industrial y la aún no efectuada parcelación de tierra, ha permitido a la memoria campesina seguir produciéndose. Nosotros, nos encontramos viviendo en transición. Todo se nos aparece provisional. Las batallas se libran dentro y fuera de nosotros. Valores desconocidos ascienden. Hay que entonarse con la hora marcada, buscar afinidades, afianzarse confiándose a algo y alguien.

Yet in spite of finding themselves, according to Alberti, as a generation of writers in a time of profound historical and social change, searching for new paths and orientations more in step with "la hora marcada," the members of this group conserve part of their original attitudes toward themselves as the artistic inheritors of a specific literary and cultural tradition:

> Entre los que más cerca de nosotros se hallan, Lope ocupa primer
> lugar. Su gran lección de temporalidad le ha hecho eterno. Es el
> Lope humano sin teologías, que ve ascender un mundo y hundirse
> otro, el que está vivo en nuestro más nuevo concepto de la historia.[1]

As proof of a Lope who wants to portray the whole spectrum of humanity, "con
su tristeza auténtica o con su risa demasiado estrepitosa," Alberti includes this
"llanto de pastor de rebaños," not cited in his previous lecture:

> ¡Ay Dios, qué noches tan bravas!
> Estas dicen que desean
> en la Corte los señores
> que duermen ensabanados
> entre algodones y olores.
> Verás como están los prados.
> ¡Ay de los negros pastores![2]

That is, Alberti initially discovers Lope's meaning for his generation in 1932, and
then rediscovers Lope in 1935. He amends but nevertheless retains his original
evaluation of Lope as the great master and model for contemporary poets in Spain.
In 1934–1935, Alberti composed an *Homenaje popular a Lope de Vega*, containing
songs of political and social content, each one introduced by and faithful to the
spirit of various *letrillas* from Lope's works.[3]

García Lorca, too, looks at the tradition of the *canción popular* with a fresh
perspective. A certain branch of that tradition now speaks to him and through him.
As an example of a song "de profunda emoción y contenido social," he sings these
verses:

> El gañán en los campos
> de estrella a estrella.
> Mientras los amos pasan
> la vida buena.

The following song, he says, "pudo servir de panfleto, de manifiesto y de estandarte":

> Qué ganas tengo
> de que la tortilla se dé vuelta;
> que los "probes" coman pan
> y los ricos coman mierda.[4]

Though Lorca never envisioned his own art as having strictly political applications, he does see the potential role for theater in the formation of a new social consciousness:

> Yo no hablo esta noche como autor ni como poeta, ni como estudiante sencillo del rico panorama de la vida del hombre, sino como ardiente apasionado del teatro de acción social. El teatro es uno de los más expresivos y útiles instrumentos para la edificación de un país y el barómetro que marca su grandeza o su descenso. Un teatro sensible y bien orientado en todas sus ramas, desde la tragedía hasta el vodevil, puede cambiar en pocos años la sensibilidad del pueblo; y un teatro destrozado, donde las pezuñas sustituyen a las alas, puede achabacanar y adormecer a una nación entera.[5]

And although Lorca never declared any specific affiliations to a political party as Alberti did, he did make his political position unreservedly clear on a number of occasions. In December of 1934:

> En este mundo yo siempre soy y seré partidario de los pobres. Yo siempre seré partidario de los que no tienen nada y hasta la tranquilidad de la nada se les niega. Nosotros—me refiero a los hombres de significación intelectual y educados en un ambiente medio de las clases que podemos llamar acomodadas—estamos llamados al sacrificio. Aceptémoslo. En el mundo ya no luchan fuerzas humanas, sino telúricas. A mí me ponen en una balanza el resultado de esta lucha: aquí, tu dolor y tu sacrificio, y aquí la justicia para todos, aun con la angustia del tránsito hacia un futuro

que se presiente, pero que se desconoce, y descargo el puño con toda mi fuerza en este último platillo.[6]

And in April of 1936:

Mientras haya desequilibrio económico, el mundo no piensa. Yo lo tengo visto. Van dos hombres por la orilla de un río. Uno es rico, otro es pobre. Uno lleva la barriga llena, y el otro pone sucio al aire con sus bostezos. Y el rico dice: "¡Oh, qué barca más linda se ve por el agua! Mire, mire usted, el lirio que florece en la orilla." Y el pobre reza: "Tengo hambre, no veo nada. Tengo hambre, mucha hambre." Natural. El día que el hambre desaparezca, va a producirse en el mundo la explosión espiritual más grande que jamás conoció la Humanidad. Nunca jamás se podrán figurar los hombres la alegría que estallará el día de la Gran Revolución. ¿Verdad que te estoy hablando en socialista puro?[7]

In 1935 the utilization of the great vein of the Spanish popular tradition by the writers and intellectuals of this generation is in the process of a final and logical transformation. Alberti concludes his talk in Havana by pointing to the changes in the future he sees lying before them:

Hasta el momento presente, nuestra influencia de Lope era caprichosa y estética, sin el contenido que requiere nuestro momento. En lo sucesivo, y ligados muchos de nosotros a ese pueblo que antes utilizábamos como tema, nuestra obra se endurecerá hasta poder hacer al Lope de *Fuente Ovejuna* el verdadero homenaje nacional que las masas populares le deben.[8]

But the appropriation of the artistic developments, as well as of the institutional apparatus, belonging to Alberti's generation for the aggrandizement of "España, una, grande y libre," was not foreseeable in 1935. Instead, the triumph of Franco's Catholic Nationalism at the end of the Civil War was to be the final curtain.

Notes

1. Havana, pp. 35–36.

2. Havana, p. 20.

3. See Robert Marrast's introduction to his edition of Alberti's *Marinero en tierra / La Amante / El Alba del Alhelí* (Madrid: Castalia, 1972), p. 44.

4. *OC*, III, pp. 581–582.

5. *OC*, III, p. 459.

6. *OC*, III, p. 614. The date according to Laffranque, p. 446.

7. *OC*, III, pp. 674–675.

8. Havana, p. 36.

Appendix
The Lesson of the Theater of
Gil Vicente and Lope de Vega

The particular talent of Gil Vicente and Lope de Vega lies in knowing how to take full advantage of the dramatic potential of popular poetry. For it is not just the ability to put a song on stage that singularizes their dramatic art, but rather the ability to squeeze out the song's inherent dramaticity. The numerous ways in which they weave popular poems and songs into their plays are pertinent to the investigation here, since their facility with this material, the seemingly effortless manipulation of traditional poetry into a full-blown dramatic process, and the capacity to bring out of the lyric its suggestive power and plasticity, are precisely the aspects of Gil Vicente's and Lope's work which catch the attention of Alberti and García Lorca.

Though Gil Vicente [1470(?)–1536] wrote nearly a century before the apogee of the *comedia* during Lope's time, his work anticipates the direction the Spanish national theater was to take. Writing primarily for the Portuguese court, Vicente's work included *autos*, numerous farces, and three *comedias*, interspliced with over fifty popular songs, over a hundred fragments of popular lyrics, and some one hundred proverbs.[1] He knew the traditional songs of both the Portuguese and Castilian traditions, and used them both, at times simultaneously:

> Ora ouvi e ouvireis
> Dizei algũa cantadella,
> Namorae esta donzella,
> E esta cantiga direis:

"Canas do amor canas,
Canas do amor.
Polo longo de hum rio
Canaval está florido,
Canas do amor."

Canta o Escudeiro o romance de "Mal me
quieren en Castilla"....[2]

Apparently this *romance* was well known to the Lisbon audience and required no more than an *incipit* to guide the performers. The lyrical composition preceding it probably originated in the oral tradition,[3] although it is possible that it is the dramatist's invention. Given Gil Vicente's extraordinary facility with the materials of popular poetry, and the fact that the majority of these songs are lost to us now, it is difficult in some cases to be certain. Dámaso Alonso posed the problem in the introduction to his 1934 edition of the poems culled from Vicente's theater:

Hay que pensar, pues, en que si algunas de estas poesías indudablemente son populares, recogidas por Gil Vicente y metidas dentro de su obra, otras bien pueden ser creación suya original.... De un modo u otro el gusto exquisito del poeta las creó o salvó del olvido....[4]

The problem loses importance on reading these lyrics. Some of the following verses are traditional; others are added or retouched by Vicente in such a way that the result renders the distinction useless:

Vanse mis amores, madre,
luengas tierras van morar.
Yo no los puedo olvidar.
¿Quién me los hará tornar?
¿Quién me los hará tornar?

Yo soñara, madre, un sueño
que me dió en el corazón:
que se iban los mis amores

a las islas de la mar.
Yo no los puedo olvidar.
¿Quién me los hará tornar?
¿Quién me los hará tornar?

Yo soñara, madre, un sueño
que me dió en el corazón:
que se iban los mis amores
a las tierras de Aragón.
Allá se van a morar.
Yo no los puedo olvidar.
¿Quién me los hará tornar?
¿Quién me los hará tornar?[5]

Gil Vicente's lyrical gifts allowed him to match the songs of tradition with his own:

> He succeeded, like a later Galician writer, Rosalía de Castro, in identifying himself with the popular genius to such an extent that some of his *cossantes* in their simplicity and natural music come as near as it is possible to come to anonymous popular poetry.[6]

In Gil Vicente's theater, we find a variety of uses of the popular lyric and *romance*, though in the early stage of dramatic integration the use is primarily as adornment and illustration. From its marginal position at the edges of the play, the *canción* moves inside the work and is performed as part of the play's development. In many instances Vicente does not copy the text of the song, as we have seen. In other cases he weaves the lines of the song into the lines of the play. In the following example, from the *Auto de los cuatro tiempos*, Vicente uses a traditional song as a point of departure for a monologue introducing the character of Winter, who enters singing:

Mal haya quien los embuelve,
los mis amores.
¡Mal haya quien los embuelve!

(*Habla.*)
¡Ora, pues eya raviar!

¡Grama de val de sogar
que ño hay pedernal
ni parejo de callentar!
Vienta más rezio que un fuele
de parte del regañón;
enfríame el coraçón,
que ño ama como suele.

(*Canta.*)
¡Mal haya quien los embuelve!

(*Habla.*)
¡La lluvia, cómo desgrana!
Doy a ravia el mal tempero;
aquesto no llieva apero
para que llegue a mañana.
¡Mal grado haya la nieve!
que mis amores, triste yo,
quando yo más firme estó
no los hallo como suele.

. . . .

(*Canta.*)
Los mis amores primeros
en Sevilla quedan presos,
los mis amores.
¡Mal haya quien los embuelve!

(*Habla.*)
¡Oh, qué friasca nebrina!
Granizo, lluvia, ventisco,
todo me pierdo a barrisco;
el cierço me desatina
mis ovejas y carneros:
de niebla no sé es qué de ellos.

. . . .

(*Canta.*)
En Sevilla quedan ambos
los mis amores.
¡Mal haya quien los embuelve!

(*Habla.*)
¡Hi de puta! ¡Qué tempero
para andar enamorado,
repicado y requebrado
con la hija del herrero!
Los borregos de mis amos,
la burra, hato y cabaña,
con la tempestad tamaña
no sé adó los dexamos.

. . . .[7]

The relationship between the song and the spoken lines is a tenuous one of association only. Another song in the same play suggests the character of Spring more directly:

En la huerta nasce la rosa.
Quiérome ir allá
por mirar al ru[i]señor
cómo cantava.

(*Habla.*)
¡Afuera, afuera, ñubrados,
nebrinas y ventisqueros!
Reverdeen los uteros,
los valles, sierras y prados.
¡Rebentado sea el frío
y su ñatío!
Salgan los nuevos vapores,

píntese el campo de flores
hasta que venga el estío.

(*Canta.*)
Por las riberas del río
limones coge la virgo:
quiérome ir allá
por mirar al ruiseñor
cómo cantava.

(*Habla.*)
Suso, suso, los garçones,
anden todos repicados.
namorados, requebrados,
renovar los coraçones.
Agora reina Cupido
desque vido
la nueva sangre venida;
ahora da nueva vida
al namorado perdido.

(*Canta.*)
Limones cogía la virgo
para dar al su amigo:
quiérome ir allá
para ver al ruiseñor
cómo cantava.

(*Habla.*)
¡Cómo me estiendo a plazer!
¡oh, hi de puta zagal!
¡Qué tiempo tan natural
para no adolescer!

. . . .

(*Canta.*)
Para dar al su amigo
en un sombrero de sirgo:
quiérome ir allá
para ver al ruiseñor
cómo cantava.

(*Habla.*)
Las abejas colmeneras
ya me zuñen los oídos,
paciendo por los floridos
las flores más plazenteras.
Quán granado viene el trigo,
nuestro amigo,
que, pese a todos los vientos,
los pueblos trae contentos.
Todos están bien conmigo.

. . . .[8]

Finally, though here the traditional song is still primarily illustration, it penetrates the play even further in the many instances in which Vicente embroiders upon the song in a subsequent elaboration or commentary of his own invention (a common poetical practice of the early *Cancioneros*, known as the *glosa*). His particular skill blurs the distinction between the song and his own creation. For instance, in the *Auto de la sibila Casandra*, presented as a Christmas play, Casandra sings:

Dizen que me case yo:
no quiero marido, no.

Más quiero bivir segura
que no estar en ventura
si casaré bien o no.
Dizen que me case yo:
no quiero marido, no.

Madre, no seré casada
por no ver vida cansada,
o quicá mal empleada
la gracia que Dios me dio.
Dizen que me case yo:
no quiero marido, no.

No será ni es nacido
tal para ser mi marido;
y pues que tengo sabido
que la flor yo me la so,
dizen que me case yo:
no quiero marido, no.[9]

The song serves as a perfect justification for the character, since the plot, such as it is, turns around her hope to be the Mother of the coming Saviour. The subsequent Nativity scene is organized around a lullaby:

Se abren las cortinas [y se descubre el lugar] donde está todo el aparato del nacimiento, y cantan cuatro *Angeles*:

Ro, ro, ro...
nuestro Dios y Redemptor,
¡no lloréis que dais dolor
a la Virgen que os parió!
Ro, ro, ro...[10]

It is this song which Alberti selects as an illustration to his 1935 lecture in order to introduce "Gil Vicente, ese otro maestro del siglo XVI," and to draw a comparison with the "Nana de Sevilla" as performed by García Lorca and La Argentinita:

Los dos poetas, Gil y Lope, han visto cómo las mujeres de las aldeas mecen a sus hijos. Las melodías son monótonas. Tienen el cabeceo aburrido de las barcas. En España se las conoce con el viejo nombre latino de *nanas*. Hoy, como hace siglos, las madres no han aprendido otro canto mejor. Desde Asturias hasta Cádiz, desde

Extremadura hasta Valencia, con el aire distinto e igual de las regiones, sigue meciéndose, insistente, en la penumbra de las alcobas.[11]

In 1522 Gil Vicente takes the idea of the *romance cantado* one step further. In the *Tragicomedia de don Duardos* he uses a *romance* for the play's theme, and works up to the text of the ballad itself in the final scene. The *romance* then for the first time enters the stage as a natural extension of the dramatic dialogue, its verses distributed between the principal characters:

[ARTADA]   En el mes era de abril,
       de mayo antes un día,
       cuando lirios y rosas
       muestran más su alegría,
       en la noche más serena
       que el cielo hazer podía,
       quando la hermosa infanta
       Flérida ya se partía,
       en la huerta de su padre
       a los árboles dezía:

[FLÉRIDA]   Quedaos adiós, mis flores,
       mi gloria que ser solía:
       voyme a tierras estrangeras,
       pues ventura allá me guía.

       . . . .
       ¡Triste, no se adó vo,
       ni nadie me lo dezía!

[ARTADA]   Allí habla don Duardos:

[D. DUARDOS] No lloréis, mi alegría,
       que en los reinos d'Inglaterra
       más claras aguas havía
       y más hermosos jardines,
       y vuessos, señora mía.

Ternéis trezientas donzellas
de alta genelosía;
de plata son los palacios
para vuessa señoría,
de esmeraldas y jacintos,
d'oro fino de Turquía,
con letreros esmaltados
que cuentan la vida mía,

. . . .

[ARTADA]   Sus lágrimas consolava
Flérida, que esto oía.
Fuéronse a las galeras
que don Duardos tenía:
cincuenta eran por cuenta;
todas van en compañía.
Al son de sus dulces remos
la princesa se adormía
en braços de don Duardos
que bien le pertenecía.
Sepan quantos son nacidos
aquesta sentencia mía:
que contra la muerte y amor
nadie no tiene valía.
. . . .[12]

Here the ballad has entered the play's interior. The *romance* provides essential information and presents the final resolution of the play in a scene which could not otherwise be represented in the theatrical space.

But the external, celebrative use of the *romance* has not been forgotten. Immediately afterward, the same *romance* is performed as simultaneous song and dance, to round off the play and bring the entire function to a close. "Este romance se dice representado y después tornado a cantar por despedida" according to Gil Vicente's instructions.[13] In repeating the song as closure, he follows the customary use of the *romance cantado*, which, along with the *jácara* or *baile*, signalled the end of the entire drama session.

The ballad of "Don Duardos" seems to have been originally Gil Vicente's invention, but given its oral style, it passed easily into a ballad of tradition. From the play it was reprinted in *pliegos sueltos* and the *Cancionero de Amberes* (c. 1550), and has since been found in the modern oral tradition of Spain, Portugal, and Morocco.[14] A version collected in central Spain in 1914 begins:

> Tan alta iba la luna
> como el sol al mediodía,
> cuando la señora infanta
> de Francia partir quería;
> de las huertas de su padre
> se anda despidiendo un día:
> —¡Adiós, adiós, agua clara,
> adiós, adiós, agua fría,
> adiós, rosas y claveles,
> los que el mi jardín tenía,
> adios damas y doncellas
> con quien yo me divertía!
> Si el rey mi padre pregunta
> por lo bien que me quería,
> direis que el amor me lleva
> y que la culpa no es mía;
> que la culpa suya era
> que soltera me tenía.—
> Veinticinco embarcaciones
> vienen a buscar la niña;
> los navios son de oro
> los remos de plata fina;
> y al son de los remecillos
> la niña se adormecía.
> . . . .[15]

Several decades passed before traditional ballads and lyrics reached a final and total integration with the *comedia*. In 1587 a relatively unknown dramatist initiated what was soon to become the *comedia nueva* in Lope's hands. In his *Farsa del obispo don Gonzalo*, Francisco Cueva y Silva incorporated five different traditional *romances* as part of the plot, at times casting them into *redondillas*,[16] and three times inserting them whole.[17] From this use of the *romance* well within the play's interior grew the idea of employing the eight-syllable assonant ballad verse as appropriate theatrical meter apart from ballad content. Lope's masterful manipulation of the natural rhythm of the *romance* form is one of the important factors contributing to his prodigious success in the "corrales" of Madrid during the early years of the seventeenth century.

Lope's early plays already show the use of many old historical and frontier ballads as themes. In the beginning, he considers the *romance* only for its value as a chronicle of national history, following the example of Juan de la Cueva, who in 1579 introduced plays on such ballad heroes as Bernardo del Carpio, the Infantes de Lara, and the Rey don Sancho, along with others on classic Hellenic heroes such as Ajax.[18] At this point the ballad *per se* is of little interest, except for its function as the basis of a *glosa* in the style of the early *cancioneros* and *pliegos sueltos*. Thus in *Los hechos de Garcilaso de la Vega y moro Tarfe*, Lope uses the frontier ballad, "Cercada está Santa Fe," both as a thematic source for the play and as the foundation for his poetic gloss.[19]

Lope uses the same *romance* as the basis for a later play, *El cerco de Santa Fe*.[20] But this time he uses another method. Working analogously but in the opposite direction to Gil Vicente's *Tragicomedia de don Duardos*, Lope reworks and plants the opening lines of the ballad at the very beginning of the play, and then proceeds to develop the play out of the ballad material.

> Cercada esta Santa Fe   de mucho lienço encerado
> y alrededor muchas tiendas   de terciopelo y damasco.
> En la más alta de todas   de brocado de tres altos
> de atadas flechas y yugos   y de coyundas bordadas
> se aloxan los nobles reyes   doña Isabel y Fernando
> y luego la demas gente   por varias tiendas del campo.
> . . . .[21]

By the time Lope writes *Las almenas de Toro*,[22] the participation of the *romance* in the interior of the *comedia* is well established. Several different historical ballads concerning the Cid and the siege of Zamora are incorporated into the plot, either through paraphrase, or through the elaboration of ballad lines into dramatic dialogue. For example, the following first two lines of the traditional ballad provoke Sancho's commentary:

> Por las almenas de Toro
> se pasea una doncella,
> pero dijera mejor
> que el mismo sol se pasea:
> ¡lindo talle, airoso cuerpo![23]

Although already considered a *romance viejo* by Lope and his contemporaries, sixteen versions of the ballad of "Las almenas de Toro" have been found in the modern oral traditions of Portugal and the Sephardic communities of Morocco and the eastern Mediterranean.[24] Several other *romances viejos* belonging to the Cid cycle are either cited and glossed, or alluded to in the play.

In Act III Lope introduces yet another innovation. He fills out each hemistich of the ballad "Rey don Sancho, rey don Sancho, no digas que no te aviso," with a verse of his own to make a single assonant rhyme:

> Rey don Sancho, rey don Sancho,
> hijo de Fernando el Bueno,
> no digas que no te aviso,
> si hubiere algún mal suceso;
> que del muro de Zamora,
> donde cerco tienes puesto,
> ha salido un gran traidor
> falso, engañoso y discreto...[25]

The verses that Lope intertwines with the lines of the ballad are simply logical extensions of the ballad's own dramatic development. Here we find the utilization of the *romance* not just as a source of the play's theme, characters, and story line, but as actual textual material. The play is constructed out of the ballad itself, producing, in effect, a three-dimensional representation of the *romance*. At this point Lope's *comedia* has become so permeable to the ballad of tradition that it is but a short step to the absorption of the *romance* eight syllable line as standard dramatic meter, not only in his plays but in the works of other Golden Age dramatists as well.

Yet not every dramatist who drew upon the *romancero viejo tradicional* as source and inspiration experienced the same degree of success as Lope. Guillén de Castro, whose plays show an even higher percentage of ballads,[26] never achieved Lope's level of integration of popular material. Castro's two best known works, Parts I and II of *Las mocedades del Cid*, constitute a veritable "antología romancística" of the Cid's life and deeds, to use Menéndez Pidal's words.[27] Yet though the plays put the Cid on stage, they fail to create the kind of theatrical life that distinguishes Lope's art.

Guillén de Castro's technique is to string the ballads together, paying strict attention to their chronological order, and filling in the transitions with his own verse. The resulting montage creates the effect of a studied documentary. Castro never strays from the information presented in the ballads as he links them together. Indeed, at times he strains to make the connection. In the scene where Xiména appears with her retinue before the Rey Fernando to complain that her father's death at the Cid's hands has gone unavenged, Castro's effort to include the ballad (which was very well known to his audience) creates an inadvertent joke:

> Escudero 1.
> > Sentado está el Señor Rey
> > en su silla de respaldo.
> Xiména.
> > Para arrojarme a sus pies
> > ¿qué importa que esté sentado?[28]

Aside from this minor embarrassment, in general Guillén de Castro's plays are valuable testimony to the importance of the *romancero* in the evolution of Spain's national theater. No other dramatist relied on historical ballads to the extent Castro did; not only as an almost exclusive source for themes, characters, and plots, but in terms of the number of actual texts dramatized. His skill lay in adapting *romances* or inserting them whole, showing the highest respect for the discourse of the ballad but little comprehension of its method. His work, however, caught the attention of Corneille, who adapted the first play of *Las mocedades* for his French version, *Le Cid*, in 1636.[29]

While the historical *romance* entered the *comedia* as recitative, used primarily for narratives and dialogue, the *romance cantado*, the *canción bailada*, and other folkloric forms of the *teatro menor* continued to participate in the *comedia's* dramatic process. Unlike Castro, Lope took full advantage of the internal narrative and lyrical aspects of popular balladry and song. And his uses were extraordinarily inventive: he employed songs directly as part of the dramatic action or to influence the action, to introduce a character, to supply information about an event taking place offstage, to interpret an event or emphasize the meaning of an action taking place onstage, to establish a mood or atmosphere, to foreshadow a tragedy, to celebrate a festivity, to introduce elements of irony, and so on.[30]

In *San Diego de Alcalá* and another related play, *Los guanches de Tenerife*, Lope uses songs and dance to incorporate the colorful, primitive culture of the people of the Canary Islands. Though both plays voice the ideals of Old Christianity within its new missionary context, Lope's attraction to what he perceives as the honest simplicity of the "barbarian" way of life is clearly evident.[31] In many respects he attributes the same virtues to the Indians of the New World and to the "guanches" of Tenerife that he finds in the Old Christian peasants of "sangre limpia" in Castile. However, the Indians offer Lope hitherto unexplored theatrical possibilities to play at primitivism. Characters enter dressed in feathers and showy headdresses, carrying bows and arrows, dancing and singing to the beat of a drum, as in this performance of "el baile canario":

> Españoles bríos,
> mirar y matar:
> volveréis vencidos,
> fan, falalán.[32]

The dance seems to have been extraordinarily popular in Lope's time. In *San Diego de Alcalá*, he uses it to fill the stage with a celebration of national pride which he projects upon the natives of the Canary Islands:

> (Canten y bailen el *canario* los bárbaros y las mujeres.)

> Canario lira,
> lilirum fa,
> que todo lo vence
> amar y callar.

> En la gran Canaria,
> isla deste mar,
> que los españoles
> quieren conquistar

para el Rey Enrique
que en Castilla está,
nacen hombres fuertes
que la guardarán;
nacen bellas damas
que les quieren dar
favores que lleven
para pelear.
Ellos, que las sirven,
cristianos trairán:
para sus cautivos
los esperan ya.

Canario lira,
lilirum fa;
que todo lo vence
amar y callar.

Quien ama callando
¿qué no alcanzará?
Todo lo merece
servir y callar.
¡Viva nuestra Reina
mil siglos y más!
Déle el sol esposo
de hermosura igual,
amor, tales hijos
que pasando el mar
conquisten a España
sin quedarse allá;
y sus bellas hembras
nos traigan acá,
para que la sangre
que en Canaria está
juntándose a España
pueda sujetar

desde el indio negro
al blanco alemán.

Canario lira,
lilirum fa;
que todo lo vence
amar y callar.[33]

In plays such as these Lope takes obvious enjoyment in the exotic aspects of the song and
dance, which add moments of surprise and notes of color that were new and different to
the crowds in the Madrid "corrales."[34] In these instances the lyric and plastic elements
have a function beyond pure adornment. They dress up the play in a different garb, and
lend atmosphere to the entire piece. They suggest a new geography. Still, the
incorporation of exotic folklore into the play does not affect interior dramatic structure.
A different procedure, however, can be seen in *Peribáñez y el Comendador de Ocaña*.

In this play Lope makes maximum use of the traditional folklore of the *campo*, not
just to create an ambience, but to saturate the entire dramatic situation. The basis of the
comedia is a *romance*:

Más quiero yo a Peribáñez
con su capa la pardilla
que al Comendador de Ocaña
con la suya guarnecida.[35]

The *romance* is first recited as a portion of Casilda's celebrated tirade against the
Comendador, in which she rejects his advances and reaffirms her love for and loyalty to
her newlywed husband, Peribáñez. Lope includes it again, with minor variants, this time
as *canción*:

La mujer de Peribáñez
hermosa es a maravilla;
el Comendador de Ocaña
de amores la requería.
La mujer es virtüosa
cuanto hermosa y cuanto linda;

mientras Pedro está en Toledo
desta suerte respondía:
"Más quiero yo a Peribáñez
con su capa la pardilla,
que no a vos, Comendador,
con la vuesa guarnecida."

The song, overheard by Peribáñez on his return to Ocaña, allays his fears, since he does not doubt for an instant the veracity of what is sung in the mouths of his *pueblo*:

Notable aliento he cobrado
con oir esta canción,
porque lo que éste ha cantado
las mismas verdades son
que en mi ausencia habrán pasado.[36]

The song thus provides the justification for the play's outcome as well, since by accepting what the song relates as truth, Peribáñez is able to take rightful action against the Comendador and not against his wife, as the conventions of honor would dictate had her fidelity been suspect.[37] Very little else goes into making up the plot of this *comedia*, which is one of the finest examples of Lope's celebrative art. As Aubrun and Montesinos observe: "Seuls le détail du tableau historique et quelques incidents accessoires semblent dérivés de sources écrites. L'essentiel de la tragi-comédie procède de la tradition orale."[38]

The play's true success is not one of intrigue but of recreation and the *recreation* of the folklore of rural Castile. The agriculture rituals of sowing, growth, and harvest provide metaphors throughout, as when Peribáñez compares Casilda's beauty to products of the tilled land ("El olivar más cargado / de aceitunas me parece / menos hermoso"; "Ni el vino blanco imagino / de cuarenta años tan fino," etc.). Casilda, in turn, answers him in simple domestic metaphors of food and clothing ("No hay pies con zapatos nuevos / como agradan tus amores"; "Pareces camisa nueva"; "pareces cirio pascual / y mazapán de bautismo," etc.).[39] The play begins with the celebration of their wedding festivities: the villagers alternately sing and dance, to musical accompaniment, a Portuguese dance known as the *folía*, a rhythmic and vigorous dance involving tambourines, rattles, and much noisy stamping of feet.

> Dente parabienes
> el mayo garrido,
> los alegres campos,
> las fuentes y ríos.
> · · · · · · · · · · · 40

The celebration is interrupted by the running of a young bull, which causes the Comendador's fall from his horse. This event provides ironic commentary to be used throughout the rest of the play; for example, the song sung to disguise the Comendador's entry into Casilda's quarters:

> Cogióme a tu puerta el toro,
> linda casada;
> no dijiste: Dios te valga.
> · · · · · · · · · · · · · · · 41

Lope also uses the song of the "Trébole" to intensify the atmosphere of hushed eroticism surrounding Casilda's door. The village harvesters who guard the entrance sing, accompanied by guitars:

> Trébole, ¡ay Jesús cómo güele!
> Trébole, ¡ay Jesús, qué olor!
>
> Trébole de la casada
> que a su esposo quiere bien;
> de la doncella también,
> entre paredes guardada,
> que facilmente engañada,
> sigue su primero amor.
>
> Trébole, ¡ay Jesús, cómo güele!
> Trébole, ¡ay Jesús, qué olor!
>
> Trébole de la soltera
> que tantos amores muda;
> trébole de la viüda

que otra vez casarse espera:
tocas blancas por defuera
y el faldellín de color.

Trébole, ¡ay Jesús, cómo güele!
Trébole, ¡ay Jesús, qué olor![42]

This song and its multiple variations, along with others belonging to the cycle of "la mañana de San Juan," have an extraordinary documentation in both the old and modern oral traditions.[43] Alberti had good reason to cite it in his as an example of the essence of popular and traditional poetry.[44]

Other miscellaneous items of popular rural culture are woven into the play. Proverbs are either referred to or quoted directly; numerous references to customary practices of speech, food, dress, and agricultural work populate the text. The *abecedario* of love Peribáñez recites to Casilda,

Amar y honrar su marido
es letra de este abecé,
siendo buena por la B,
que es todo el bien que te pido.

Haráte cuerda la C,
la D dulce, y entendida
la E, y la F en la vida
firme, fuerte y de gran fe.
                                    45
. . . .

appears in *Don Quijote* and other literary works of the times.[46] It exists still in the modern oral tradition,[47] and is related to a group of songs which enumerate the months of the year and the cycles of nature, or which list the physical attributes of a beloved lady.[48]

The celebration of life in the countryside was a common theme in the Renaissance, but in Lope's hands the subject is given a realism and robust vitality that is lacking in the pastoral and bucolic visions of Juan del Encina and other artists. The difference stems primarily from Lope's methods of using the materials of popular tradition, in this case, to amplify the theatrical space.

> Pour la peinture de d'ambiance rustique, le poète a recouru, comme d'habitude, à sa connaissance étonnante des chansons, danses, ballets, grâce à quoi il comble les lacunes d'une mise en scène très primitive....se mêlent les mots et les expressions populaires de toutes les régions de l'Espagne...ils chantent, dansent, discutent des travaux des champs, se querellent, en un mot, suggèrent un milieu que ne saurait évoquer le décor élémentaire.[49]

Lope's method differs from that of Guillén de Castro and other dramatists of the age in that he does not merely append the popular song to his play: he thoroughly integrates it. The presence of this poetry in his work is seamless. A play such as *Peribáñez* shows Lope's level of integration at its best.

The other dimension of Lope's art lies in knowing to look within the materials of tradition for the dramatic impetus inherent in the traditional method of representation. In *El caballero de Olmedo*, Lope discovers the dramatic potential for the play in a brief *cantar*,[50] which he bursts open into a full-length poetic tragedy. According to E. Anderson Imbert, "*El caballero de Olmedo* es esto: una dramatización del misterioso proceso de la poesía tradicional."[51] The "mysterious" song which Lope dramatizes,

> Que de noche lo mataron,
> al caballero,
> la gala de Medina,
> la flor de Olmedo.[52]

had been current in the tradition some years before; it related a true incident, a murder which occurred on the road to Olmedo in 1521.[53] Antonio de Cabezón (1510–1565) composed musical variations on it, called the "Differencias sobre el canto llano del Caballero,"[54] and an unknown dramatist wrote a *comedia* with the same title in 1606.[55] Beyond the common title, this *comedia* bears little resemblance to Lope's work; it is unlikely Lope knew of its existence when he wrote his version, sometime between 1620–1625.[56] A different, danced version of the song was also popular at the time. Called the "Baile del Caballero," it was the basis of another work attributed to

Lope, the *Baile famoso del Caballero de Olmedo*, published in 1617.[57] Proof of Lope's attraction to the *cantar* can also be seen in two other works, in which he gives it a religious treatment, *a lo divino*. For instance, in his *Auto de los Cantares*:

> Que de noche le mataron
> al caballero,
> a la gala de María,
> la flor del cielo.[58]

Gonzalo Correas includes the song, which he considers already "vieja," in his *Arte de la lengua española castellana* (1625), and it appears together with variations in various *entremeses* and *mojigangas* of the following years.[59]

A "cancionero manuscrito" of 1615 contains this glossed version:

> Esta noche le mataron
> al caballero,
> a la vuelta de Medina,
> la flor de Olmedo.

> Esta noche le mataron
> los seis traidores:
> bien es, señora mía,
> la muerte llores
> del caballero,
> a la [vuelta de Medina,
> la flor de Olmedo.]

> Esta noche le mataron
> con emboscada,
> con escopetas fieras,
> no con espadas,
> al caballero,
> . . . .[60]

The specific details stitched into the *glosa* may well be the product of popular imagination, which characteristically strives for verisimilitude through the concrete representation of events. These details are not matched by the historical accounts, which describe the killing as a result of a personal dispute.[61]

The version Lope uses for *El caballero de Olmedo* is accompanied by a traditional *glosa* which, though thematically related, can stand apart from the parent text.[62] Lope takes advantage of the song's bipartite structure to gradually introduce the *canción* into the dramatic action. The scene takes place at night on the road from Medina to Olmedo. The song is sung offstage, at a distance, by a chorus of voices; the *glosa*, carried by one voice, then enters the stage space and confronts Don Alonso, the Caballero.

> (Canten desde lejos en el vestuario y véngase acercando
> la voz como que camina.)
>> Que de noche le mataron
>> al caballero,
>> la gala de Medina,
>> la flor de Olmedo.

> D. Alonso.
>> ¡Cielos! ¿Qué estoy escuchando?
>> Si es que avisos vuestros son,
>> ya que estoy en la ocasión,
>> ¿de qué me estáis informando?
>> Volver atrás, ¿cómo puedo?
>> Invención de Fabia es,
>> que quiere, a ruego de Inés,
>> hacer que no vaya a Olmedo.

> La Voz (Dentro.)
>> Sombras le avisaron
>> que no saliese,
>> y le aconsejaron
>> que no se fuese
>> el caballero,
>> la gala de Medina,
>> la flor de Olmedo.

> (Sale un Labrador.)[63]

The intervening space between the song and the *glosa* is filled with the Caballero's fear and apprehension, which burst out of him with sudden intensity. The heightened emotion is explained by his previous encounter with a "sombra" only minutes before:

> (Al entrar Don Alonso, una Sombra con una máscara negra y
> sombrero, y puesta la mano en el puño de la espada, se le ponga
> delante.)[64]

Indeed, the impact of the song is not fortuitous: Lope has prepared us for this ominous warning with utmost care. In *Las almenas de Toro* we saw how he planted the *romance* in the very first scene, and built the play out of the ballad. Here he works in reverse. He buries the *canción* in the third act, at the very heart of the play, and carefully constructs the action toward it.

References to the road between Olmedo and Medina, the site of the tragedy, are strung like beads throughout the work. Tension is set up between the two poles by tying Don Alonso's identity to "el Caballero de Olmedo" and by identifying Doña Inés with the city of Medina (Fabia declares at the beginning of Act I, "pienso que doña Inés / es de Medina la flor."[65] The fatal attraction between the two lovers works like a magnet, drawing them together over the distance. When Don Alonso describes his first glimpse of Inés for the benefit of the go-between, Fabia, the warning is implicit:

> Mirándome sin hablarme,
> parece que me decía:
> "No os vais don Alonso, a Olmedo,
> quedaos agora en Medina."[66]

The constant comings and goings along the road increase the tension to the point where it deserves the servant Tello's question, "¿No te cansa y te amohina / tanto entrar, tanto partir?," and provokes his explicit warning:

> Temo que se ha de saber
> este tu secreto amor;
> que con tanto ir y venir
> de Olmedo a Medina, creo

que a los dos da tu deseo
que sentir, y aun que decir.[67]

Gradually Don Alonso's interior state is divided between the two poles as well, as we see in these *quintillas*,[68] spoken the night of his last departure for Olmedo:

Yo lo siento, y voy a Olmedo,
dejando el alma en Medina
No sé como parto y quedo
. . . .
Así parto muerto y vivo
. . . .
Tengo, pensando perderte,
imaginación tan fuerte,
y así en ella vengo y voy,
que me parece que estoy
con las ansias de la muerte.
. . . .
porque tengo, Inés, por cierto
que si vuelvo será muerto,
pues partir no puedo vivo.
Bien sé que tristeza es;
pero puede tanto en mí,
que me dice, hermosa Inés:
"Si partes muerto de aquí,
¿cómo volverás después?
Yo parto, y parto a la muerte....[69]

The conflict is, by this time, so well established that the *conceptismo* between "muerto" and "vivo" arises quite naturally in Don Alonso's speech as a complement to the general atmosphere of fear and uncertainty that permeates the play. (Several scholars have noted Lope's intention to create similarities, both thematic and contextual, between *El caballero de Olmedo* and the uncertain world of *La Celestina*.)[70]

Lope does not simply insert the song at a key moment in the dramatic structure; he prepares us for it by weaving the song's imagery into the text from the beginning. The play is filled with quiet references to flowers and night. Before the end of the first act, the metaphor for the approaching night bites into the text and becomes menacing:

> ...La vecina
> noche, en los últimos fines
> con que va expirando el día,
> pone los helados pies.[71]

In Act II, Inés relates her imaginary conversation with flowers, verbally setting them against the night:

> Bajaba al jardín ayer
> . . . .
> a las fuentes, a las flores
> estuve deciendo amores,
> y estuve también llorando.
> "Flores y aguas, les decía,
> dichosa vida gozáis,
> pues aunque noche pasaís,
> veis vuestro sol cada día."
> Pensé que me respondía
> la lengua de una azucena
> (¡qué engaños amor ordena!):
> "Si el sol que adorando estás
> viene de noche, que es más,
> Inés, ¿de qué tienes pena?"[72]

The passage is echoed by Don Alonso's account to Tello at the close of the same act:

> Hoy, Tello, al salir el alba,
> con la inquietud de la noche,
> me levanté de la cama,
> abrí la ventana aprisa,
> y mirando flores y aguas
> que adornan nuestro jardín,
> sobre una verde retama

> veo ponerse un jilguero,
> cuyas esmaltadas alas
> con lo amarillo añadían
> flores a las verdes ramas.

Don Alonso's initial uneasiness is reinforced when the beauty of this landscape is suddenly and violently disrupted:

> Y estando al aire trinando
> de la pequeña garganta
> con naturales pasajes
> las quejas enamoradas,
> sale un azor de un almendro,
> adonde escondido estaba,
> y como eran en los dos
> tan desiguales las armas,
> tiñó de sangre las flores,
> plumas al aire derrama.[73]

The death of the "jilguero" (which, like the Caballero, is a "flower" against the green branches) is clearly an omen presaging his own death. From the *Romancero tradicional* Lope has borrowed not only the ballad meter and one of the powerful ballad formulae for death omens (the "azor" is the functional equivalent of the "garza" in "El sueño de doña Alda," for instance), he has used the ballad's own method of representation. He brings the event to life before our eyes; we mentally visualize it taking place. Lorca, who learned much from Lope, could easily have written the last two lines himself.

In *El caballero de Olmedo* Lope takes the traditional song one step further and uses it as the nucleus of the play. The *cantar* and its *glosa* generate the rest of the dramatic structure from their position at its core. In the textual weaving of the song and in the use of its inherent dramaticity, Lope reaches a maximum level of integration of popular song with the dramatic text, that of complete fusion.

The methods of Gil Vicente and Lope de Vega were what Lorca and Alberti admired most from their stance at the forefront of the Generation of 1927. As we shall see, the presence of these Golden Age models is perceptible in the works of Lorca and Alberti as a constant background, but the twentieth-century poets arrive at the same techniques by various roads. They admire Lope, but they do not imitate Lope. Lope's theater helps them to understand "lo popular" and to comprehend his distinctive artistry in both using and creating it. Yet Lorca and Alberti find out through their own experiments just what their own perception is. Through the theatrical art of their "maestros" and the discovery of "lo popular" in their own milieu, they come to know and understand what they already recognize.

Notes

1. Aubrey F. G. Bell, *Gil Vicente* (Oxford: Oxford University Press, 1921), p. 38.

2. *Farça de Inez Pereira*, in vol. III of *Obras de Gil Vicente*, eds. J. V. Barreto Feio and J. G. Monteiro (Hamburg: Langhoff, 1834), p. 143.

3. Even Eugenio Asensio, in "Gil Vicente y las cantigas paralelísticas 'restauradas'; ¿Folclore o poesía original?," agrees that its stylistic features "parecen apuntar a una cantiga paralelística ya conocida de los circunstantes y añeja." See *Poética y realidad en el cancionero peninsular de la Edad Media* (Madrid: Gredos, 1970), p. 170. Asensio finds three different functions for the songs in Gil Vicente's plays: 1) to establish an "ambiente" or setting for the action; 2) to define the social status or personality of the character; and 3) to duplicate the dramatic action "en plano épico o lírico." See pp. 164–167.

4. *Poesía de Gil Vicente* (México: Séneca, 1940), p. 14. First published in *Cruz y Raya*, 10 (1934), pp. 1–46. More recently reprinted in *De los siglos oscuros al de oro* (Madrid: Gredos, 1958). Pedro Henríquez Ureña encountered the same difficulty in *La versificación irregular en la poesía castellana*, 2nd ed. (Madrid: Centro de Estudios Históricos, 1933), p. 111: "La transcripción y la imitación se mezclan en él a tal punto que se dificulta distinguirlas."

5. *Poesías de Gil Vicente*, p. 62. The techniques of the *glosa popular* are analyzed by Margit Frenk, "Glosas de tipo popular en la lírica antigua," in *Estudios sobre lírica antigua*, pp. 267–308. On p. 273, "En la utilización de glosas de tipo arcaico ningún dramaturgo español, contemporáneo o posterior, iguala a Gil Vicente."

6. Bell, p. 43.

7. Thomas R. Hart, ed., *Gil Vicente: Obras dramáticas castellanas* (Madrid: Espasa-Calpe, 1968), pp. 73–75.

8. Hart, pp. 76–78.

9. Hart, pp. 49–50. See also the commentary of Humberto López Morales, *Tradición y creación en los orígenes del teatro castellano* (Madrid: Ediciones Alcalá, 1968), pp. 121–122.

10. Hart, p. 64; Havana, p. 16. López Morales, p. 121, notes that in this *auto*, "Las canciones y las danzas están distribuidas con una asombrosa mezcla de funcionalidad teatral y sentido artístico...."

11. Berlin, p. 92; Havana, p. 16. In Berlin Alberti does not cite Gil Vicente's lullaby, though he traces the same relationship between the modern and old traditions.

12. Hart, pp. 225–227.

13. Hart, p. 227.

14. *Romancero hispánico*, II, p. 104 and pp. 216–217. See, for instance, the 11 unpublished versions of "Flérida y don Duardos" listed in *El Romancero judeo-español en el Archivo Menéndez Pidal*, II (Madrid: Cátedra Seminario Menéndez Pidal, 1978), pp. 181–184.

15. Ramón Menéndez Pidal, "Los 'Estudos sobre o Romanceiro peninsular' de Doña Carolina," *Miscelánea de Estudos em honra de D. Carolina Michaëlis de Vasconcellos* (Coimbra: 1933), p. 496. Other published versions can be seen in José Leite de Vasconcellos, *Romanceiro portuguez*, Biblioteca do Povo e das Escolas, 121 (Lisboa: David Corazzi, 1886), pp. 442–446. The history of the ballad and its relation to the play are studied by I. S. Révah, "Edition critique du 'romance' de don Duardos et Flérida," *Bulletin d'Histoire du Théâtre Portugais*, 3, no. 1 (1952), pp. 107–139. A separate study of the ballad has been done by Manuel da Costa Fontes, "*D. Duardos* in the Portuguese Oral Tradition," *Romance Philology*, 30, no. 4 (1977), pp. 589–608. In addition to the versions collected and published by Costa Fontes—see his *Romanceiro da Ilha de S. Jorge* (Coimbra: Universidade da Coimbra, 1983)—see Armando Cortes-Rodrígues, *Romanceiro Popular Açoriano* (Ponta Delgada: Instituto Cultural de Ponta Delgada, 1987), pp. 323–326.

16. The *redondilla*, a quatrain of eight-syllable verses with consonant rhyme, was popularly used in the classic *comedia* for animated conversations and amorous dialogue. The assonance of the ballad could be matched easily in the *redondilla* rhyme scheme, normally *abba*.

17. See Diego Catalán, "Don Francisco de la Cueva y Silva y los orígenes del teatro nacional," *Nueva Revista de Filología Hispánica*, 3 (1949), pp. 130–140.

18. See *Romancero hispánico*, II, pp. 107–108.

19. Jerome A. Moore, *The "Romancero" in the Chronicle-Legend Plays of Lope de Vega* (Philadelphia: University of Pennsylvania, 1940), pp. 9–16.

20. Written before September, 1598, according to S. Griswold Morley and Courtney Bruerton, *Cronología de las comedias de Lope de Vega* (Madrid: Gredos, 1968), p. 44.

21. *El cerco de Santa Fe*, in *Biblioteca de Autores Españoles*, 214 (Madrid: M. Rivadeneyra, 1849; rpt. Madrid: Atlas, 1945), pp. 438ff.

22. Probably written between 1610–1613, according to Morley and Bruerton, p. 276.

23. *Las almenas de Toro*, Act I. Lope de Vega, *Obras escogidas, III: Teatro*, ed. Federico Carlos Sainz de Robles (Madrid: Aguilar, 1962), p. 772.

24. See *Catálogo general del Romancero*, vol. 2 (1982), pp. 121–126.

25. *Las almenas de Toro*, Act III, pp. 794–795. See also *Romancero hispánico*, II, p. 175, and Moore, p. 122.

26. *Romancero hispánico*, II, p. 172.

27. *Romancero hispánico*, II, p. 176. The ballads used by Guillén de Castro can be found in Agustín Durán's *Romancero general o Colección de romances anteriores al siglo XVIII*, I, *Biblioteca de Autores Españoles*, X, nos. 725–729, 732, 734–739, 742–744, 749 and 767.

28. *Las mocedades del Cid*, Part I, Act II. I use the edition by Víctor Said Armesto (Madrid: Clásicos Castellanos, 1913), p. 89.

29. Corneille's play, in five acts instead of three, is written in the longer Alexandrine verse of twelve to fourteen syllables of consonant rhyme; consequently Corneille was not interested in translating the texts of the *romances*. Other changes Corneille made to the original, including the compression of the dramatic time from over three years in the Spanish play to the twenty-four hours required by Aristotelian convention, are summed up by William E. Wilson, *Guillén de Castro* (New York: Twayne, 1973), pp. 77–82.

30. An entire gamut of the functions popular lyrics have in Lope's plays has been admirably summed up by Gustavo Umpierre, *Songs in the Plays of Lope de Vega* (London: Tamesis, 1975). Basing his study on more than one hundred plays, Umpierre notes that most plays use two to four songs; some use up to twelve (p. 2).

31. See Joseph Silverman's "Cultural Backgrounds of Spanish Imperialism as Presented in Lope de Vega's Play *San Diego de Alcalá*," in a special issue, ed. David Ringrose, of *The Journal of San Diego History*, 24, no. 1 (Winter, 1978), pp. 7–23. This volume includes the proceedings of the symposium, "From Lope de Vega to San Diego: The Backgrounds of Spanish Colonization in the Californias," held at the University of California, San Diego, in October, 1976.

32. *Los guanches de Tenerife*, Act II, in *Obras escogidas*, III, pp. 1277–1278. Umpierre notes in his discussion of the Indian songs: "when deemed necessary for artistic reasons, European instruments are employed by the Indians, e.g., 'Salen indios músicos delante con unos tamborillos y *por ser fuerza para cantar, con sus guitarras...*,' in *Arauco domado*" (Umpierre's emphasis), *Songs in the Plays of Lope de Vega*, p. 97.

33. Act II. I use the edition by J. E. Hartzenbusch, in *Biblioteca de Autores Españoles*, IV (Madrid: M. Rivadeneyra, 1860), p. 523.

34. The New World was also a subject of interest to the *entremés*, *mojiganga*, and other theatrical forms which continued to accompany the *comedia* throughout the seventeenth century. Antonio Pages Larraya notes in his insightful study, "Bailes y mojigangas sobre el Nuevo Mundo en el teatro español del siglo XVIII," *Cuadernos Hispánoamericanos*, 109 (1977), pp. 246–263: "Así se anuncia, sorprendemente, el Mundo Nuevo como una aparición curiosa, alegra, divertida.... Lucen algunos de esos donaires en la *Mojiganga del Mundi Nuevo*. Veremos en ella bailes de portugueses, valencianos, indios y negros. Cada uno posee una bien perfilada singularidad folklórica. Los distintos grupos salen vestidos con trajes regionales y cantan en su propio idioma. Dentro del conjunto sobresalen por su gracia el baile y la canción de América" (p. 250 and p. 254).

35. All references are to Charles V. Aubrun and José F. Montesinos, eds., *Peribáñez y el Comendador de Ocaña* (Paris: Librairie Hachette, 1943). Lope locates the song at the exact center of the play, Act II, scene iii, p. 90.

36. Act II, scene vii, p. 108. In their prologue to the play, Aubrun and Montesinos note the unifying force of traditional song: "En introduisant dans son *Peribáñez* la voix populaire sous la forme d'un romance, il nous fait sentir profondément le caractère de cette communauté rurale castillane. Le protagoniste en est l'expression la plus accomplie; et les autres personnages, faites de la même argile, prolongent pour ainsi dire la conscience du héros, dont ils se savent solidaires et dont ils partagent les anxiétés. Cette solidarité, d'ailleurs, s'est réalisée et traduite en action...," p. xxi.

37. Marsha Swislocki brings out this point in "Ballad Formation in the Plays of Lope de Vega," *El Romancero hoy: Historia, comparatismo, bibliografía crítica* (Madrid: Cátedra Seminario Menéndez Pidal, 1979), p. 69.

38. In their prologue, p. xvi.

39. Aubrun and Montesinos, Act I, scene i, pp. 3–6.

40. Act I, scene i, pp. 6–7. Aubrun and Montesinos take their description of the dance from Covarrubias. See also J. F. Montesinos, *Letras para cantar*, pp. 140–142.

41. Act III, scene v; Aubrun and Montesinos, p. 154. Also *Letras para cantar*, pp. 147–148.

42. Aubrun and Montesinos, Act II, scene ii, p. 82.

43. See, among others, Montesinos, *Letras para cantar*, p. 146; Torner's *Lírica hispánica*, pp. 19–22; Henríquez Ureña, p. 235; Alín, pp. 172–177; Dámaso Alonso and José Manuel Blecua, *Antología de la poesía española. Lírica de tipo tradicional*, 2nd ed. (Madrid: Gredos, 1964), p. 81, p. 101, p. 199; Frenk, *Lírica española de tipo popular*, p. 170.

44. See the discussion of "Traditional Aesthetics" in Chapter 1.

45. Aubrun and Montesinos, Act I, scene i, p. 22.

46. In "El Curioso impertinente," chap. XXXIV of *Don Quijote*, Part I: "dicen que han de tener los buenos enamorados…todo un abecé entero…agradecido, bueno, caballero, dadivoso, enamorado, firme…." I use the edition by Martín de Riquer (Barcelona: Juventud, 1966), p. 351. Torner cites a *Loa famosa de las letras del A. B. C.* (1612), included in Cotarelo's *Colección de Entremeses*.

47. Eduardo M. Torner's *Lírica hispánica* documents the persistence of the *abecedario* from the fifteenth through the twentieth centuries, pp. 162–165.

48. Examples of these songs can be found in F. Olmeda, *Folk-lore de Castilla o Cancionero popular de Burgos* (Sevilla: 1903), pp. 70–71; Manuel García Matos, *Cancionero popular de la provincia de Madrid* (Barcelona-Madrid: 1952), p. 172.

49. Aubrun and Montesinos, Prologue, pp. xix–xx. According to the authors, the villagers' collective performance of song and dance serves the same function as the chorus of classical theater. The same observation was made by Menéndez y Pelayo. See p. xxi.

50. Henríquez Ureña classifies it as a "cantar viejo" in *Versificación*, pp. 154–155.

51. "Lope dramatiza un cantar," *Asomante*, 8, no. 2 (1952), p. 17. The author uses the *misterio* of traditional poetry to mean "Misterio de una expresión al mismo tiempo individual y colectiva, circunstancial y perenne, flúida como una conversación y encerrada en una forma endurecida, afición del vulgo y también actividad aristocrática, elemental y, sin embargo, tan compleja como la idea de que todos los hombres somos el mismo hombre."

52. *El caballero de Olmedo*, Act III. I refer to José Manuel Blecua's edition (Zaragoza: Clásicos Ebro, 1943), p. 107.

53. The story and legend surrounding the song has continued to interest historians and memorialists up to the twentieth century. Antonio de Prado y Sancho provides this date in his *Novenario de Nuestra Señora de la Soterraña, con siete recuerdos históricos, panegíricos y morales* (Valladolid: 1906). See the preliminary study by Eduardo Juliá Martínez, *Comedia de El Caballero de Olmedo* (Madrid: Consejo Superior de Investigaciones Científicas, 1944), pp. 9–16; also see Blecua, p. 15.

54. Included in the *Obras de música para tecla, arpa, vihuela…recopiladas y puestas en cifra por Hernando de Cabezón, su hijo* (Madrid: 1578). According to Jesús Bal y Gay, these are "de las primeras variaciones que se han escrito en el mundo," in *Treinta canciones de Lope de Vega*, a special issue in commemoration of Lope by the *Revista de la Residencia de los Estudiantes* (Madrid: S. Aguirre, 1935), p. 106. Music, pp. 59–62; reproduced in Blecua, pp. 119–123.

55. Edited by E. Juliá Martínez (see above), who attributes it to Cristóbal de Morales.

56. According to Morley and Bruerton, p. 296.

57. The text of the *Baile* is given in Juliá Martínez, pp. 211–213.

58. Cited by Blecua, p. 24, and Alín, p. 740.

59. Alín, pp. 739–740.

60. The manuscript text, belonging to Antonio Rodríguez Moñino, was published by Margit Frenk, "Glosas de tipo popular en la lírica antigua," in *Nueva Revista de Filología Hispánica*, 12 (1958), pp. 301–334; reproduced in her *Estudios sobre lírica antigua* (Madrid: Castalia, 1978), pp. 267–326, with the note: "esta pieza, que prueba a maravilla el hecho de que en el siglo XVI seguían componiéndose glosas de confección tradicional," p. 287. Also in Alonso and Blecua, p. 246.

61. See Blecua, p. 15. I have not yet seen the article by Fidel Fita, "El Caballero de Olmedo y la Orden de Santiago," *Boletín de la Real Academia de la Historia*, 56, p. 398,

which suggests that the Caballero was killed for having supported the king against the rebellion of the *comuneros*.

62. "Nótese que la glosa constituye un texto aparte, que presupone el del villancico, pero que no toma de él, en este caso, ni una sola palabra; lo que hace es continuar por su propia cuenta el relato inicial, en el mismo metro, con el mismo tono narrativo." Frenk, *Estudios sobre lírica antigua*, p. 293.

63. Blecua, *El caballero de Olmedo*, Act III, pp. 107–108.

64. Blecua, p. 104.

65. Blecua, p. 31.

66. Blecua, *El caballero*, Act I, p. 34.

67. Blecua, *El caballero*, Act II, p. 59.

68. The *quintilla* is a strophe of five octosyllabic lines with a variety of rhyme schemes, usually *ababa* or *aabba*, which is used to express deep emotion of a lyrical or pathetic nature. My omission of certain lines disrupts the rhyme in places.

69. Blecua, *El caballero*, Act III, pp. 102–103.

70. The counterpart of *La Celestina* in *El caballero de Olmedo* is Fabia. Lope consciously tries to reproduce the atmosphere of the fifteenth century, setting the time of the play during the reign of Juan II and Don Alvaro de Luna. As Blecua notes in his prologue, p. 16: "Describe con una habilidad extraordinaria, como ya señaló Menéndez y Pelayo, el ambiente de magia, de fatalismo y de violencia en que se mueven los personajes de esta época. Como en *La Celestina*, un ansia de vida y de juventud corre por las páginas iniciales de la obra, hasta chocar con la trágica idea de la muerte, y de la fatalidad, tan típica del siglo XV." Inés calls Tello 'Sempronio'; he calls her 'Melibea' and refers to Alonso as 'Calisto' during Act I, making the relation overt.

71. Blecua, *El caballero*, p. 49.

72. Blecua, *El caballero*, p. 64.

73. Blecua, *El caballero*, p. 88.

References

Primary Sources

Alberti, Rafael. *La arboleda perdida*. Barcelona: Bruguera, 1980.

_____. *Fermín Galán. Romance de ciego, en tres actos, diez episodios y un epílogo.* Madrid: Chulilla y Angel, 1931.

_____. *Imagen primera de....* Madrid: Ediciones Turner, 1975.

_____. *Lope de Vega y la poesía contemporánea, seguido de La Pájara Pinta.* Prologue by Robert Marrast. Paris: Centre de Recherches de l'Institut d'Etudes Hispaniques, 1964.

_____. *Marinero en tierra. La Amante. El Alba del Alhelí.* Ed. Robert Marrast. Madrid: Castalia, 1972.

_____. *El poeta en la España de 1931, seguido del Romancero de Fermín Galán y los sublevados de Jaca.* Buenos Aires: Editorial Araújo, 1942.

_____. "La poesía popular en la lírica española contemporánea." In *Prosas encontradas (1924–1942).* Ed. Robert Marrast. Madrid: Ayuso, 1970, pp. 87–103.

Alonso, Dámaso and José Manuel Blecua, eds. *Antología de la poesía española. Lírica de tipo tradicional.* 2nd ed. Madrid: Gredos, 1964.

Castro, Guillén de. *Las mocedades del Cid.* Ed. Víctor Said Armesto. Madrid: Clásicos Castellanos, 1913.

Catalán, Diego, et al., eds. *Catálogo General Descriptivo del Romancero Pan-Hispánico.* 4 vols. Madrid: Seminario Menéndez Pidal and Gredos. Vol. 1.A, 1984. Vol. 1.B, 1988. Vol. 2, 1982. Vol. 3, 1983.

_____. *La Flor de la Marañuela.* 2 vols. Madrid: Seminario Menéndez Pidal and Gredos, 1969.

_____. *Romancero tradicional de las lenguas hispánicas.* Madrid: Seminario Menéndez Pidal and Gredos, 1978. Vol. V, 1971. Vol. X, 1978.

Cervantes, Miguel de. *Don Quijote de la Mancha.* Ed. Martín de Riquer. Barcelona: Editorial Juventud, 1966.

_____. *Entremeses.* Ed. Eugenio Asensio. Madrid: Castalia, 1970.

Cortes-Rodrígues, Armando. *Romanceiro Popular Açoriano.* Ponta Delgada: Instituto Cultural de Ponta Delgada, 1987.

Costa Fontes, Manuel da. *Romanceiro da Ilha de S. Jorge.* Coimbra: Universidade de Coimbra, 1983.

Durán, Agustín, ed. *Romancero general o Colección de romances castellanos anteriores al siglo XVIII.* 2 vols. In *Biblioteca de Autores Españoles,* X and XVI. Madrid: M. Rivadeneyra, 1849 and 1851. Rpt. Madrid: Atlas, 1945.

Frenk, Margit. *Corpus de la antigua lírica popular hispánica (Siglo XV a XVII).* Madrid: Castalia, 1987.

_____. *Lírica española de tipo popular.* Madrid: Cátedra, 1978.

García Lorca, Federico. *Amor de Don Perlimplín con Belisa en su jardín.* Ed. Margarita Ucelay. Madrid: Cátedra, 1990.

_____. *Cartas, postales, poemas y dibujos.* Ed. Antonio Gallego Morrell. Madrid: Editorial Moneda y Crédito, 1968.

_____. *Colección de canciones populares españolas,* recogidas, armonizadas e interpretadas por Federico García Lorca (piano) y La Argentinita (voz). Producción de Pedro Vaquero Sánchez. Patrocinado por la Casa-Museo Federico García Lorca. Madrid: Sonifolk, 1990, no. J-105.

_____. *Conferencias.* Ed. Christopher Maurer. 2 vols. Madrid: Alianza, 1984.

_____. *Epistolario.* Ed. Christopher Maurer. 2 vols. Madrid: Alianza, 1983.

_____. *Obras completas.* 3 vols. Ed. Arturo del Hoyo, 22nd ed. 3 vols. Madrid: Aguilar, 1986.

_____. *Obras de Federico García Lorca.* Ed. Mario Hernández. Madrid: Alianza. 1. *Romancero gitano,* 1981. 5. *Primeras canciones. Seis poemas galegos. Poemas sueltos. Canciones populares,* 1981. 6. *Canciones 1921–1924,* 1982. 7. *La zapatera prodigiosa. Fin de fiesta,* 1982. 13. *Bodas de sangre,* 1984.

Hernández de Soto, Sergio. "Juegos infantiles de Extremadura." In *Biblioteca de las tradiciones populares.* Ed. Antonio Machado y Álvarez. Sevilla: Alejandro Guichot, 1884. Vol. II, pp. 101–195; Vol. III, pp. 85–298.

Olmeda, Federico. *Folk-lore de Castilla o Cancionero popular de Burgos.* Sevilla: María Auxiliadora, 1903.

Olvarría y Huarte, Eugenio de. "El Folk-lore de Madrid." In *Biblioteca de las tradiciones populares.* Ed. Antonio Machado y Álvarez. Vol. II. Sevilla: Alejandro Guichot, 1884, pp. 5–100.

Petersen, Suzanne, et al., eds. *Voces nuevas del Romancero castellano-leonés.* In *Archivo Internacional Electrónico del Romancero.* 2 vols. Madrid: Seminario Menéndez Pidal and Gredos, 1982.

Rodríguez Marín, Francisco. *Cantos populares españoles.* 5 vols. Sevilla: Francisco Álvarez, 1882–1883.

Torner, Eduardo Martínez. *Lírica hispánica: Relaciones entre lo popular y lo culto.* Madrid: Editorial Castalia, 1966.

Unpublished materials, collected from the oral tradition and stored in the Archives of Menéndez Pidal in Madrid.

Vega Carpio, Lope de. *Las almenas de Toro.* In *Obras escogidas.* Ed. Federico Carlos Sainz de Robles. Madrid: Aguilar, 1962. Vol. III: *Teatro,* 765–799.

———. *El caballero de Olmedo.* Ed. José Manuel Blecua. Zaragoza: Clásicos Ebro, 1943.

———. *El cerco de Santa Fe.* In *Biblioteca de Autores Españoles,* 214. Madrid: M. Rivadeneyra, 1849. Rpt. Madrid: Atlas, 1945, pp. 438–446.

———. *Letras para cantar.* In *Poesías líricas.* Ed. José F. Montesinos. Madrid: Clásicos Castellanos, 1925. Vol. I, 131–196.

———. *Peribáñez y el Comendador de Ocaña.* Eds. Charles V. Aubrun and José F. Montesinos. Paris: Librairie Hachette, 1943.

———. *San Diego de Alcalá.* In *Comedias escogidas de Frey Lope Feliz de Vega Carpio,* IV. Ed. Juan Eugenio Harztenbusch. In *Biblioteca de Autores Españoles.* Madrid: M. Rivadeneyra, 1860, pp. 515–533.

———. *Treinta canciones de Lope de Vega.* Ed. Jesús Bal y Gay. Special issue of the *Revista de la Residencia de Estudiantes.* Madrid: S. Aguirre, 1935.

Vicente, Gil. *Farça de Inez Pereira.* In *Obras de Gil Vicente.* Eds. J. V. Barreto Feio and J. G. Monteiro. Hamburg: Langhoff, 1834. Vol. III, 136–151.

———. *Obras dramáticas castellanas.* Ed. Thomas R. Hart. Madrid: Clásicos Castellanos, 1968.

———. *Poesías de Gil Vicente.* Ed. Dámaso Alonso. *Cruz y Raya,* 10 (1934), 1–46. Rpt. México: Séneca, 1940.

Secondary Sources

Alín, José María. *El Cancionero español de tipo tradicional.* Madrid: Taurus, 1968.

Alonso, Dámaso. *Ensayos sobre poesía española.* Madrid: Revista de Occidente, 1944.

Anderson, Andrew A. "De qué trata *Bodas de sangre?*" *Hommage/Homenaje a Federico García Lorca.* Toulouse: Université de Toulouse-Le Mirail, 1982, pp. 53–64.

_____. "García Lorca's *Bodas de sangre*: The Logic and Necessity of Act Three." *Hispanófila*, núm. 90 (1987), pp. 21–37.

_____. "Representaciones provinciales de dramas de García Lorca en vida del autor." *Segismundo*, nos. 41–42 (Madrid, 1985), pp. 269–281.

Arbeloa, Víctor Manuel. "Iglesia y República: Diálogo imposible." *Historia 16*, Año VI, no. 60 (April, 1981), pp. 70–77.

Armistead, Samuel G., Antonio Sánchez Romeralo, and Diego Catalán, eds. *El Romancero hoy: Historia, comparatismo, bibliografía crítica.* Vol. IV of *Romancero y poesía oral.* Madrid: Editorial Gredos, 1979.

_____. *El Romancero judeo español en el Archivo Menéndez Pidal.* 3 vols. Madrid: Cátedra Seminario Menéndez Pidal, 1978.

Asensio, Eugenio. *Poética y realidad en el Cancionero peninsular de la Edad Media.* Madrid: Gredos, 1970.

Baroja, Pío. "Carteles de feria y literatura de cordel." *Revista de Información Médico Terapeútica*, Año 22, nos. 21–22 (1947), pp. 1024–1033.

Bayo, Manuel. "Una obra escénica inédita de R. Alberti." *Revista de Occidente*, 128 (November, 1973), pp. 151–158.

Bell, Aubrey F. G. *Gil Vicente.* Oxford: Oxford University Press, 1921.

Bergman, Hannah, ed. *Ramillete de entremeses y bailes (Siglo XVII).* Madrid: Castalia, 1970.

Blanco Aguinaga, Carlos, Julio Rodríguez Puértolas, and Iris M. Zavala. *Historia social de la Literatura española.* Vol. II. Madrid: Castalia, 1978.

Byrd, Suzanne. "The Puppet Theater as Genesis of Lorcan Drama." *García Lorca Review*, 6 (1978), pp. 139–149.

_____. "The Twentieth Century *Fuente Ovejuna* of Federico García Lorca." *García Lorca Review*, 5, no. 1 (Spring, 1977), pp. 34–39.

Cano, José Luis. *García Lorca: Biografía ilustrada.* Barcelona: Ediciones Destino, 1962.

Caro Baroja, Julio. *Ensayo sobre la literatura de cordel.* Madrid: Revista de Occidente, 1969.

Castillejo, José. *Wars of Ideas in Spain.* London: John Murray, 1937.

Catalán, Diego. "Don Francisco de la Cueva y Silva y los orígenes del teatro nacional." *Nueva Revista de Filología Hispánica*, 3 (1949), pp. 130–140.

_____. *Por campos del Romancero.* Madrid: Gredos, 1970.

Catalán, Diego, Samuel G. Armistead and Antonio Sánchez Romeralo, eds. *El Romancero hoy: Poética.* Vol. III of *Romancero y poesía oral.* Madrid: Editorial Gredos, 1979.

Costa Fontes, Manuel da. "*D. Duardos* in the Portuguese Oral Tradition." *Romance Philology*, 30, no. 4 (1977), pp. 589–608.

Couffon, Claude. *Granada y García Lorca.* Buenos Aires: Losada, 1962.

Devoto, Daniel. "Las zapateras prodigiosas." *Lecciones sobre García Lorca.* Ed. Andrés Soria Olmedo. Granada: Comisión Nacional del Cincuentenario, 1986, pp. 67–78.

Díaz, Joaquín. *100 Temas infantiles.* Valladolid: Centro Castellano de Estudios Folklóricos, 1981.

Díaz Roig, Mercedes. *El Romancero y la lírica popular moderna.* México: El Colegio de México, 1976.

Díez-Canedo, Enrique. *Artículos de crítica teatral. El teatro español de 1914–1936.* 4 vols. México: Joaquín Mortiz, 1968.

Eisenberg, Daniel. "Dos conferencias lorquianas (Nueva York y La Habana, 1930)." *Papeles de Son Armadans*, 79, no. 236–237 (1975), pp. 196–212.

Espina, Antonio. "Estreno en el Teatro Beatriz." In *Federico García Lorca.* Ed. Ildefonso-Manuel Gil. Madrid: Taurus, 1973, pp. 469–473.

Fichter, William L. "A Great Spanish Educational Institution: The Residencia de Estudiantes (1910–1936)." *Homenaje a Juan López-Morillas.* Eds. J. Amor y Vázquez and A. David Kossoff. Madrid: Castalia, 1982, pp. 209–220.

Frenk, Margit. *Entre folklore y literatura.* México: El Colegio de México, 1971.

_____. *Estudios sobre lírica antigua.* Madrid: Castalia, 1978.

_____. "'Lectores y Oidores.' La difusión oral de la literatura en el Siglo de Oro." Actas del Séptimo Congreso de la Asociación Internacional de Hispanistas. August, 1980. Rome: Bulzoni, n.d., pp. 101–123.

Fuentes, Víctor. *La marcha al pueblo en las letras españolas, 1917–1936.* Madrid: Ediciones de la Torre, 1980.

García de Enterría, María Cruz. *Sociedad y poesía de cordel en el Barroco.* Madrid: Taurus, 1973.

García Lorca, Francisco. *Federico y su mundo.* Ed. Mario Hernández. Madrid: Alianza Editorial, 1980.

_____. Prologue to *Three Tragedies by Federico García Lorca.* New York: New Directions, 1955, pp. 1–29.

García Matos, Manuel. *Cancionero popular de la provincia de Madrid.* 3 vols. Barcelona-Madrid: Consejo Superior de Investigaciones Científicas, 1951–1960.

Gerould, Gordon H. *The Ballad of Tradition.* New York: Oxford University Press, 1957.

Gibson, Ian. *Federico García Lorca. I. De Fuente Vaqueros a Nueva York, 1898–1929.* Barcelona: Grijalbo, 1985. *II. De Nueva York a Fuente Grande, 1929–1936.* Barcelona: Grijalbo, 1987.

Gil, Ildefonso-Manuel. *Federico García Lorca*. Madrid: Taurus, 1975.

González-del-Valle, Luis T. "Perspectivas críticas: horizontes infinitos. *La Niña que riega la albahaca y el Príncipe preguntón* y las constantes dramáticas de Federico García Lorca." *Anales de literatura española contemporánea*, vol. 7 (1982), pp. 253–264.

González Martín, Jerónimo Pablo. *Rafael Alberti*. Madrid: Júcar, 1978.

Henríquez Ureña, Pedro. *La versificación irregular en la poesía castellana*. 2nd ed. Madrid: Centro de Estudios Históricos, 1933.

Herr, Richard. *An Historical Essay on Modern Spain*. Berkeley: University of California Press, 1971.

Jiménez Fraud, Alberto. *La Residencia de Estudiantes*. Barcelona: Ariel, 1972.

Juliá Martínez, Eduardo, ed. *Comedia de El Caballero de Olmedo*. Madrid: Consejo Superior de Investigaciones Científicas, 1944.

Laffranque, Marie. "Bases cronológicas para el estudio de Federico García Lorca." In *Federico García Lorca*. Ed. Ildefonso-Manuel Gil. Madrid: Taurus, 1973, pp. 411–459.

Lapesa, Rafael. "Menéndez Pidal, creador de escuela: El Centro de Estudios Históricos." In *¡Alça la voz, pregonero! Homenaje a Don Ramón Menéndez Pidal*. Madrid: Cátedra Seminario Menéndez Pidal and the Corporación de Antiguos Alumnos de la Institución Libre de Enseñanza, 1979, pp. 43–79.

Lazarillo de Tormes. Ed. Angel González Palencia. Zaragoza: Clásicos Ebro, 1953.

Lázaro Carreter, Fernando. "Apuntes sobre el teatro de García Lorca." *Papeles de Son Armadans*, 28, no. 52 (July, 1960), pp. 9–33.

Ledesma, Alonso de. "Juegos de Noches Buenas a lo divino" (Barcelona: Sebastián Cormellas, 1605). In *Romancero y cancionero sagrados*. Ed. Justo de Sancha. Vol. XXV of *Biblioteca de Autores Españoles*. Madrid: M. Rivadeneyra, 1872.

Ledesma, Dámaso. *Folk-lore o Cancionero salmantino*. Madrid: Imprenta Alemana, 1907.

Leite de Vasconcellos, José. *Romanceiro portuguez*. Biblioteca do Povo e das Escolas, 121. Lisboa: David Corazzi, 1886.

León, María Teresa. *Memoria de la melancolía*. Buenos Aires: Losada, 1970.

Longhran, David K. "Lorca, Lope and the Idea of a National Theater: *Bodas de sangre* and *El caballero de Olmedo*." *García Lorca Review*, 8, no. 2 (Fall, 1980), pp. 127–136.

López Estrada, Francisco. "El romance de 'Don Bueso' y la cancion de 'La peregrinita' en el cancionero folklórico de Antequera." *De los romances-villancico a la poesía de Claudio Rodríguez.* Ed. J. M. López de Abiada and A. López Bernasocchi. Madrid: Gráficas Sol, 1984, pp. 253–263.

López Morales, Humberto. *Tradición y creación en los orígenes del teatro castellano.* Madrid: Ediciones Alcalá, 1968.

Mainer, José Carlos. *La Edad de Plata (1902–1939).* 2nd ed. Madrid: Cátedra, 1981.

Mairena, Antonio. *Las confesiones de Antonio Mairena.* Ed. Alberto García Ulecia. Sevilla: Universidad de Sevilla, 1976.

Marrast, Robert. *Aspects du théâtre de Rafael Alberti.* Paris: Société d'Edition d'Enseignement Supérieur, 1967.

Mena Benito, Francisco. *El tradicionalismo de Federico García Lorca.* Barcelona: Rondas, 1974.

Menarini, Piero. "Federico y los títeres: Cronología y dos documentos." *Boletín de la Fundación Federico García Lorca,* III, no. 5 (June, 1989), pp. 103–128.

Menéndez Pidal, Jimena. *Auto de Navidad.* Madrid: Aguilar, 1971.

Menéndez Pidal, Ramón. "Algunos carácteres primordiales de la literatura española." *Bulletin Hispanique,* 20, no. 4 (October-December, 1918), pp. 205–232.

———. "Cómo vivió y cómo vive el Romancero." In *Estudios sobre el Romancero.* Vol. XI of *Obras completas de R. Menéndez Pidal.* Madrid: Espasa-Calpe, 1973, pp. 403–462.

———. "Los 'Estudos sobre o Romanceiro peninsular' de Doña Carolina." In *Miscelánea de Estudos em honra de D. Carolina Michaëlis de Vasconcellos.* Coimbra: 1933.

———. *Flor nueva de Romances viejos.* 20th ed. Madrid: Espasa-Calpe, 1965.

———. *La primitiva poesía lírica española.* Madrid: Ateneo Científico, Literario y Artístico, 1919.

———. *Romancero hispánico.* 2nd ed. Vols. IX and X of *Obras completas de R. Menéndez Pidal.* Madrid: Espasa-Calpe, 1968.

Montesinos, José F. *Ensayos y estudios de literatura española.* Ed. Joseph H. Silverman. México: Ediciones de Andrea, 1959.

Moore, Jerome A. *The "Romancero" in the Chronicle-Legend Plays of Lope de Vega.* Philadelphia: University of Pennsylvania, 1940.

Moreno Villa, José. *Los autores como actores.* México: El Colegio de México, 1951.

Morla Lynch, Carlos. *En España con Federico García Lorca.* Madrid: Aguilar, 1958.

Morley, S. Griswold, and Courtney Bruerton. *Cronología de las comedias de Lope de Vega.* Madrid: Gredos, 1968.

Olrik, Axel. "Epic Laws of Folk Narrative." In *The Study of Folklore.* Ed. Alan Dundes. Englewood Cliffs, NJ: Prentice-Hall, 1965, pp. 129–141.

Onís, Federico de. "La Argentinita." *Revista Hispánica Moderna*, 13, nos. 1–2 (January-April, 1946), pp. 182–187.

———. "Lorca, folklorista." In *Federico García Lorca (1899–1936)*. New York: Hispanic Institute, 1941, pp. 113–149.

Pages Larraya, Antonio. "Bailes y Mojigangas sobre el Nuevo Mundo en el teatro español del siglo XVIII." *Cuadernos Hispánoamericanos*, 109 (1977), pp. 246–263.

Paucker, Eleanor Krane. "Cinco años de misiones." *Revista de Occidente*, Extraordinario I, nos. 7–8 (November, 1981), pp. 233–268.

Petersen, Suzanne. "Cambios estrucurales en el Romancero tradicional." In *El Romancero en la tradición oral moderna*. Eds. Diego Catalán, Samuel G. Armistead and Antonio Sánchez Romeralo. Madrid: Cátedra Seminario Menéndez Pidal and the Rectorado de la Universidad de Madrid, pp. 167–179.

Popkin, Louise B. *The Theatre of Rafael Alberti*. London: Tamesis, 1975.

Ramos-Gil, Carlos. *Claves líricas de García Lorca*. Madrid: Aguilar, 1967.

Révah, I. S. "Edition critique du 'romance' de don Duardos et Flérida." *Bulletin d'Histoire du Théâtre Portugais*, 3, no. 1 (1952), pp. 107–139.

Rico Godoy, José. "No pudimos convencer a Galán." *Historia 16*, Año VI, no. 60 (April, 1981), p. 85.

Río, Angel del. "Vida y obra." In *Federico García Lorca (1899–1936)*. New York: Hispanic Institute, 1941, pp. 7–74.

Rodrigo, Antonina. *García Lorca el amigo de Cataluña*. Barcelona: Edhasa, 1984.

———. *García Lorca en Cataluña*. Barcelona: Planeta, 1975.

———. *Mariana de Pineda*. Madrid: Alfaguarra, 1965.

———. "Mariana de Pineda, Federico García Lorca: Relación personaje-autor." *Hommage/Homenaje a García Lorca*. Toulouse: Université de Toulouse-Le Mirail, 1982, pp. 39–51.

Rodríguez Moñino, Antonio, ed. *Las Fuentes del Romancero general de 1600*. 12 vols. Madrid: Real Academia Española, 1957.

———. "Textos sobre literatura de cordel (Siglos XVI–XX)." In *Diccionario bibliográfico de pliegos sueltos poéticos (Siglo XVI)*. Madrid: Castalia, 1970, pp. 85–126.

Ruíz, Juan, Arcipreste de Hita. *El Libro de buen amor*. 2 vols. Ed. Julio Cejador y Frauca. Madrid: Clásicos Castellanos, 1913.

Sáenz de la Calzada, Luis. *"La Barraca": Teatro Universitario*. Madrid: Biblioteca de la Revista de Occidente, 1976.

Salinas de Marichal, Solita. *El mundo poético de Rafael Alberti*. Madrid: Gredos, 1968.

Sánchez, Roberto G. *García Lorca: Estudio sobre su teatro.* Madrid: Ediciones Jara, 1950.

Sánchez Romeralo, Antonio. *El villancico. Estudios sobre la lírica popular en los siglos XV y XVI.* Madrid: Gredos, 1969.

Sánchez Romeralo, Antonio, Diego Catalán, and Samuel G. Armistead, eds. *El Romancero hoy: Nuevas fronteras.* Vol. II of *Romancero y poesía oral.* Madrid: Editorial Gredos, 1979.

Silverman, Joseph. "Cultural Backgrounds of Spanish Imperialism as Presented in Lope de Vega's Play *San Diego de Alcalá.*" *Journal of San Diego History,* ed. David Ringrose, 24, no. 1 (Winter, 1978), pp. 7–23.

Styan, J. L. *Drama, Stage and Audience.* London: Cambridge University Press, 1975.

Swislocki, Marsha. "Ballad Formation in the Plays of Lope de Vega." *El Romancero hoy: Historia, comparatismo, bibliografía.* Madrid: Cátedra Seminario Menéndez Pidal, 1979, pp. 63–73.

Tinnel, Roger D. *Federico García Lorca: Catálogo-Discografía de las "Canciones populares antiguas" y de música basada en los textos lorquianos.* Plymouth, NH: Plymouth State College of the University of New Hampshire, 1986.

Tuñón de Lara, Manuel. *Medio siglo de cultura española.* Barcelona: Bruguera, 1982.

Umpierre, Gustavo. *Songs in the Plays of Lope de Vega.* London: Tamesis, 1975.

Unamuno, Miguel de. *En torno al casticismo.* Barcelona: Antonio López, 1902.

Velloso, José Miguel. *Conversaciones con Rafael Alberti.* Madrid: Sedmay, 1977.

Vilar, Pierre. *Historia de España.* Trans. Manuel Tuñón de Lara. Paris: Librairie Espagnole, 1963.

Villalón, Fernando. *Poesías.* Ed. José María de Cossío. Madrid: Hispánica, 1944.

Wilson, William E. *Guillén de Castro.* New York: Twayne, 1973.

Zavala, Iris M. *El texto en la historia.* Madrid: Nuestra Cultura, 1981.